Steven Brooks
Editor

Mark Coleman
Art Director

Christopher Bradshaw
Airport Diagrams

Writers
David Athay
Claire Bolgil
Steven Brooks

Map Design
Barna Ban

Michael J Kinghorn
Contributing Photographer

Stephanie Larson
Proofreading

Adventus Media LLC
4731 N. Highway A1A
Vero Beach, FL 32963
(772) 361-6577
sbrooks@adventusmedia.com

The *Florida Flying Guide*
is published annually by
Adventus Media LLC.

CONT

ABOUT THIS GUIDE

This book was written for you, the pilot, who would like to fly someplace interesting for a meal, a day or a weekend escape.

Did you know you can fly into a resort in the the the Keys **that has its own airport?** Or that there is a place in Northern Florida that you can **swim with the Manatees?** Or that there is an airport you can fly to and **walk to a Yankees or Red Sox baseball game?** Or that you can fly into the airport where the Piper factory is located and **get a tour?**

From Central Florida, a pilot in a typical Cessna or Piper can **fly to just about any destination in two and a half hours or less.** For example, Orlando to Key West, or Orlando to the scenic Apalachicola are both less than two hours direct.

If you live in the north or south part of Florida, there are many destinations within

an hour or two of you, and everywhere in the state is within reach of a tank of gas.

No matter where you are flying from, this guide will help you pick special places to fly that you would have missed, **and have special experiences and memories.**

For each destination we have selected some unique things to do, places to stay, and restaurants to visit.

Let us know what you think.

Blue Skies,

S Brooks

THE $100 HAMBURGER

If you are on the hunt for a new or interesting place to fly for breakfast, lunch or dinner, this guide lists 27 destinations in Florida.

As private pilots, we are all looking for a great excuse to get up in the air. And what better excuse than an early morning run for breakfast or a lunch flight?

We have made the locations of airports with restaurants on or adjacent to the field easy to find by placing a food icon on the top left side of the destination page.

In fact, some of the destinations have been selected almost solely because of the availability of an easy meal.

No doubt you have a few places you fly to for a meal time and time again. But I urge you to stretch your wings and try some new

places. Just recently I was flying with a high time pilot who has lived in south/central Florida for many years. Yet he had never eaten at Ft. Lauderdale's famous Jet Runway Café. We flew in for breakfast, and it is now his favorite place.

The excellent restaurant at the private Spruce Creek airport community outside Daytona is open to all, and it is an hour or less flight in most airplanes from as far north as Jacksonville, as far south as Palm Beach and as far west as Tampa.

So spread your wings and eat! And please send any suggestions for your favorites that we may have missed to: sbrooks@adventusmedia.com

Bon appétit!

FLORIDA EVENTS AND FESTIVALS

There are thousands of events in Florida every year. We have listed a few that might spark you to fly in for a day or a weekend.

JANUARY

Florida Keys Seafood Festival. Second weekend in January. Fun excuse to fly down to Key West. Unlike most festivals, there are no food vendors here — all the food is caught and cooked by the local commercial fishermen. You'll find grilled Florida lobster, fried fish, stone crab claws, Key West shrimp, conch fritters, conch ceviche, Key Lime pie tarts and more.

Gasparilla Pirate Festival in Downtown Tampa. Very close to Peter O'Knight airport. Kicking off the last weekend in January with the Pirate Fest Stage Street Festival, there is the invasion, brunch and parade on Saturday.

Gasparilla Ship at the Gasparilla Pirate Festival

U.S. Sport Aviation Expo. End of January. Held on the Sebring airfield, it showcases dozens of affordable light aircraft including LSAs, Experimental and even refurbished airplanes. They open a control tower during the show.

New Smyrna Beach Chowder Festival. Low key Sunday afternoon event on the last weekend of January. This progressive chowder cook-off has been going on for over 20 years. Featuring more than 40 chowders at locations along Flagler Avenue, the event benefits the Florida Sheriff's Youth Camp. You can buy your tickets ahead of time online. www.nsbchowder.com

FEBRUARY

Speed Weeks. These are the first three weeks in February at Daytona, leading up to the Daytona 500.

Mount Dora Art Festival. Typically the first weekend in February. Ranked in the Top 100 art shows in the nation, the Mount Dora Art Festival attracts about 250,000 visitors each year to the two-day street festival featuring artists that create oil painting, watercolors, acrylics, clay, sculpture and photography. The event also offers musical entertainment and a wide array of festival food.

Swamp Cabbage Festival. Last weekend in February. The location is La Belle, just east of Fort Myers. Attractions include live entertainment, rodeo, car show, fishing tournament and a parade. The Festival honors the official state tree, the sabal (cabbage) palm, by eating it. The heart of the cabbage palm is prepared into swamp cabbage or fritters which are Florida Cracker delicacies. Fly in to La Belle Municipal (X14)

Everglades City Seafood Festival. Second weekend in February. This town of 500 people puts on a big event. Typically 50,000 people attend the weekend event for fresh seafood, country music, carnival rides and crafts booths. Considered the "stone crab capital," this old Florida town is worth visiting. The event is about a 10 minute walk from the Everglades City airport.

Carlisle Winter Autofest at SUN 'n FUN. Typically the last weekend in February. A combination of car show, car auction, food and flea market make this a fun fly in. Park your airplane right next to the event. KLAL, Lakeland.

MARCH

Sanibel Shell Show. Held the first week of March. This event has been happening for over 80 years. The show runs for three days on the first weekend in March.

Florida Strawberry Festival. Typically the first two weeks in March, this annual event takes place in Plant City. The festival lasts 11 days, and generates an attendance of about half a million people The festival has flea market style craft sales, various free entertainment acts/events, a large midway, plus twice-daily "big name" musical concert performances. Tickets are required for these concerts. Fly in to Lakeland (KLAL) for a 15 minute drive to the festival.

TICO Warbird Air Show. Typically the second weekend in March, it is held at KTIX. They have first class performers. Past shows have included the Aeroshell Aerobatic Team and the USAF Thunderbirds. Flights in the UH-1 Huey and the AH-1 Cobra Helicopter are offered during the show.

Daytona Bike Week. This 9-day event runs during the first two weeks in March. The 'World's Largest Motorcycle Event' has been going on for over 75 years. Join over 500,000 motorcycle enthusiasts for Bike Week.

Sunnyland Antique Boat Festival. Held toward the end of March, this 3-day weekend event is located in Tavares next to Mt. Dora. It is a 24 minute ride from X23 Umatilla Municipal airport.

APRIL

Springtime Tallahassee is an annual event typically held on the first weekend in April. Celebrating Tallahassee's history and culture, there are over 100 colorful units and floats, marching bands, dance groups, Springtime Krewe floats and much more. Music, food, arts and crafts abound. Arts and Crafts booths showcase over 250 local, regional and national vendors.

Sun 'n Fun International Fly-In & Expo. Historically the first week in April starting on a Tuesday. Lakeland, Florida. You know what it is!

Conch Republic Independence Celebration. Usually the last week in April. With activities ranging from a wacky bed race to a lighthearted sea battle featuring tall ships, the Conch Republic's 10-day birthday party showcases the independent and eccentric spirit that characterizes the Florida Keys. For more information

visit http://www.conchrepublic.com/schedule. htm or call 305-296-0213.

Annual Isle of Eight Flags Shrimp Festival. Amelia Island at Fernandina Beach. The Festival is an annual tradition that has been going on for over 50 years. This huge festival attracts over 100,000 people during the weekend. Usually the last weekend in April or the first weekend in May.

Pensacola Crawfish Festival. Usually the last weekend in April on Pensacola Bay. Get your Cajun on with over 16,000 pounds of boiled crawfish. Cajun dishes such as red beans and rice, boudin balls, seafood gumbo, jambalaya, and Cajun pasta are served. They also have less exotic fare including hot dogs, chicken tenders, and funnel cakes. In addition to food, there is music from artists representing New Orleans instrumental jazz, R&B, rock and traditional Cajun music.

MAY

Pensacola Crawfish Festival

Florida Folk Festival. Last weekend in May. Over 60 years old, this three-day celebration offers the music, dance, stories, crafts and food that make Florida unique. The Festival is held along the Suwannee River at Stephen Foster Folk Culture Center State Park. A 25 minute drive from Suwannee County Airport.

Rock By The Sea. Celebrated for over 10 years, this music festival is designed to raise money to assist deserving charities who provide direct services to those in need. The three-day engagement features dozens of touring troubadours, bands performing live by the beach as well as beer tents, fresh fare and a golf tournament.

Nine minutes from Saint George's Island Airport (F47).

The Blue Crab Festival. Always Memorial Day weekend in Palatka. (Northwest of Daytona) This is a big event that has been going on for almost 30 years. Its got everything. Carnival rides, live music, arts and crafts, commercial vendors, and more along the St. Johns River in downtown Palatka. It even has a Memorial Day parade featuring marching bands and various other floats and units. Saturday night there are fireworks. Admission and parking are free, with free live entertainment throughout the the day and night. Fly into Palatka Municipal Airport (28J) Nice new FBO. A 20 minute ride to the event via cab or Enterprise Rental Car.

JUNE
St. Augustine Music Festival. Typically in June. The St. Augustine Music Festival is an annual classical music concert series featuring musicians from the Jacksonville Symphony Orchestra performing a variety of classical compositions. All concerts are free and start at 7:30 p.m. in the St. Augustine Cathedral Basilica. No tickets are required.

Monticello Watermelon Festival. Third weekend in June. Originally the festival was started to recognize the watermelon growers in Jefferson County. This festival has enjoyed 65 plus years of watermelon, music, children's theater, pageants, street dance, arts and crafts vendors, food, a 5K run, car show, art show, ghost tours, seed spitting contest, watermelon carving contest, softball tournament, beer garden, parade and much more.

Downtown Venice Street Craft Festival. Mid June. For over a quarter century, crafters have lined the streets of downtown Venice. Historic downtown Venice will be full of booths filled with paintings, photography, stained glass, handmade soaps, handmade baskets and more. There are food vendors too.

Silver Spurs Rodeo. The rodeo is held twice a year: June and February. The Silver Spurs Rodeo is the largest rodeo east of the Mississippi. Since 1994, it has been the official state rodeo of Florida. While the rodeo is wild, you won't be roughing it here. The events happen in the

indoor climate controlled Silver Spurs Arena with 8,300 seats and 12 luxury skyboxes. 15 minutes from Kissimmee airport.

JULY
Christmas in July. Mid-July. If you are craving the holiday spirit, Venice puts on this event in the middle of July. Not a big event, but fun. The merchants and restaurants have sales, specials and prizes! Summer Santa and Mrs. Claus visit, and the trolley takes you around. Fly in to do early holiday shopping. Mid July.

Pensacola Beach Air Show. Held in the beginning of July, it always features the home team: the Pensacola based Blue Angels. Beach Trolley service will be running to help you get around. Find the schedule at visitpensacolabeach.com/trolleytracker.

Hemingway Days Festival. Mid-July. Celebrating his time living in the Keys in the 1930s, the events in Key West typically include a look-alike contest, readings and book signings, a museum exhibit of rare Hemingway memorabilia, a zany "Running of the Bulls" and a three-day marlin tournament recalling Hemingway's devotion to the deep-sea sport.

AUGUST
Key West Lobsterfest. Mid-August. When lobster season opens, Key West throws the biggest party of the summer. Events include the Duval Crawl on Friday night after the nightly sunset celebration at Mallory Square, a free concert and street fair on Saturday and a decadent Sunday brunch.

Annual Wausau Possum Festival. First Saturday in August. This town of 400 claims it is the "Possum Capital of the World." The festival has more than 10,000 people turn out for the Possum Parade, Possum Auction and old-fashioned square dancing. The square dance and other 'throwback' aspects of the festival, include cross-cut saw contests, sack races and greasy pole contests, making this family-friendly, heritage-style event.

SEPTEMBER
Key West BrewFest Labor Day Weekend. Events from beer dinners, beer brunches, happy

hour parties, pool parties, late-night parties, seminars and the Signature Tasting Festival Event are some of the activities on tap for you! Try tasting close to 200 beers in one weekend! keywestbrewfest.com

Annual Pirate Invasion in Cedar Key. Mid-September Pirate Festival with vendors on Thieves' Row at the City Park. Musical performers Friday and Saturday. "Parlay with Pirates" dinner party on Friday. They even sell pirate wares so you can look the part.

Wings & Wheels Wakulla Fly-In Festival. Mid-September. Started just a few years ago, this one-day event is held at Wakulla County Airport (2J0). This is a combination BBQ Cookoff and car, airplane, and motorcycle show. wakullawingswheels.com

Florida Scallop & Music Festival. Last weekend in September. The annual Scallop Festival draws big crowds to Port St. Joe. Sample scallops cooked many ways plus a variety of great southern foods. Live music, arts and crafts, a kids zone all overlooking beautiful St. Joseph Bay. Fly into Costin Airport (A51). scallopfestfl.org

OCTOBER
Cedar Key Seafood Festival. Mid-October. Almost 50 years old, the festival features over 200 arts and crafts exhibits, live music, a parade on Saturday morning, and amazing local seafood. Saturday offers tours to Seahorse Key Lighthouse from 8:30 a.m.-1:30 p.m.

Boggy Bayou Mullet Festival. Mid October. The annual festival in Niceville has fine art and home hand-crafts, carnival rides, games, attractions, exhibits, and a lot of food concessions. Over the last 40 years, the Boggy Bayou Mullet Festival has become one of the South's best known country music events featuring nationally known country acts in a small, festival atmosphere. 15 minutes from Destin-Ft Walton Beach airport (KVPS).

Fort Lauderdale Boat Show. Late October. They say it is the largest in-water boat show in the world. Spread over six locations in Fort Lauderdale, there is everything from boats and yachts to anything a boater or fisherman could need.

Biketoberfest. Mid-October. Known as the "little brother" of the spring Daytona Bike Week, it attracts 75,000 to 100,000 motorcycle fans. Festivities include street festivals, concerts, charity rides, expos, seminars and celebrity appearances.

Lakeland Zombie Fest. Mid October. Held right on the Sun 'n Fun campus, you can fly in and experience the closest thing to a zombie apocalypse as tens of thousands of bloody, ashen-faced, hollow-eyed zombie wannabes slither through the area. Kids can hit the "safe zone" if they're not fans of the walking dead people, and food vendors, dance and costume competitions lighten the mood.

NOVEMBER
Fort Lauderdale International Boat Show. First weekend in November. More than $4 billion worth of boats and yachts of all kinds and sizes, along with products, accessories, marine art and jewelry will be on display in three million square feet of exhibition space. showmanagement.com

Florida Seafood Festival. First weekend in November. Fodor's travel guide named it one of "America's best 15 small-town events." The Florida Seafood Festival is a two-day event annually drawing tens of thousands of visitors to the historic town of **Apalachicola.** There are music and events like oyster-eating and oyster-shucking contests, blue crab races, photo contest, parade, 5k Redfish Run, the Blessing of the Fleet, and Tonging For Treasure. floridaseafoodfestival.com

NAS Pensacola Open House — Blue Angels Homecoming Air Show. Mid November. Day performances on Friday and Saturday plus a spectacular Friday Night Air Show, complete with nighttime aircraft and performers, capped off by the largest fireworks display in the Pensacola area.

Ribfest, St. Petersburg. Fly into Albert Whitted field (KSPG) and you can walk to the event in Vinoy park, right on the bay. (Or you can take the trolly for 50 cents!) Ribfest features the best BBQ ribbers in the world, and national touring bands playing classic and southern rock and country hits on the Main Stage. On Saturday and Sunday, fun activities for kids - in the Family Fun Zone, hosted by Great Explorations Children's Museum. You might want to get tickets ahead of time. Second weekend in November. ribfest.org

Carlisle Fall Autofest at SUN 'n FUN. This Thursday through Sunday event is typically the second weekend of November. It's one of the largest automotive swap meets in the region. In addition, there are classic cars and trucks on display within the car corral and a collector car auction presented by Carlisle Auctions. The onsite museum will be open during the event. Fly in to Lakeland and you are at the event.

Annual Sponge Docks Seafood Festival. 3-day event on the second weekend in November that's been going on for 30 years. Historic Tarpon Springs is famous not only for the world's finest sponges, but also for some of the finest Greek restaurants, markets, and bakeries in the Country, so this seafood festival has a slightly different "flavor." There are also crafts and music. Fly into either KPIE or Clearwater Airpark. It is about a 30-minute drive from each, and both have car rentals. spongedocks.net

Mount Dora Scottish Highland Festival. Mid-November. Celtic music, Highland games, Scottish country dancing, Tartan parade, vendors, Clan heritage tents, Border collies and more. Third weekend in November. mount-dora.fl

American Sandsculpting Championships on Fort Myers Beach starts the third weekend in November and runs for 9 days. Features world-class master sand sculptors, speed sculpting, demonstrations and lessons, a state championship contest, and a kids activity area with bounce houses and slides. fmbsandsculpting.com

Sarasota Medieval Fair. Taking place over the first three weekends in November, this is quite a spectacle. The food, activities and entertainment is different than you'll find at most events.

DECEMBER

When Pigs Fly South. First Saturday in December. Located on the SUN 'n FUN campus, this has really grown since the inaugural event a few years ago. Fly in to Lakeland (KLAL), park your airplane and you are there. There is competition BBQ, lots of food, cars, motorcycles and airplanes, including warbirds. Weekend camping is also available. Check for the event NOTAMs.

Colonial Night Watch St Augustine. First Saturday in December. This popular annual event re-creates historic Night Watches in garrison towns, where any citizens still on the streets after the gates were locked were required to carry a light so that they could be seen and identified by the Night Watch. The highlight of the event is the Grande Illumination parade. The costumed Spanish and British troops lead the parade with torches and period-costumed people walk the route. Beginning at 7 p.m. at the Castillo de San Marcos, the parade will proceed west to the City Gate, where the public is invited to join in and follow the parade south to the Plaza de la Constitución. Parade participants will be greeted with a welcoming speech at the Government House, followed by the firing of the "Volley of Joy" by the soldiers and militia and Christmas caroling in the Plaza. The best place to view the parade is in the Plaza to the Cathedral Basilica. NOTE: All day Saturday before the parade reenactors will be on hand for weapons demonstrations, flag raisings, and other historical presentations on the grounds of the Castillo.

Snow Fest Sarasota. Mid-December. A 3-day event that lets everyone enjoy the thrill of playing in the snow in 80 degree weather. Every day it snows. Lots for kids to do, from giant snow slides to pony rides, pictures with Santa, snowman building, and a giant snow globe. There are also live shows including Candy Cane Hula Hoopers and Jelly Bean Jugglers, a Kids Amusement Area, DJ Grinch, Vendors and much more! snowfestsarasota.com

Sarasota Medieval Fair

SPRING TRAINING IN FLORIDA

15 baseball teams come to Florida for Spring Training. While workouts tend to start in the middle of February, games start the first week of March.

Atlanta Braves
They play in Champion Stadium at the sports complex in Disney World. 700 S. Victory Lane, Lake Buena Vista, Disney World. Fly in to Kissimmee (KISM) for your visit. It is a 26 minute drive to the stadium.

Baltimore Orioles
After its recent renovation, this small ballpark is now one of the nicest in the Grapefruit League. 2700 12th Street (12th Street and Tuttle Avenue), Sarasota, FL 34237 12 minute drive from KSRQ.

Boston Red Sox
JetBlue Park at Fenway South in Ft. Myers is home to the Red Sox. 11500 Fenway South Drive, Fort Myers, FL 33913. The stadium is partially based on Fenway Park, including a Green Monster in left field. Fly to Fort Myers (KFMY) for a 20 minute drive to the park.

Detroit Tigers
The Tigers have been training in Lakeland since 1934 at Joker Marchant Stadium. Al Kaline Dr., 2301 Lake Hills Blvd., Lakeland, FL 33805. Fly to Lakeland (KLAL). It is a 16 minute drive to the stadium.

Houston Astros
Check out their new stadium in West Palm Beach. "The Ballpark of the Palm Beaches," has 6400 fixed seats and room for 1,000 more on the berm. Shared with the Washington Nationals, The Ballpark of the Palm Beaches offers an immersive spring-training experience. Fans walkthrough training fields and workout facilities before they even set foot in the ballpark. 5444 Haverhill Rd, West Palm Beach, FL 33407. Fly to F45, North Palm Beach County airport for a 16 minute drive to the stadium.

Miami Marlins
The Marlins share Rodger Dean Stadium with the St. Louis Cardinals. 4751 Main St., Jupiter, FL 33458. The closest airport is North Palm Beach County General Aviation airport (F45) which is 20 minutes away.

Minnesota Twins
Hammond Stadium is the winter home of the Twins. 14100 Six Miles Cypress Pkwy., Ft. Myers, FL 33912. Just down the street from the Red Sox, Hammond Stadium is a 15 minute drive from Fort Myers (KFMY).

New York Mets
The Mets have trained in Tradition Field since 1988. 525 NW Peacock Boulevard, Port St. Lucie, FL 34986. It is a 24 minute drive from St Lucie County International (KFPR).

New York Yankees
Steinbrenner Field has been the spring-training home of the New York Yankees since it opened. This is a nice stadium that was recently refreshed. 3802 Dr Martin Luther King Jr Blvd., Tampa 33614. It is a 22 minute drive from Peter O'Knight Airport (KTPF).

Philadelphia Phillies
Bright House Field is one of the best ballparks in spring training. 601 Old Coachman Road, Clearwater, FL 33765. It is only 14 minutes from KPIE, St. Pete-Clearwater International.

Pittsburgh Pirates
They play at McKechnie Field, which was built in 1923 and last renovated in 2012 for a good mix of old school charm and modern amenities. 1611 9th Street W. Bradenton, FL 34208. It is a 14 minute drive from Sarasota-Bradenton (SKRQ) airport.

St. Louis Cardinals
They share Rodger Dean Stadium with the Miami Marlins. 4751 Main St., Jupiter, FL 33458. The closest airport is North Palm Beach County General Aviation airport (F45) which is 20 minutes away.

Tampa Bay Rays
While the Rays play their regular season in an air conditioned stadium in St. Petersburg, for spring they move out of town to Port Charlotte. Charlotte Sports Park. 2300 El Jobean Road, Port Charlotte, FL 33948. The stadium is about 28 minutes from Punta Gorda airport (KPGD) and 33 minutes from Venice airport (KVNC).

Toronto Blue Jays
A great little stadium that you can walk to from downtown Dunedin. Florida Auto Exchange Stadium. 373 Douglas Av., Dunedin, FL. The field is an 11 minute ride from Clearwater Air Park (KCLW).

Washington Nationals
Sharing their new stadium in West Palm Beach with the Houston Astros, the Nationals and their fans enjoy a much upgraded experience. Particularly nice for the fans is the extra shade during the game. 5444 Haverhill Rd, West Palm Beach, FL 33407. Fly to F45, North Palm Beach County airport for a 16 minute drive to the stadium.

FLYING IN THE SUMMER

The main concern about flying in the summer is the frequency with which thunderstorms develop during the day. You need a strategy to keep flying.

Flying in Florida during the summer months means doing a little more flight planning, leaving earlier in the day before the convection builds, and having one or more "outs" if the weather does not go as planned. Sometimes it means you cancel your flight altogether or take the car to your destination.

Turbulence

The first thing to be aware of is that as the intense summer sun heats the land, convection starts. One of the main causes of turbulence is convective currents. Turbulence ranges from bumpiness, which can annoy you and your passengers, to much worse.

Since we are flying for pleasure, the easiest way to avoid the bumps is to fly early in the morning. By 10 or 11 a.m. on a sunny day, you will start to have bumps at low altitudes. Ordinarily, this can be avoided by flying at higher altitudes. When the larger convection currents form cumulus clouds, you will typically find smooth air above the cloud level.

When convection extends to greater heights, it develops larger, towering cumulus clouds and cumulonimbus which can turn into thunderstorms.

Kinds of Thunderstorms

The FAA's classic weather guide, *Aviation Weather,* makes the point that there are two kinds of thunderstorms: (1) *Air Mass Thunderstorms* and (2) *Steady State Thunderstorms.*

Air Mass Storms

Air mass storms result from surface heating. When the storm matures, rain falls through or immediately beside the updraft which retards the updraft and reverses it to a downdraft. The storm is self-destructive and usually has a life cycle of about an hour. Air mass thunderstorms are also called an "ordinary" or "single cell" storms.

Since air mass thunderstorms generally de-

Avoid Turbulence Caused by Convection Currents by Flying Above the Cloud Level

velop from surface heating, they pop up from nowhere, and they reach maximum intensity and frequency over land during middle and late afternoon.

Steady State Storms

Steady state storms are associated with weather systems such as fronts, converging winds, and troughs of low pressure which often form into squall lines. Afternoon heating intensifies them.

In the mature state, updrafts become stronger and last much longer than in air mass storms, hence the name steady state. Steady state storms can last for hours and be intense.

Summer Flying Strategy

Unless the forecast is for heavy cloud cover, depart early in the day. Very early.

As discussed above, the thunderstorm's convective currents are powered by the heat of the day. By 10 a.m. the earth begins heating and vertical air currents begin to build. By 1 p.m. areas of convection are identifiable on NEXRAD imagery. By 4 p.m. storms will generally be in the mature phase, and by 5 to 7 p.m. thunderstorms fully develop.

By starting your flight early, you avoid the dangerous times. In addition, you have a chance to get weather updates during a mid-morning en route stop. By then, the weather models will give you a more developed idea of what to expect for the rest of the day.

With the arrival of the iPad in the cockpit, many pilots now have access to data-linked NEXRAD radar images. This is a great tool to look ahead and see what is developing, but remember because of the 5 to 20-minute delay assembling the images and uploading them, NEXRAD shows where the weather *was,* not where the weather *is.*

Thunderstorms are dynamic, and can grow at rates of 5,000 FPM or higher. Old data can lead you to fly into areas that look clear, only to encounter a rapidly developing thunderstorm.

Data link weather is, however, a great tool for strategic decision-making.

Pilots should consider observing the following rules for any flight potentially near actual or possible thunderstorm activity:
- Never go closer than 5 miles to any visible storm cloud with overhanging areas.
- Strongly consider increasing that distance at least 10 nautical miles.
- If the tops are above the tropopause (about 30,000 feet), avoid by at least 20 miles.
- Do not attempt flight beneath thunderstorms, even when visibility is good, because of the destructive potential of shear turbulence in these areas.

Smooth Flight Above Clouds on an Early Summer Morning

HOW TO FLY THROUGH MOAs
AND RESTRICTED AREAS

Florida is littered with *Military Operations Areas* (MOAs) and *Restricted Areas* throughout the center of the state as well as in the "panhandle" to the west. Offshore there are *Warning Areas*. As a group, these are called "Special Use Areas." Some pilots aren't sure what the difference is between these, and when or if they can fly through those areas.

As a result of this confusion, they try to entirely avoid these areas, when a 30-second call to ATC could save them significant time.

The short answer is you can fly though MOAs *any time* (but if you are wise you will check for military activity before you do). You can only fly through Restricted Areas when they are *not in use*. (Pilots generally say the area is "cold" if it is not in use)

There are several Warning Areas offshore of Florida. Warning areas are similar to restricted areas; however, the United States government does not have sole jurisdiction over the airspace. Treat them the same as Restricted Areas and consider flying through them only when the controlling agency says they are "cold."

Planning to enter a MOA

A MOA is an airspace where military aircraft train. When "hot" (meaning they are actively in use), it means military aircraft are conducting training activities that generally involve acrobatic or abrupt flight maneuvers, so VFR flights should avoid the area. (IFR traffic may be cleared through a MOA if IFR separation can be provided by ATC)

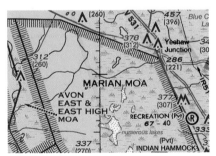

MOA as depicted on a VFR chart

For planning purposes, there are two easy ways to find out what the MOA schedule will be. First, pilots can contact any Flight Services Station (FSS) within 100 miles of the area to obtain accurate real-time information concerning the MOA hours of operation. Some charts actually print the FSS frequency in a box. When on the ground, call FSS at 800-WX-BRIEF.

The second way to find out what area is hot or cold is to go to the special use airspace website **sua.faa.gov.** It is a great resource.

Entering a MOA

Even after you have checked with FSS or the FAA's special use airspace website, when you are in the air approaching the MOA, you should contact the controlling agency (not Flight Services) to make sure it is still cold. Typically the controlling agency will be a Center, such as Miami Center (abbreviated Miami Cntr). MOAs can go hot at any time, typically when a planned operation in another area doesn't have the weather for their mission. Again, you don't have to make this call, but you should.

Entering a Restricted or Warning Area

Restricted and Warning areas typically add additional dangers to pilots, such as live fire gunnery ranges and bombing runs. The restricted airspace is designated with a "R" followed by a number (e.g., R-2901A). Warning areas are designated with a "W" followed by a number (e.g., W-174A).

Unlike the MOA, you may not operate an aircraft in a restricted area unless the controlling agency has designated it as "cold."

Even if you have checked the FAA special use airspace website, *you still have to make a radio call* to ATC (or the controlling agency) before entering the Restricted Area.

Finding the Controlling Agency

You can find the controlling agency for MOAs, Restricted Areas and Warning Areas on the frequency section of the sectional chart (Typically on the lower left side of the back

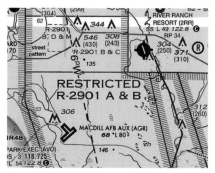

Restricted Area

Warning Area

of the chart).

You can also find the appropriate ATC and their frequency on some GPS units. Also, some iPad electronic flight charts will give you the information by touching on the area to bring up information.

If you are not in the habit of contacting Centers, you may be surprised when you discover the controlling agency on the sectional chart (for example Miami Cntr), there is no frequency printed. Due to the large area they cover, Centers have remote broadcast stations. These stations have different frequencies. You need to pick an ATC frequency that works with the ATC antenna that is closest to your location. This information is on the IFR enroute charts but not on the Sectionals. If you have flight planning software, it is possible you have IFR charts available to you. The frequency is printed in a box that looks like a postage stamp with wavy edges.

There are two other easy ways to locate the best Center contact frequencies. First, you can check the airport diagram page of a nearby airport. For example, if you were flying to a MOA or Restricted Area near Sebring, check the Sebring airport diagram in this book and the nearest Miami Center frequency (127.2) will be printed there.

If you can't find the frequency to use, contact any flight service station (FSS). The universal frequency is 122.2. Give your location to the (FSS) specialist who answers your call. Once the FSS specialist knows where you are, they will give you the correct frequency to contact Center.

Summary

With a quick call radio call to the controlling agency, there is no reason to avoid both MOAs and Restricted areas if they are cold. You'll save time and gas.

A WORD OF CAUTION TO PILOTS USING THIS GUIDE

Florida Pilots Guide is a **planning tool** for your adventures.

The information is collected from many sources and may not always be accurate. When you are ready to fly, all critical flight information must be verified by the user with official sources at the airport and by reference to official charts and publications.

We can not guarantee the accuracy of the material published nor guarantee against changes to airport facilities, frequencies or data, and assume no responsibility for the use of the contents of this manual.

Please be proactive and get all available information before your flight (FAR 91.103). Make sure you have current charts (electronic or paper) on board and use them. The guide is not intended to be used for navigation. *Fly safely!*

Amelia Island

Amelia Island and its town of Fernandina Beach has a colorful history of Pirates, Casinos and Brothels. Today it is a charming Victorian town with majestic sand dunes and a Civil War Fort.

Amelia Island has a lot of history. It is the only place in the state to have been claimed by eight different countries! The island is the first glimpse of Florida that southbound aviators and boaters see when they navigate down the coast from Georgia.

Depending on what you are looking for, Amelia Island can offer you a romantic getaway, a family vacation, championship golf, spectacular beaches, wonderful fishing, and even the option to ride horses on the beach.

Amelia Island holds the title of Florida's first resort, due to its location at the nexus of the railroads in the 1800s. Today, the Victorian buildings of that era in Fernandina Beach combine with bed and breakfasts, cozy shops, and galleries to make this a charming Victorian seaport village.

Well known for the **Amelia Island Plantation** resort started in 1971, the island's claims to fame are many. Classic car collectors all know about the annual **Amelia Concours d'Elegance** that has been taking place every spring for 20 years.

Fernandina Beach

The cozy village of Fernandina Beach is just a 10 minute drive north of the airport (KFHB), and the famed Amelia Island Plantation resort is only 10 minutes to the south.

Flying There

Flying from southern Florida can be a beautiful flight for the pilot and passengers. A GPS direct course can put you just off the coast all the way to KFHB. Note that 13 miles south of KFHB there are high and low MOAs around Mayport Naval Station KNRB. For transition contact them on 118.75. (NAS Jacksonville)

Flying from the north, maintaining an altitude of 3000 or higher will assure that you avoid a prohibited (P-50) area over the Kings Bay Naval Base in southeastern Georgia. P-50 has a 2-nm radius centered on the Brunswick vortac's 198-degree radial at 15.4 nautical miles, extending up to but not including 3,000 feet.

From the west you will encounter Jacksonville's semi-circular Class C airspace. Contact JAX approach (127.0) for a transition.

McGill Aviation *(904) 261-7890,* located east of

the terminal on taxiway A, has tie downs, Avgas and Jet fuel as well as a courtesy car available on a first come first served basis.

Getting Around

A walk to town from the airport would take an hour and a half, but driving time is only 10 minutes, so alternate means of transportation are necessary. If you are staying at one of the resorts and don't plan to venture off the property, they will most likely send a driver to pick you up.

Hertz *(904) 261-3728* rental cars are available at McGill Aviation.

The other on-airport car rental company is **Thrifty/ Dollar Car Rental** *(904) 261-3728.*

Multiple taxi and car services are available including **First Coast Transportation** *(904) 261-1130,* **Affordable Transportation** *(904) 469-0459,* and **Island Hopper Taxi** *(904) 624-5568.*

Scooter rentals are also available from **Amelia Island Adventure Rentals** *(904) 672-5512.* You should ideally call 24 to 48 hours ahead to reserve. They can deliver the scooters to the airport.

Walking Distance Activities

There is nothing really close enough to walk to.

What to See

A great place to start exploring is walking around Fernandina's 50 block historic district. The Silk Stocking district comprises over half of the historic district and has an elegant collection of over 400 structures built before 1927. Pick up a self-guided tour map at the chamber of commerce in the old train station.

Walking around the historic district you'll see, arguably, the country's finest collection of Victorian, Queen Anne, and Italianate homes.

Centre Street is the core of the historic commercial district. It ends at the shrimp dock. Gathering there at sunset to see the boats coming in is a local ritual as well as a photo opportunity.

The old brick commercial buildings are now the homes of gift shops, antique shops and restaurants. One place to stop is the **Palace Saloon.** Built in 1879, and a bar since 1903, you'll see the same bar front and mosaic tile floor today that patrons saw at the turn of the century. Florida's oldest continually operating bar — you can also stop in for lunch or dinner.

The Museum of History, *(904) 261-7378 Ext 105* just off Centre Street on 3rd, is a great place to learn about the history of the area. They have guided tours of the museum as well as walking tours of the town (book ahead). They even have a cell phone walking tour of the historic district available. For information call.

Fort Clinch State Park is just an 8 minute drive north of Fernandina's historic district. The fort was built in 1847 and was used by Confederate as well as Northern troops during the Civil War. Bought by the State of Florida in 1935 and restored during the depression by the Civilian Conservation Corps, it brings history to life. Park rangers wear Civil War uniforms. There are daily tours by period reenactors depicting garrison life. Candlelight tours are given on Saturday night. Once a month volunteers join the rangers to do a large scale reenactment. In addition to the well preserved fort, visitors can make a day out of the visit by fishing (surf and from the pier), exploring the 6-miles of trails on foot or bike, swimming and even camping.

Near the park is **Amelia Island Lighthouse.** Built in 1832, it is the oldest existing lighthouse in the state. It is only open two Wednesdays a month.

Beaches abound on the island. The **Main Beach Park** is probably the most popular

Downtown Fernandina Beach

and is a good destination for families. There are picnic tables, pavilions, a playground, barbecue grills, a boardwalk, outdoor showers, sand volleyball courts, restrooms and more. In addition there is a casual restaurant and bar on the beach. Next to the beach is a skate park and a miniature golf course (Putt-Putt) that serves refreshments.

Peters Point Beach is less than 2 miles from the airport. It is quieter than Main Beach Park and gives you access to the beautiful sand dunes enjoyed by the patrons of the Ritz Carlton. Fishing is allowed, and there are indoor showers, outdoor showers, tables and a picnic area. In season, there are also lifeguards.

What to Do
Being a tourist destination, there are a great number of activities available to you.

Kayaking
Kayak Amelia *(904) 251-0016* has guided nature tours that leave from several different locations.

Segway™ Tours
You can explore park trails on a **Segway™ tour** organized by **Kayak Amelia** *(904) 251-0016*.

Amelia's Wheels *(904) 277-5120* offers guided Segway™ tours through the Amelia Island Plantation's grounds giving you a view the ocean, forests, and marsh waterways. The tour is open to the public as well as to resort guests.

Ride a Horse on the Beach
Kelly Seahorse Ranch *(904) 491-5166* has Florida's only ranch on the beach. Located within Amelia Island State Park, they offer a one-hour guided beach horseback ride starting at their ranch.

Another stable offering this experience is **Ride the Beaches of Amelia Island** *(904) 277-7047*. They meet you at Peters Point Beach with horses and give you a friendly, relaxed experience.

Fernandina's historic district has two companies offering

Fernandina

tours. **Old Towne Carriage Company** *(904) 277-1555* offers a 30 minute tour. **Amelia Island Carriages** *(904) 556-2662* offers both standard tours and private tours that will allow you to design your own unique tour.

In Shore and Offshore Fishing
You can fish from the beach at the state parks and even the pier at Fort Clinch State Park. **Amelia Island Charters** *(904) 335-1162* has a shallow draft (8") boat for backwater fishing as well as a 24' catamaran style boat for venturing farther out. They also do wildlife

and sightseeing tours.

AC Charters *(904) 261-9481* has two well equipped sport fishing boats for offshore fishing and a flats boat for inshore fly fishing.

Golf
For golfers, Amelia Island has 117 holes of championship caliber golf.

Fernandina Beach Golf Club *(904) 310-3175* is one of the most popular municipal golf facilities in the country. Located next to the airport to the east, it features 27 holes. You fly directly over it landing on runway 27 or taking off on runway 9. If you book your tee time online, you will get a better rate.

Amelia River Golf Club *(904) 491-8500* is adjacent and south of the airport with holes 1, 5 and 13 paralleling two runways.

Omni Amelia Island Plantatation Resort has two golf courses. One was designed by Pete Dye and the other by Bobby Weed. If you are not staying at the resort, the only way to book a tee time is on golfnow.com. Select the "Jacksonville" area.

The Golf Club of Amelia Island is a private club with an oceanfront course. Guests at the Ritz-Carlton, Amelia Island receive playing privileges.

Where to Eat
Hola! Cuban Cafe *117 Centre St, North 2nd, Behind the Palace Saloon, Fernandina Beach, Amelia Island, FL 32034 (904) 321-0163* Great sandwiches and perhaps the best coffee in Fernandina Beach. Friendly service. They bake all their breads in-house. Only 4

tables inside but a large outdoor patio. Open 9am - 4pm. Closed Tuesday and Wednesday. $

España Restaurant & Tapas *22 S 4th St, Fernandina Beach, Amelia Island, FL 32034-4272 (904) 261-7700.* Located in historic downtown Fernandina Beach, it features traditional flavors from Spain and Portugal. It has a European feel with limited outdoor seating in a lovely garden area; an enclosed section looking out to the garden through windows; a small bar reminiscent of those in Spain and Portugal; and the main, cozy dining room. Open for dinner. $$

Le Clos *(904) 261-8100* is a charming, romantic French restaurant in an intimate converted 1906 cottage at 20 S. 2nd St. Opened in 1996, patrons say it is still one of the best restaurants in the area. Candlelite dinner Mon - Sat. $$$

Joe's 2nd Street Bistro *14 S. 2nd St. (904) 321-2558* is in a restored 1900's home. While the name and exterior seem rather plain, the inside is quiet and classy and the food gets rave reviews. They prepare almost everything in house including the mozzarella. There is also outdoor seating with umbrellas. Lunch and dinner. Closed Tuesday. $$

Salt *(904) 277-1100* is located in the Ritz-Carlton. Innovative cuisine, great views of the ocean and excellent service. They have a 300 bottle wine list. Reserve a seat in the kitchen to watch the chefs cook. Reservations are a must. Dinner. Closed Monday. $$$$

Where to Stay

Fairbanks House *227 S 7th St. (904) 277-0500* is a restored Italianate villa in the historic area. This B&B is set back from the road and is a quiet and romantic place to stay. It combines period details like claw foot tubs and 14 foot ceilings with contemporary comforts like a pool, iPhone docking station, Wi-Fi and flat screen TVs. Complimentary evening drinks and hors d'oeuvres. Of course you also get breakfast. $$$

Residence Inn Amelia Island *2301 Sadler Road, Fernandina Beach, FL 32034 (904) 277-2440* features modern suites with kitchens. Pet friendly. Not close enough to walk to the historic area, but has a shuttle that will take you where you want to go. Short walk to the beach. Full breakfast, pool, hot tub, free Wi-Fi, putting green and bike rentals. $$

Omni Amelia Island Plantation Resort and the Villas of Amelia Island Plantation *39 Beach Lagoon Road, Amelia Island, FL 32034 (800) 597-2155* A recent $85 million "re-imagination" created beautiful oceanfront beach club pools. Many amenities including three golf courses, a spa, restaurants and family friendly activities. With 1,350 acres, getting around may require their shuttle or golf cart. The Villas get mixed reviews. $$$

The Ritz-Carlton, Amelia Island *4750 Amelia Island Parkway, Amelia Island, FL 32034 (904) 277-1100* Beautiful grounds and beachfront location. An elegant resort with the renowned Ritz-Carlton service from their staff of 700 ladies and gentlemen. Heated indoor and outdoor pools. Golf course access, spa, fitness center, tennis, and the outstanding Salt restaurant. $$$$

Elizabeth Pointe Lodge *98 S. Fletcher Avenue, Fernandina Beach, Amelia Island, FL 32034 (904) 277-4851* is a modern B&B built to resemble the historic feel of the area. Located on the oceanside beach, it is very popular with guests although some find it pricy for what it is. The Lodge is known for friendly service, excellent breakfast and complimentary wine and hors d'oeuvres in the evening. Unlike most B&Bs, there is a lunch menu and 24-hour room service. Free Wi-Fi and parking. $$$$

Fairbanks House

Fernandina Beach Municipal, *Amelia Island* KFHB

UNICOM ©122.7

AWOS 118.075 904-277-7323

JACKSONVILLE App/Dep ®127.2

GCO 121.725 (Jacksonville Clnc AND
Gainesville FSS)

Elevation	Traffic Pattern	Flight Service Station
16' MSL	816' MSL (800')AGL)	800.WX.BRIEF

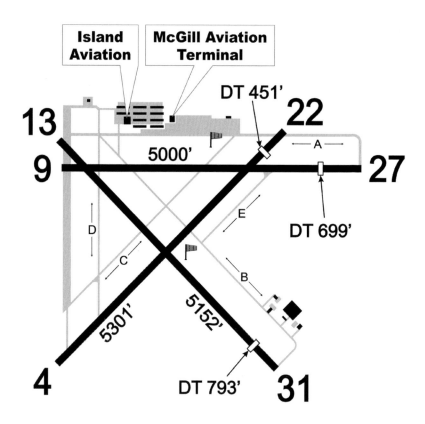

Not for navigation or inflight use | © 2017 Adventus Media LLC

Apalachicola

Apalachicola was established as a customs station in 1823. Today this town on Florida's "Forgotten Coast" attracts visitors seeking "Old Florida" with its restored houses and old New England flavor.

Apalachicola is in its fifth rebirth. Located at the mouth of the Apalachicola River, it first grew to prominence as a shipping center for King Cotton. When the cotton boom faded, sponge harvesting took over until there were hardly any sponges left. Next the lumber boom brought wealth to the town. As lumbering faded in the 1920s, oystering took over.

Today Apalachicola harvests 90% of all oysters in Florida representing 10% of the nation's total production. Shrimp, blue crab and a large variety of other fish come from its waters, making it great for lovers of fresh seafood to visit. This supports the city's newest development: tourism.

Just north of the town is the beginning of the Apalachicola National Forest stretching across four counties.

Flying There

Flying to Apalachicola Regional Airport (KAAF) takes you through Tyndall AFB's MOAs. Whether you will be on instrument plan or VFR, you will talk to Tyndall AFB as

Apalachicola

your final ATC contact. Flying VFR, they ask that you make radio contact with them as you first enter their MOAs (which cover the entire Panhandle). For Tyndall Approach use 124.15 to the south or 125.2 to the north for communication. On weekends or off hours when Tyndall is closed, contact Jacksonville Approach on 120.82. From the west, request transition of Pensacola's Class C airspace on 128.65, 118.6 or 119.0.

Be aware that there are at least four other airports on the two Unicom frequencies for KAAF and nearby F47, so you need to listen carefully.

Crystal Air *(850) 653-1366* has tie downs, fuel, free Wi-Fi, and a courtesy car. It is located on the south part of the field on the ramp off runway 32.

Getting Around

A walk to town from the airport would take an hour, but driving time is only eight minutes.

Car rental is limited here. The best best option is the car rental service at **Crystal Air.** *(850) 653-1366.*

Taxi service in Apalachicola is provided by **Croom's Transportation** *(850) 653-8132.*

Walking Distance Activities

Nothing of note.

What to See and Do

The town is a postcard picture waiting to be photographed with its elegant historic homes and its colorful oyster and fishing fleet.

In February 2007, Southern Living published a feature article called "Florida's Quiet Side." Author Wanda McKinney wrote:

"Morning comes gently to Apalachicola. Oyster boats and shrimp boats begin their daily pilgrimages into the seafood-rich bay as the sun rises on the Northwest Florida coast. The lights twinkle on in this fishing village, its residents ready for another day in unspoiled paradise. If you ever wondered if such a place still exists, yes, old Florida lives here. A lone blinking yellow light directs the downtown traffic. Come and stay awhile in this wonderful, walkable, watery hamlet."

Walking is easy in this town laid out in a compact grid. Pick up a walking map from the chamber of commerce. While you are wandering around town, explore over seven art galleries and many shops. Not to miss is the homage to Apalachicola's sponging past at the **Apalachicola Sponge Company,** *31 Avenue E. (850) 653-3550.*

The John Gorrie State Museum honors the physician who invented the first ice making machine in 1851. His goal was to help cool his yellow fever patients. While the northern natural ice lobby kept him from successfully marketing the machine, the museum, located on 6th street, has a replica of the machine on display.

Apalachicola Maritime Musuem, *103 Water Street, Apalachicola, FL 32320* provides a good background on the history of the area. They have a 58' Herreshoff Ketch, as well as a 75' paddle wheeler they are restoring. In addition the museum features a boat-building program for small boats, and you might see people doing some actual building. They also have a variety of boat tours available.

The Raney House Museum, *128 Market Street, Apalachicola* is one of the city's favorite attractions. The antebellum Greek Revival House was built in 1838 and is furnished in the style of the mid-1800s. The tour brings history to life and lets you visualize life as it was back in that time. Free, but donations accepted. *(850) 653-1700*

Orman House Historic State Park, *177 Fifth Street, Apalachicola, FL 32320* Built in 1838 by Thomas Orman, a cotton merchant, this antebellum home overlooks the Apalachicola River, and was used for both business and social gatherings. The grounds are beautiful and enchanting. The

Apalachicola National Forest

grounds also feature the Three Soldiers Detail, a bronze replica of the Vietnam memorial statue in Washington, D.C. $2

Chestnut Street Cemetery, *Ave E and 8th St., Apalachicola, FL 32320* Very old Southern cemetery (some graves dating from the 1700s) with lots of iron fencing, unique grave makers and historical plaques. See the names of the area's founders like Raney, Orman, and Coombs. Live oaks dripping with moss give it extra charm. Ghost tours are hosted by the Apalachicola Historical Society in May and October.

Where to Eat

The Owl Café *15 Avenue D, Apalachicola, FL 32320-1719 (850) 653-9888* is prominently located in a large clapboard building. A consistently popular place to eat with an innovative daily menu and a reliable everyday menu. Check the different dining areas like the Tap Room next door, and the wine room which has character and ambiance. The second floor dining room has a balcony so you can dine looking over the Apalachicola River. $$

Apalachicola Seafood Grill & Steakhouse, *100 Market St., Apalachicola, FL 32320 (850) 653-9510* This downtown restaurant is known for the "World's largest fried fish sandwich." Both tourists and locals eat here. Homey feel. Check out the flamingo painted on the ceiling. $$

Up the Creek Raw Bar, *313 Water St., Apalachicola, FL 32320-1427 (850) 653-2525* Informal place with a laid back atmosphere. Serves much more than raw oysters. There are outside tables available with a beautiful view of the river. $$

Hole In The Wall Seafood, *23 Ave D, Apalachicola, FL, (850) 653-3222* Located downtown, this small place has a limited menu, but to keep everything fresh and focused. It has a real Florida feel and is decorated with seashells and a wall of hats behind the bar. $$

Papa Joe's Oyster Bar & Grill, *45 Ave D, Apalachicola, FL 32320 (850) 653-1189* Used to be located on the water, but is now downtown. Not very fancy looking on the outside, but nice on the inside. Locals and visitors alike praise the food. $$

Tamara's Cafe Floridita, *71 Market St., Apalachicola, FL 32320 (850) 653-4111* Open for breakfast, lunch and dinner. Located in the historic district, the 1920's building has a stamped tin ceiling, original brick walls and a fresh bright color scheme. Nice change from the normal coastal restaurant menu. Still featuring seafood but with a latin influence. Has a tapas menu on Wednesday night. $$

Where to Stay

Riverwood Suites, *29 Avenue F, Apalachicola, FL 32320 (786) 574-9208* Serene place with a wonderful atmosphere and ambiance in the renovated historic Baltimore House built in 1908. They transformed the second floor of this building into 4 unique and beautiful suites. Downstairs there is a spa and an organic market. Its quiet location on the edge of this small town makes it easy to walk to local establishments. $$

The Consulate, *76 Water Street, Apalachicola, FL 32320 (850) 653-1515* This building was built in 1880 by the JE Brady Co, as a hardware and ships store. The second floor, in the early 1900s, housed the French Consulate, the Captain of the Port and the U.S. Customs office. Today the second floor (the former French Consulate) has been refashioned into four luxury suites overlooking the Apalachicola River. All of the suites have fully-equipped kitchens, flat screen TVs with Blu-ray players, internet access, laundry facilities and balconies. $$$

Gibson Inn *51 Ave. C, Apalachicola, FL 32320 (850) 653-2191* Listed on the National Historic Register of Historic Places, The Gibson Inn is a fine example of Florida "Cracker" Architecture. Built in 1907, it is in the heart of downtown. The rooms are smaller with no amenities like a coffee maker or refrigerator. The three story building also has no elevator. There are comfy wrap around porches and ornate woodwork. There is a grand lobby and a wonderful old bar with the charm of a sophisticated upscale bar. $$

Coombs House Inn, Bed and Breakfast, *80 Sixth Street, Apalachicola, FL 32320. (850) 653-9199* Romantic Victorian B&B consisting of three mansions with period antique decorations and very well appointed common areas and rooms. All rooms have private bathrooms (7 feature jacuzzis). Some 2 to 3 room suites are available, and a few come with kitchenettes and private verandas. Free Wi-Fi internet, in-room coffee and flat screen cable TVs. No elevator. Guests report that rooms facing US 98 can suffer from traffic noise. $$$

Apalachicola Regional, *Apalachicola*　　KAAF

UNICOM ©122.8

Airport Manager Phone
(850) 653-2222

ASOS 119.925 (850) 653-8271

®TYNDALL App/Dep 125.2 (North above 5000)

®TYNDALL App/Dep 124.15 (South above 5000)

Elevation 20' MSL	Traffic Pattern 820' MSL (800')AGL)	Flight Service Station 800-WX-BRIEF

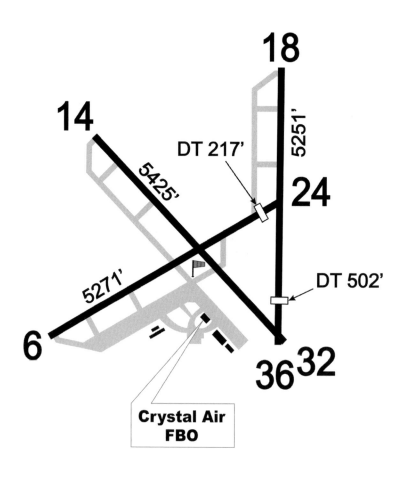

DT 217'

DT 502'

5251'

5425'

5271'

18

14

24

6

36 32

Crystal Air FBO

Cedar Key

A very out-of-the-way pilot's favorite is one of Florida's most charming towns with great seafood and friendly residents. This old Victorian town of 900 once used its barrier island location to bypass the Union's blockade during the Civil War.

Cedar Key Airport

Cedar Key is actually a group of islands called the Cedar Keys, the largest of which is Cedar Key. It is rich in small town flavor. One of the oldest ports in the state, in the 1800's, it was a bustling center of commerce. When Florida's first railroad connected it to the east coast, it became a major supplier of seafood and timber products to the northeast.

Its cedar trees lured pencil makers Eagle and Eberhard Faber to build mills there. But a 1896 hurricane flattened everything and put an end to manufacturing on the islands.

Cedar Key's industry today is tourism and seafood. It has also become a haven for artists and writers who find the unspoiled environment inspirational to their work.

In addition to excellent fishing, birdwatching and nearby nature trails, guides are available to take parties for off-shore trips to the outer islands. A public marina with boat docking is available.

Federally protected sanctuaries, the Cedar Keys form a chain of barrier islands ideally suited to a vast range of migratory and shore birds, including the elusive white pelican, roseate spoonbill and bald eagle. The variety of natural habitats, from salt marshes to Indian shell mounds, makes this truly a nature lover's paradise.

Flying There

No surrounding controlled airports impede the approach to Cedar Key. Set right on the Gulf, it is just northeast of the Cedar Keys National Wildlife Refuge. Aircraft are requested to keep 2,000 feet above the refuge.

The runway is the shortest paved runway of Florida's public airports, measuring only 2,355 feet long by 100 feet wide. Landing on Runway 5, the landing distance available is the full 2,355 feet. A displaced threshold shortens Runway 23 by 338 feet, so you only end up with 2,017 feet. If you don't touch down in the first 1/3 of the runway, go around.

The entire airport perimeter is fenced with a 4-foot tall chain-link fence. There is a walk-through gate near the normal aircraft parking area. The combination to the gate is 5-2-3.

With erratic runway lights, no beacon and no instrument approach, Cedar Key is best used as a daytime or overnight destination.

Getting Around

Town is just a mile from the airport so it is about a 30 minute walk into town. Judy's Taxi's well known white Checker Cab has been replaced by a mini-van, but Judy *(352) 949-2127* is still the way many pilots choose to get to town. Since cell service is unreliable at the airport, most pilots call Judy for a pickup on CTAF 122.9 about 5 miles out.

If you want to use a golf cart to get around town, the **Gulf Kart Company** *(352) 477-0041* can set you up with two to six passenger carts. With advanced notice they can also meet you at the airport with a cart.

Walking Distance Activities

There is nothing adjacent to the field, but town is just a 30 minute walk away. **Cedar Key Paddling,** *12292 State Road 24, Cedar Key, FL (352) 665-1276* will launch kayaks at two locations right next to the airport.

What to See and Do

Cedar Key Historical Society Museum *2nd Street and SR24, 609 2nd Street, Cedar Key, FL 32625 (352) 543-5549* Good first stop when visiting Cedar Key. Lots of information. You can get brochures detailing self-guided tours of the historic district. The museum features two buildings recounting the history of Cedar Key and nearby islands. $2.

The Cedar Key Chamber of commerce. *450 Second St., Cedar Key, FL (352) 543-5600* Excellent source of information about what to do and where to eat and shop while visiting Cedar Key. The Chamber is closed on Tuesday and Wednesday.

Cedar Keys National Wildlife Refuge is a group of coastal islands just off the village of Cedar Key, Florida. Established in 1929 the Refuge contains natural and cultural resources from pre-historic and historic times. The Refuge consists of 13 islands totaling 762 acres. Ancient Indian cultures once used these off-shore islands as camps, later creating living areas. In more recent history, the Faber Pencil Mill was located on Atsena Otie Key where its remains can be seen today.

Wading birds, shorebirds, fish, manatees, bald eagles, crabs, and even reptiles are some of the species of wildlife that inhabit the islands and marshes that make-up Cedar Keys National Wildlife Refuge. The Refuge has a major seabird rookery and an 1850's lighthouse on Florida's highest coastal elevation. Access is by boat.

Boat Tour and Rental

Tidewater Tours, *#4 Dock Street, Cedar Key City Marina, Cedar Key, FL 32625-4742 (352) 543-9523* has a tour that will take you around the is-

lands.

If you want to go on your own, you will need to rent a boat. Most public use at Cedar Keys is focused on Atsena Otie Key. Here visitors will find a pier, toilet facility, and a walking trail to a 19th century cemetery. Tidewater Tours (see above) also rents pontoon and skiffs for you to captain.

Kayaking

You can also kayak from the marina to Atsena Otie Key. It is only 0.6 miles. Once there you can beach your kayak and hike the trail past the remains of the old pencil mill, the cistern and the civil war cemetery. **Kayak Cedar Keys,** Next the marina. *1st St. and A St., Cedar Key, FL 32625 (352) 543-9447* has rentals available.

Fishing

Fishing in the Gulf is popular. There are a number of charter captains available.

A popular captain is Jim Keith and his son, Jimbo at **Saltwater Assassin Fishing Charters,** *Dock Street, Cedar Key, FL 32625 (352) 535-5083*

Voyles Guide Service, *8070 A St, Cedar Key Boat Dock, Cedar Key, FL 32625. 352-339-2034.* Captain Dennis is polite, funny, kind, patient and above all the man knows how to put you on the fish. Inshore from trout to tarpon, offshore from grouper to goliath grouper, you won't be disappointed.

A J Brown Charters, *Dock St., Boat Ramp, Cedar Key, FL 32625, 352 543 9701* Captain AJ Brown will make sure you have a good time. He is a lifelong fisherman in the Cedar Key Area and uses that knowledge and experience to

The best clam chowder in New England is served at Tony's Seafood Restaurant

help you catch fish.

Where to Eat

Kona Joe's Island Cafe, *4051 D Street, Near the corner of SR24 and 6th Street, Cedar Key, FL 32625 (352) 543-9898* Extremely popular small cafe on the salt marsh, located away from touristy bustle of the Gulf-side strip. Open for breakfast and lunch. $

Tony's Seafood Restaurant, *597 2nd St., Cedar Key, FL 32625 (352) 543-0022* The best clam chowder in New England is served here in Cedar Key. Tony famously took his clam chowder to New England's Great Chowder Cook-off and won the competition in 2009, 2010 and 2011 before retiring into the Great Chowder Cook-off Hall of Fame. This small, popular restaurant is open for lunch and dinner. $$

Annie's Cafe, *6th Street, Cedar Key, FL 32625 (352) 543-6141.* Lovely, quirky little place serving breakfast and lunch. Always full, mostly with local residents. Great food and water views. $

Steamers Clam Bar & Grill, *420 Dock St, Cedar Key, FL 32625-5168 (352) 543-5142.* This restaurant is on a pier on the gulf with great views — especially at sunset. Very fresh seafood. Open for lunch and dinner. $$

Where to Stay

Low-Key Hideaway, *12050 State Road 24, Cedar Key, FL 32625 (352) 543-0700* Calling themselves a "Couple's Retreat," this adults only destination has a motel, RV campground and Tiki Bar. It is the perfect place to get away from it all, kick back and relax. It is about a mile or so from downtown, but there are beach cruiser bicycles you can use. $$

Faraway Inn, *847 Third Street, Cedar Key, FL 32625 (888) 543-5330* Peaceful location on the waterfront. Spacious rooms. Very pet friendly. The location is within walking distance of Dock St. and the restaurants, pier and grocery store. Bikes, kayaks and grills are available for your use. They also have four-seat golf cart rentals for $65/day. $

Pirates Cove Bayside Cottages *13633 State Rd 24, Cedar Key, FL 32625* for a real "Old Florida" experience, this place has it in spades. There are six cottages of which two have attached screened-in porches that look over the water. Each cottage has a microwave and a small refrigerator. Well-maintained and within walking distance to most things. $

Cedar Key Runway 23 Approach

George T Lewis, *Cedar Key* | KCDK

CTAF ©122.9

Airport Manager Phone
[352] 486-5216

Elevation	Traffic Pattern	Flight Service Station
11' MSL	800 MSL	800-992-7433

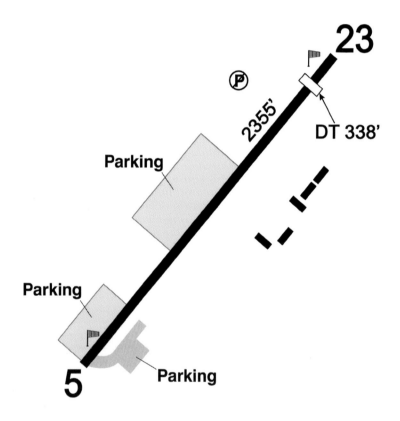

Not for navigation or inflight use | © 2017 Adventus Media LLC

Clearwater

With a name like "Clearwater," it's surely no surprise that almost all the attractions focus on the water. There are beaches and boat tours galore. Oh and check out the Sim Center where you can fly an F-16, a Boeing 737, or the 3D space simulator.

When you realize that Clearwater holds a record in the Guinness Book of World Records for the most consecutive days of sunshine (361 days!) in a year, you know that this is the place to go for fun in the sun. The west coast of Clearwater is lined with white sand beaches and busy marinas, where you can find many days worth of entertainment in swimming, boating or fishing.

The settling of the area revolved around Fort Harrison, built in 1835 to protect the harbor. As the population grew, the reputation of the beaches made it a popular vacation spot even in the late 1800s. Today, the population of Clearwater is around 110,000 and the city is pretty much contiguous with the larger metropolitan area of Tampa. Celebrities like Lisa Marie Presley, Kirstie Alley and Hulk Hogan have all lived in Clearwater at some time, owning some spectacular beach-front property.

Though mainly known for its beaches, there really is more

Sunset at the Beach in Clearwater

to do in Clearwater than just sunbathe. Many coastal areas have been designated as protected parks, where you can see the more natural side of Clearwater. Sand Key Park and Moccasin Lake Nature Park are two of the best.

Clearwater is small enough for easy transportation as you see the sights, but large enough that you can find just about anything you might need during your travels.

Flying There

KPIE is surrounded by airports in the busy Tampa/St. Petersburg airspace. Flying from north the easiest approach is to come down the coast staying under Tampa International's 3000 foot class B floor. As you turn east to approach KPIE, you will have to keep under a lower 1,200 foot floor from Tampa International. Flying from south or east Florida, it is probably best to call Tam-

Pier 60

pa approach on 125.3. Note: 20 miles to the east there are several TV towers up to 1,670 feet to avoid.

Also note the heavy fast military traffic to the northeast and south of MacDill Air Force Base (KMCF) from 1,000 to 2,500 feet over Tampa Bay.

While the airport is big and handles large jets like Alegiant Air's MD80s, the FBOs are happy to handle small aircraft. Both FBOs are on the west side of the field.

Signature Flight Support *(727) 531-1441* has Starbucks coffee, popcorn and cookies for pilots as well as a pilot shop.

Sheltair *(727) 530-3453* also has refreshments, shuttle services and crew cars available.

Getting Around

If you are going straight to a hotel on the beach or a B&B, the easiest way to do it might be taking the **Super Shuttle** *(727) 572-1111* from the airport, although that means you will be sharing a ride with others. **Sheltair** *(727) 530-3453* has **Hertz** rental cars available. **Signature** *(727) 531-1441* features **National** car rentals.

If you're looking to get

around the various beaches of Clearwater, the **Suncoast Beach Trolley** is the way to go. It runs every half hour, 5 a.m. until 10 p.m. and seven days a week. For more urban travel, the **Pinellas Suncoast Transit Authority** (PSTA) runs a complete network of buses all across Clearwater. Fare is $2, or you can explore the city all day for a $4.50 GO card.

main terminal in about five minutes where you can eat at the **Sam Adams Grille.** Its second floor location gives you a great view of the airport and Old Tampa Bay. They are open for breakfast, lunch and dinner.

What to See and Do

SimCenter *483 Mandalay Ave, Clearwater Beach Clearwater, FL 33764 (727) 643-1781* For a little high-tech thrill seeking, the SimCenter offers a range of automotive and flight simulator experiences. Do a few laps in a Formula 1 race car, or take an F-16 up into combat. There is also a Boeing 737 simulator, F-35 simulator and a new 3D Space simulator. It's about a 25 minute drive from the airport, but you need to call ahead to book your simulator time.

Clearwater Marine Aquarium *249 Windward Passage, Clearwater, FL 33767 (727)*

Fly the Full Size, Very Realistic Boeing 737 Cockpit Simulator at the SimCenter

Walking Distance Activities

The airport is on the east side of Clearwater, and unfortunately most of the beaches are on the other side of town. You can walk from FBO **Signature Flight Support** to the

441-1790 is one of the biggest attractions in town. Their exhibits include sea turtles, otters, sharks, stingrays and countless tanks of fish from around the world. Of course, they are famous for their dolphin residents as well. Winter's

Dolphin Tale Adventure is a new exhibit at the aquarium, and provides a more detailed look at dolphin life and the "Dolphin Tale" movie.

Fishing

Sport fishing is a popular activity around Clearwater, and there is no shortage of charter opportunities. **Above Average Charters** is at *25 Causeway Blvd. at Slip #28 (727) 365-7931*. They know where to find the big fish, like grouper, barracuda and king mackerel. **Gulfstream II Fishing Charters** is at the same marina, but at *Slip #34 (727) 442-6339* and their 50-foot Gulfstream yacht can take you up to 100 miles offshore to find grouper, red snapper and several other large sport fish.

Fishing from shore is popular at **Pier 60,** the 1,080 foot concrete pier. *Memorial Causeway, Clearwater, FL (727) 462-6466*. Bring your own fishing gear or rent at the on-pier bait shop, then try your luck fishing in the Gulf from the outer pier - day or night. Daily fishing fees: Adults: $8.00, Seniors: $6.75 Children 15 and under: $5.25. Rent a pole for additional $8.

Beaches

Clearwater is most famous for its lovely beaches, and you can take your pick from several excellent spots. The main one is **Clearwater Beach** at the end of State Road 60, 1 Causeway Blvd. The white sand is smooth and clean, and there are lots of shops and restaurants around. It's across town from the airport, but right near the Aquarium. You can also stroll along the shores at **Sand**

Key Park, *1060 Gulf Blvd*. It's much more peaceful, and perfect for relaxing.

On the other hand, you can have a more entertaining time along the boardwalks of **Pier 60,** on the Memorial Causeway. There, you can walk along the coast and check out musical performers, vendor stalls and lots of food stands. Sunset at Pier 60 is a daily tradition for visitors and locals to gather to see the bay front sunsets. The action starts about two hours before sunset. Friday and Saturdays they have "Sunset Cinema" at Pier 60 where they show free outdoor movies on the grass near the entrance to the Pier. Bring your own blankets or chairs.

Dolphin Experiences

If you didn't get enough dolphin action at the Aquarium, there are places in Clearwater where you can get even closer and more personal. **Encounters with Dolphins,** *25 Causeway Blvd., Clearwater, FL 33767 (727) 466-0375* will take you out on their 40 foot excursion boat to see dolphins in the wild. You can also take in a little shell collecting or snor-

keling during your tour. At the same marina, you can book a similar dolphin tour with **Little Toot Dolphin Adventures** *(727) 446-5503*. What makes Little Toot different is that they use an authentic 40 foot tug boat. It's wake makes a large wave, allowing the dolphin to jump and play in it.

Boat Tours

Besides the dolphin tours, there are other ways to get out on the water to see the sights of Clearwater. **Captain Memo's Pirate Cruise,** *Clearwater Marina (727) 446-2587* is particularly fun if you enjoy a swashbuckling theme as you sail around the bay. For a little bit of everything, **Dream Catcher Explorations** at Slip #32 will take you on a superb boat tour along the coast that includes some dolphin watching, tube riding, and a stop at the **3 Rooker Bar Wildlife Preserve.**

Where to Eat

Cristino's Coal Oven Pizza *1101 South Fort Harrison Avenue, Clearwater, FL 33756 (727) 443-4900* While not in the beach area, this extremely popular restaurant is open from

Having a Close Encounter with a Dolphin

Captain Memo's Pirate Cruise

early breakfast until well after dark so you can get a fine meal of classic Italian cuisine anytime. Though they're famous for their wide menu of real brick oven pizzas, you can get all sorts of other dishes at Cristino's too. The atmosphere is small and cozy, and the servers are very friendly. Nice, shaded, outside patio-style tables are also available. $$

Clear Sky Beachside Cafe *490 Mandalay Ave., Clearwater, FL 33767 (727) 442-3684* The menu is a varied mix of casual snacks and international cuisine, including a nice range of very fresh seafood. Have a quick lunch or kick back on the outdoor patio and linger over some drinks. $

Salt n Pepper Bistro *1757 Clearwater-Largo Road, Clearwater, FL 33756 (727) 585-3500.* The Salt n' Pepper Bistro is one of the most popular eateries in Clearwater, so you should try to have at least one meal there while you're in town. It will be an elegant night of excellent French cuisine. Certainly not the cheapest place to eat in Clearwater, but you'll enjoy every bite. The

atmosphere is classy, but they don't expect you to get dressed up. $$$

Mano's Bakery Cafe *1971 Drew Street, Clearwater, FL 33765 (727) 614-9748* When you're in the mood to indulge in something sweet, make a stop at Mano's Bakery. They serve up a range of traditional Greek pastries, like bougatsa and spanakopites. There is also plenty of fresh bread, salads and sandwiches if you want a meal for lunch. Top it off with a coffee or espresso. $

Frenchy's Original Cafe *41 Baymont St, Clearwater, FL 33767 (727) 446-3607* There are several different Frenchy's in Clearwater, but this location is the one that Chef Alton Brown featured on his show. He states his favorite dish in Clearwater is their french fries covered in snow crab! He also called their grouper sandwich one of the best that he's had.

Where to Stay

Sandpearl Resort *500 Mandalay Avenue, Clearwater, FL 33767 (727) 441-2425* For some high-class accommodations, the Sandpearl Resort will

make an impression. There is a full-service spa, top-notch dining options and some spectacular beach views. It might be a bit extravagant for some, but it's worth checking out.

Holiday Inn St. Petersburg North/Clearwater *3535 Ulmerton Road, Clearwater (877) 859-5095* If you are looking for accommodations near the airport, this hotel is on the airport grounds. Since it is located across the field from the terminal and FBO, they will pick you up. Staff gets great reviews for being responsive and friendly.

Laughing Lizard Bed and Breakfast *2211 Gulf Blvd., Clearwater, FL (727) 595-7066* For a more personal experience, the Laughing Lizard is a cozy B&B that will make you feel at home. Walk across the street to the small town beach. The rooms are bright and very colorful, and having been built in the past 10 years, you'll have modern amenities. Visitors report the rooms are quiet. They serve a hearty breakfast every morning in the common dining room. The wine tasting event each afternoon at 5:30 is a nice touch.

St Pete-Clearwater International | KPIE

TOWER ©**118.3**
(0600-2300)

GROUND CONTROL 121.9

Control Tower Phone
(727) 539-6867

Airport Manager
(727) 453-7800

ASOS (727) 531–3456

ATIS 134.5

®TAMPA APP/DEP CON 125.3

CLNC DEL 120.6

UNICOM 122.95

Elevation 10' MSL	Traffic Pattern 800' MSL (810'AGL)	Flight Service Station ST PETERSBURG 122.1R 122.2 122.45 123.6 116.4T

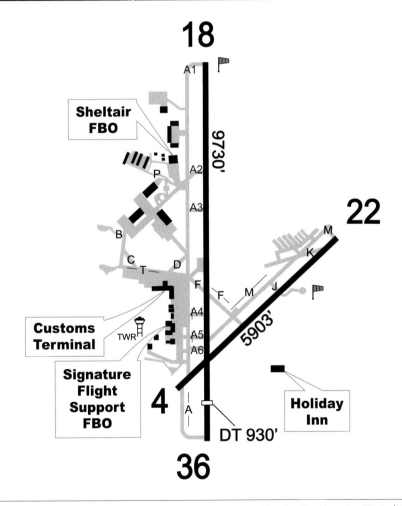

18

A1

Sheltair
FBO

9730'

P   A2

A3

B

C T   D

F

F   M   J

22

M

K

Customs
Terminal

TWR

A4

A5

5903'

A6

Signature
Flight
Support
FBO

4

A

Holiday
Inn

DT 930'

36

KCGC

Crystal River

It's all about the manatees! If you'd like to find the right spot to see these gentle giants out in the wild, then plan your flight to Crystal River. Rent a boat or kayak and paddle the clear waters of Crystal River. You never know what you might see!

Famous for its manatee population, **Crystal River** is a destination for anyone who enjoys seeing unspoiled nature at its finest.

There were Native American settlements in the Crystal River area as far back as 500 BC. By the time Europeans moved in, the area was mysteriously abandoned. Not long after the Civil War, the region began to see wealth and development from citrus farming that was started after residents found many wild trees that grew from seeds left by Spanish explorers. The fruit industry collapsed in 1894 due to a brutal cold spell that paved the way for other industries to move in, and the town flourished.

These days, Crystal River is a magnet for tourists who want to see the manatees that flock to the river and the bay every year to enjoy the clear warm waters. They are such peaceful animals that you can safely swim in the water with them, and it's quite an experience. Dozens of tour companies in Crystal River will rent boats

Manatees

and charter tours to watch these animals every year.

If you are coming to Crystal River for the manatees, keep an eye on the calendar. Though they're around all year, the best time for viewing is in the winter. Plan on visiting sometime between October and April.

Flying There

There are no surrounding controlled airports impeding the approach to Crystal River. Set just east of the Gulf,

it is 20 nautical miles north of Tampa's Class B airspace. **The Crystal River National Wildlife Refuge** is just to the north west, and aircraft are requested to keep 2,000 feet above the refuge.

The paved runway is an ample 4555 feet long. There is also a 2665 turf runway. **The Crystal Aero Group** *(352) 795-6868* is the FBO, and they have a nice, clean facility with a friendly staff. **Enterprise Rental Car,** *(352) 563-5511* is just 100 yards away.

Crystal River

Walking Distance Activities

If you would like to fly in for a **Blizzard**® shake, an ice cream cone (or some fast food) there is a **Dairy Queen** right next to runway 18! A ten-minute walk to the north will bring you to a Greek restaurant/diner called **The Olive Tree** *(352) 563-0075* Open 6:30 a.m. to 9 p.m. every day, they serve breakfast all day long including a $1.99 special with eggs, hash browns and toast. Many Greek dishes are served for lunch and dinner.

On the other side of the grounds, the **Seven Rivers Golf Club** *(352) 795-2100* is now open to non-members if you are looking for a new place for a round of golf or to enjoy the bar and grill.

What to See and Do

Crystal River National Wildlife Refuge *1502 S.E. Kings Bay Dr., Crystal River, FL 34429 (352) 563-2088* Not to be confused with the larger **Crystal River Preserve State Park** (which is south of the city), this wildlife refuge is one of the protected manatee areas. If you're not interested in taking a guided manatee tour, a visit to this refuge is a great option. Not only can you see manatees, but there are enclosures of alligators as well as a large number of wild birds.

Crystal River Archaeological State Park *(352) 795-38117* For a different kind of outdoor experience, you can visit a site of **Native American burial mounds**. This is probably the longest continuously occupied place in Florida having been used as an Indian ceremonial center from 200 BC to 1400 AD. The visitor's center

Yulee Sugar Mill Ruins State Historic Site

has a whole gallery of artifact exhibits as well as the history of the site. The walk among the mounds is peaceful, and you'll get some nice views of the surrounding countryside. The center may be closed on Tuesdays and Wednesdays, so plan your trip accordingly.

Yulee Sugar Mill Ruins *3400 N. Museum Pointe, Crystal River, FL (352) 795-3817* Take a smaller step back in time to see some more modern history at the ruins of the Yulee Sugar Mill. If you're heading south toward the Chassahowitzka River and Coastal Swamps Park, then you should make a quick detour to see the sugar mill ruins site. The remains of a big old sugar press are still there, surrounded by the stone walls and chimney of the old factory.

Three Sisters Springs *Kings Bay Dr., Crystal River, FL 34429* There are dozens of springs that all feed Kings Bay, but the **Three Sisters Springs** claim to be the loveliest of them all. It's near the refuge so you're almost guaranteed to see pods of manatees slowly swimming through the clear water. Many visitors say this is the best place of all to see the manatees.

Manatee Tours

The big draw in Crystal River is being able to see the large population of local manatees — *and swim with them* (an activity rarely allowed anywhere else). Seeing manatees in the wild is something uniquely Floridian, and this is one of the best places in the state to do it. Just plan your visit between October and April to have the best sightings.

Manatee Fun *PO Box 1226, Crystal River, FL (352) 601-6576* offers excellent private tours if you don't like the crowds. Not only can you watch manatees swim from the houseboat, but also you'll get the opportunity to swim or snorkel with them.

Manatee Paddle *544 N Citrus Avenue, Crystal River, FL 34428 (352) 564-0901* keeps it simple and lets you take a personal paddle board out among the manatees for a very unique and personal encounter. The **River Ventures Manatee Tour Center** *498 S.E. Kings Bay Drive, Crystal River, FL 34429 (352) 564-8687* is just a short drive up Hwy 19 from the airport, and they can help you arrange the right type of tour. They have group tours on houseboats but they also rent out kayaks if you want a smaller craft.

If you prefer to see the sights on your own, you can just rent a kayak at **Captain Mike's Kayak Rental** *1610 SE Paradise Circle (352) 364-5557* and go paddling around the Bay.

Where to Eat

The Olive Tree mentioned in "walking distance activities," is the closest restaurant.

Grannie's Restaurant *1712 SE US Highway 19, Crystal River, FL 34429 (352) 795-8884* Less than a mile north of the airport (16 minute walk), this is anther spot to go for breakfast or brunch. All the locals know it's the best place in town for all-day breakfasts. It's nothing fancy, but the taste is all Southern home cooking. You can get your usual breakfast dishes, including grits and

Three Sisters with Kayakers

biscuits with gravy. They open extra early at 5 a.m. but close at 3 p.m. $

Vintage on 5th *114 NE 5th St., Crystal River, FL 34429 (352) 794-0004* Not quite as close to the airport as the first two, but very convenient once you're in the downtown area. Vintage on 5th looks like a lovely little cottage from the outside, so you can imagine that the dining room is going to be comfortable and cozy. The style is actually quite elegant, and in the evenings it is a busy wine bar. $$

Burkes of Ireland *564 N Citrus Ave., Crystal River, FL 34428 (352) 795-0956* For a fun casual downtown night out, grab a pint at Burkes of Ireland. Beer aficionados will love the diverse selection of brews on tap, and the crowd is always friendly as are the husband and wife owners. The decor is classic "pub," and they have patio seating outside. This is where you want to go after a long day of walking or sight-seeing. $$

Where to Stay

Plantation on Crystal River *9301 West Fort Island Trail, Crystal River, FL 34429 (352) 765-1368* For luxury surroundings without the price

tag, the grand Plantation delivers. It really does look like an old Southern plantation estate house, complete with columns at the front entrance and nicely groomed grounds. The rooms are comfortable, and you'll be within walking distance of the Bay and marina if you are planning any manatee tours. $$

Hampton Inn Crystal River *1103 N Suncoast Blvd., Crystal River, FL 34429 (352) 564-6464* If you want a handy place to stay that's just moments from the airport, then get a room at the Hampton Inn Crystal River. The hotel is newly built, so you won't have to worry about run-down grounds or dated rooms. There's a pool, fitness center, free Wi-Fi, and though they don't have a restaurant, they do offer a free hot breakfast bar. $$

Crystal Cove B&B *244 NE 2nd Court, Crystal River, FL (352) 586-3532* The Crystal Cove is a friendly little B&B that is just steps away from the marina and boat tours. There is a spring right on the property, and there are great waterfront views from the rooms. Not a lot of amenities, but the rooms are very pretty and clean, and they do have private bathrooms. $$

Crystal River

KCGC

UNICOM ©**122.725**

Airport Manager Phone
[352] 795-6868

AWOS-3 118.325 [352] 563-6600

JACKSONVILLE ®App/Dep 118.6

Elevation	Traffic Pattern	Flight Service Station
9' MSL	800' MSL [791']AGL)	800-WX-BRIEF

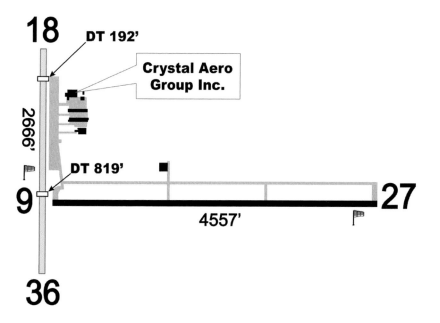

18

DT 192'

Crystal Aero Group Inc.

2666'

DT 819'

9

27

4557'

36

KDAB

Daytona Beach

Daytona Beach really needs no introduction. Its famous beach is legendary though you may be just as familiar with the Daytona Speedway. Back in the day, the long stretches of beaches were actually used as a raceway, which is where the city's love of motorsports was born.

The long uninterrupted stretches of sandy beaches drew automobile racers as far back as the early 1900s, starting what would become a long history of racing in Daytona. Land speed records were frequently set in Daytona Beach, and eventually a race track was built in 1958. The Daytona International Speedway is still famous today.

Though the annual Daytona 500 race is one of the biggest events of the year, late October brings Biketoberfest as well. More than 100,000 motorcycle enthusiasts descend on the city for a huge rally.

Daytona Speedway From the Air

Flying There

Arrival from the north, down the coast, presents the fewest challenges, with only the two Class D airports of Flagler and Ormond Beach along the way.

From the west, consider arriving via Gainesville and then flying east to the St. John's River to avoid the Palatka 1 and 2 Military Operations Areas, which contain several Restricted Areas. If you want to fly through the Palatka MOAs and restricted areas, the controlling authority to see if they are hot is SEALORD on 134.65.

Pilots flying in from the southwest below or through Orlando's Class B airspace should be alert for a pair of 1,700-foot tall towers in the Deltona area, as well as the R-2910B and C Restricted Areas and Sanford's Class C airspace.

Coming up the Indian River from the south, following the

V 3 airway from Melbourne to Ormond Beach will ensure clearance from Orlando's Class B to the west and the Restricted Areas of Cape Canaveral to the east. IFR traffic on V 3 flies at odd thousands northbound and even thousands southbound.

DAB is a hive of flight training activity, with mainline commercial air service and business aviation traffic in the mix as well. After receiving ATIS on 120.05, contact Daytona Beach Approach

Ponce de Leon Lighthouse

control for arrival instructions and sequencing to the airport. At 3,500 feet and below, use 125.80 from the north or 125.35 from the south within 20 nm of DAB. From 4,000 feet to 7,500 feet, 127.075 from the north or 118.85 from the south.

On the ground, you may be asked to stay on the right side of the taxiway to permit other small aircraft to taxi in the opposite direction.

Consistent with the size of the airport and the amount of traffic, all three FBOs offer high levels of service, including crew cars. Minimum fuel purchase and facility fees vary depending on class of aircraft.

Yelvington Jet Aviation is located south of the main runway (7L/25R) across from the commercial terminal and just west of the control tower. They offer full- and self-serve 100LL fuel and full-service jet A. Hertz car rental available. Open 7 a.m. to 9 p.m. Call them at *(386) 257-7791* or *(888) DAB-JETA,* on private radio frequency 129.70, or email csr@yjeta.com.

ATP Jet Center is a full-service FBO operated by the ATP flight school on the southeastern ramp, east of runway 16/34. Full-service 100LL and jet A and self-serve 100LL. Open 0800-2000 (SS 100LL 24/7). After-hours jet A by reservation. *(386) 385-8880* or *(877) ATP-JETS,* UNICOM 122.95, or dab@atpjetcenter.com.

Sheltair offers full-service 100LL and jet A, and is located on the north ramp east of runway 16/34. Hertz car rental available. Open 5:30 a.m. to 11 p.m. *(callout fee after hours).* Telephone *(386) 255-0471.*

Getting Around

There is a great public bus system in Daytona (Votran) *(386) 424-6800* that can take you all over the city. Single fares are $1.50 or an all-day pass goes for $3.50. Routes 18 and 19 serve the airport and will take you right downtown or to the beaches. These bus stops are a nine minute walk from **Sheltair** and are located in front of the **Residence Inn.** For a little more convenience, call yourself a cab from **Day-** tona Taxi *(386) 257-7777* or **Tri-Stars Taxi** *386-860-8888* for a pick-up to your hotel or to head straight out to the beach.

You can also arrange for a rental car. **Shetair** has Hertz, **Yelvington Aviation** has Enterprise and Hertz. The commercial terminal has eight different car rental agencies.

Walking Distance Activities

One of the best attractions in Daytona is actually located right on the airport grounds. **The Daytona International Speedway** is literally just moments from the runways. You can walk to the entrance of the Speedway (and the **Richard Petty Driving Experience**) from Sheltair in 18 minutes. Along the way you will pass six restaurants ranging from Cajun and Island themed to Mexican and sub shops.

What to See and Do

Daytona International Speedway *1801 West International Speedway Blvd., Daytona Beach, FL 32114 (877) 306-7223* This is a must-visit for any motorsport enthusiast. Take a behind-the-scenes tour of the speedway, and learn everything there is to know about racing in Daytona. You'll see the pits, the garages, and get a close-up of the finish line. If you are going to be there in February, you might want to get tickets to the Daytona 500. Check their schedule though, as there are many other races throughout the year too. The speedway is an 18 minute walk from the **Sheltair** FBO, and a perfect destination for a quick fly in.

And if you enjoy speed try

the **Richard Petty Driving Experience** *(386) 947-0507* at the Speedway. Fly around the track in a NASCAR racer for an experience of a lifetime! Plan ahead, since they only do the experiences at certain times of the month.

Daytona Lagoon *601 Earl Street, Daytona Beach, FL 32118 (386) 254-5020* For a fun and playful afternoon, spend some time at the Daytona Lagoon. A mix of water slides, arcade games, go-karts, mini golf and junk food makes it the ideal place to relive your childhood, or bring the kids or grandchildren with you. Take

Daytona International Speedway

advantage of all the facilities for a full day for $50, or stick to the water park only for $24.

Museum of Art and Science *352 South Nova Road, Daytona Beach, FL 32114 (386) 255-0285* This is a huge museum installation. Their collections are a fascinating mix of art, history and science. Walk outdoors through the 90-acre wildlife preserve, or stick to the indoor exhibits. The museum has the largest collection of Cuban art outside of Cuba, Chinese artwork, lots of Coke memorabilia and an extensive Americana collection. There is a massive 13 foot tall 13,000 year old Giant Ground Sloth skeleton on display as well as African Art, early American art and more. They are closed on Mondays and general admission is $12.95 with discounts for kids, students and seniors.

Tuscawilla Park *1000 E Orange Ave., Daytona Beach, FL 32114* Find a little green space just a few minutes from the airport at Tuscawilla Park. Simply take a walk to recharge your batteries, or have a little more fun on one of the forest ziplines. Bring some food for a picnic, and you're set. The park is free, but tickets for the Zoomair zipline run start at $18 per person.

Halifax Historical Museum *252 South Beach Street, Daytona Beach, FL 32114 (386) 255-6976* If you want to see more of Daytona than the beach, then take a look back through the city's past. Set in a gorgeous old bank building with original Tiffany windows. Exhibits cover all eras of Daytona's history, including the Native American population, pioneer settlers and the Victorian period. There are also Daytona Beach race exhibits. The museum is closed on Mondays and Sundays, and admission is $5 (except on Thursdays when it's by donation).

The Beach. You can't talk about Daytona Beach without mentioning the beach itself. It's 23 miles of soft white sand and warm blue waters. The currents can be strong for swimming but the surfing is often spectacular.

There is a fun stretch of boardwalk in the center portion of the beach (15 minutes from the airport by car) *1200 Main, Daytona Beach, FL 32118 (386) 253-1212,* where you can find snacks, shops and a classic beach-side amusement park. Spend a bit of time on the Ferris wheel or trying to win a prize at the arcade games.

At the very southern tip of the beach is the **Ponce de Leon Lighthouse,** which is a local landmark worth seeing if you're down that far. And if you do want to see the entire stretch of beach, you can actually take your (rental!) car for a unique drive along the sand.

Where to Eat
Bahama Breeze *1786 W.*

International Speedway Blvd., Daytona Beach, FL 32114 If you want to eat near the airport this is a nice place. It is across from the Speedway so it is a 17 minute walk from **Sheltair.** Part of a small chain, Bahama Breeze's menu has a nice variety of Caribbean dishes. Choices range from lunch specials, salads, soups, complete dinners, appetizers and little meals. Fish dishes consist mostly of shrimp, Mahi, and tilapia. They also have choices like shrimp and grits or Chipotle Beef over yellow rice, also with corn, beans, sour cream and salsa. $$

The Cellar Restaurant *220 Magnolia Ave., Daytona Beach, FL 32114 (386) 258-0011* You might want to get a little dressed-up when dining at the Cellar, though it's not a pretentious eatery at all. The cuisine is Italian, with dishes like porcini risotto, caprese salad and osso buco. You can always find the perfect pairing with your meal from their lengthy wine list. The Cellar is open for dinners only and they're closed on Mondays. $$$

Daytona Brickyard *747 W International Speedway Blvd., Daytona Beach FL 32114 (386) 253-2270* A good meal at a casual sports bar can be perfect after a day out on the town. The Brickyard Lounge & Grill is in the center of downtown Daytona, and still only a 10 minute drive from the airport. Burgers, fries, hearty sandwich platters, chicken wings and beer are on the menu. $$

Bay Street Seafood Market & Grill *141 Bay St., Daytona Beach, FL 32115 (386) 255-8650* Looking at this restaurant from the outside you may be unimpressed, but the food is great. The atmosphere is pretty casual. You'll get all your favorite seafood comfort foods, like steamed shrimp, fried oysters, grilled scallops and huge grouper sandwiches. Everyone raves about the onion rings so be sure to try them. The restaurant is near the river and right downtown. There is a patio for outdoor dining and they have free Wi-Fi too. $$

Where to Stay

If you want to stay at the airport there are three hotels right on the grounds. All are about a 10 minute walk from Sheltair, but of course they will most likely pick you up if you call. (1) **Hilton Garden Inn Daytona Beach Airport,** *189 Midway Avenue, Daytona Beach, FL 32114 (386) 944-4000* (2) **Residence Inn Daytona Beach Speedway/Airport,** *1725 Richard Petty Blvd., Daytona Beach, FL 32114 (386) 252-3949* (3) **Hampton Inn Daytona Speedway-Airport,** *1715 W International Speedway Blvd., Daytona Beach, FL 32114. (386) 257-4030*

River Lily Inn Bed & Breakfast *558 Riverside Drive, Daytona Beach, FL 32117 (386) 253-5002* This beautiful six-room B&B is one of the nicest places to stay in Daytona if you're trying to get away from the chain motels. It's downtown on the western shores of the Halifax River, so you're overlooking the water without the hassle of being right down on the beaches. The hosts are always fun and friendly, and the rooms have Wi-Fi, flat-screen TVs and there is a pool. $$

Shores Resort and Spa *2637 South Atlantic Avenue, Daytona Beach, FL 32118 (866) 934-7467* Even a resort right on the beach is a reasonable price in Daytona. The Shores Resort is a four-star facility, with a fitness center, full-service spa, swimming pool, large rooms as well as suites and there is an outdoor tiki bar for drinks by the pool. There is a private stretch of beach with personal cabanas so you should enjoy some personal space when sunbathing out on the sand. $$

Daytona Bikeweek in March

Daytona Beach International   KDAB

TOWER Ⓒ120.7, 118.1

Ground Control **121.9**

Control Tower Phone
(386) 226-3900

Airport Manager Phone
(386) 248-8030

ASOS (386) 253-7469

ATIS 120.05

DAYTONA App ®125.72 (8000–11000')
®118.85 (South 4000–7500)
®125.35 (South 3500 and below)
®125.8 (North 3500 and below)

DAYTONA Dep 123.9

UNICOM 122.95

Elevation 34' MSL	Traffic Pattern 999' MSL (965' AGL)	Flight Service Station 800-WX-BRIEF

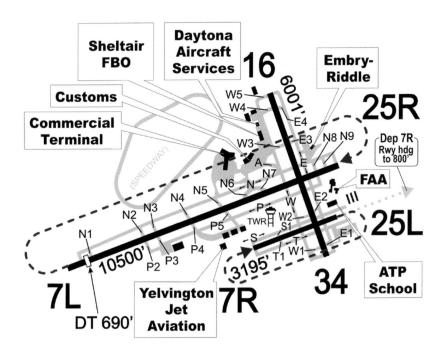

Not for navigation or inflight use | © 2017 Adventus Media LLC

KDED

DeLand

Halfway between Orlando and Daytona Beach, DeLand is a good destination because there is a lot to do right at the airport, including two restaurants. The rest of the city has plenty of charm too, and some natural attractions like the Hontoon Island State Park. DeLand would make a fun weekend or day trip destination.

The small airport in DeLand was once a military station where pilots trained, and the facility is still a popular destination for private pilots due to the skydiving DZ and Naval Air Station museum. Add in some restaurants, and you don't even have to leave the airport.

DeLand has something most people don't expect in Florida — rolling hills and big pine trees. The downtown historic district still has many buildings from the early years of the city and is called "The Athens of Florida."

Every year, the Fall Festival of the Arts takes over the town for two days. Held the weekend before Thanksgiving, the town comes alive with hundreds of artists from around the country, to show their works at a mix of locations around the city. It's all free for the public, and they host artistic workshops and live entertainment all weekend long.

Downtown DeLand

Flying There

Approaching DeLand from the west is not recommended due to multiple Restriced Areas and the Palatka 1 and 2 Military Operations Areas. Consider flying over Gainesville and proceeding east until clear. If you want to fly through the Palatka MOAs and restricted areas, the controlling authority to see if they are hot is SEA-LORD on 134.65.

From the southwest, in addition to the Orlando Class B and Sanford Class C airspace, pilots should be alert for a pair of 1,700-foot tall towers in the Deltona area.

From the southeast, V 3 is a well-travelled path that ensures clearance from the Orland Class B as well as the restricted airspace over Cape Canaveral.

DeLand Muncipal is heavily utilized for flight training, sky diving, and various types of sport flying. Listening to AWOS on 119.575, and monitoring CTAF/UNICOM on 123.075 as early as possible will help you sequence your arrival with whatever else may be happening at the time.

Traffic pattern altitude is 1,080 feet MSL and runway 5 is the preferred calm-wind runway. Standard left-hand traffic patterns are in use for all runways. Visit www.delandairport.com for additional useful information.

DeLand Aviation is located on the south side of the field and provides FBO services, including full-service 100LL and Jet A fuel. Self-serve 100LL is available 24/7 by credit card. *(386) 740-1955* or www.delandaviation.com.

Getting Around
Volusia County (Votran) runs bus service through DeLand, but there is really only one route that will take you down through town, and it doesn't directly come to the airport. For a little less responsibility, just call a cab. **DeLand Taxi** *(368) 734-8484* or Steve's Taxi *(386) 734-0013*.

Walking Distance Activities
There aren't too many things you can walk to from the airfield. However, there are a few things going on at the airport itself, like **Skydive DeLand** and the **DeLand Naval Air Station Museum.** There are also two good restaurants near the terminal buildings. You can easily spend an afternoon at the DeLand airport and never leave

the grounds.

What to See and Do
Skydive DeLand *1600 Flightline Blvd., DeLand FL 32724 (386) 738-3539* Go up to 14,000 feet in a Twin Otter or a Pac 750 XL, and leap out in a tandem dive at 120 mph. Rates for a tandem dive are $179 per jump, but if you are already a trained skydiver, you can get a jump alone for only $23. Make sure you arrange to get a video, especially if this is your first time skydiving. For the regulars, check out their big gear store for any equipment you need or just a new T-shirt. You can jump 365 days a year.

Skydive DeLand

DeLand Naval Air Station Museum *910 Biscayne Blvd., DeLand FL (386) 738-4149* Several old planes and military memorabilia are on display at the DeLand Naval Air Station Museum, also located on the airport grounds near the terminal area. See their TBF Avenger torpedo bomber and T-33 Shooting Star, both have been restored to pristine flight condition. A sleek PT boat is also

out on display. The focus is on WWII, when the airport was a military training facility. The museum is open Wednesday through Saturday, from noon until 4 p.m., and admission is by donation. The Annex is only open Wednesday from noon until 4 p.m.

Stetson Mansion *1031 Camphor Lane, DeLand, FL 32720* This beautiful historic house is lavishly decorated in period style, and one of the most popular attractions in DeLand. This amazing blend of Gothic, Polynesian, Moorish and Tudor styles was designed by architect George Pearson. There are 10,000 sq ft to explore in the main mansion and smaller buildings like the school house and carriage house nearby. The outdoor gardens are just as impressive for a peaceful afternoon walk. You'll have to head across town to get here, but it's still only 12 minutes from the airport. A tour of the mansion is $20, except during the Christmas decorating season (November to January) when it's $25.

Blue Heron River Tours *2317 River Ridge Rd., DeLand, FL 32720 (386) 873-4843* Across town is the Hontoon Island State Park, and you can enjoy a fabulous river boat tour with Blue Heron River Tours. You'll head out on the water in a classic pontoon river boat, and see the river and surrounding wetlands. There is the opportunity for great bird-watching all along the St. John River, and keep your eyes open for herons, kingfishers and even bald eagles. The water holds alligators and a new population of manatees that were never found here before. Tours are

Blue Heron River Tours

2 hours long, and tickets are $22 for adults.

Reptile Discovery Center *2710 Big John Drive, DeLand, FL* If you're squeamish about snakes, it might not be the best place to visit, but if you're interested in exotic reptiles from around the world, you should go. Rattlesnakes, cobras and a mix of other snakes, lizards and turtles are on display. They do venom collection at the center as well (for making anti-venom and other medical products) and you can watch "snake milking" demonstrations every day. Admission tickets are $10.50 for adults. They're open Thursday through Sunday (closing at 1 p.m. on Sundays though).

Where to Eat

Airport Restaurant & Gin Mill *1120 Airport Terminal Dr., DeLand, FL 32724 (386) 734-9755* This is one of two places you can eat right at the airport, and watch both the planes coming and going as well as the skydivers coming down for a landing. If nothing is going on out on the field, they have several big TVs and free Wi-Fi. Lunch could be a burger and fries, but they also serve a fine rib-eye if you're here for dinner. You can also just hang out with other pilots for late-night drinks as the place is open until 2 a.m. $

The Perfect Spot *1600 Flightline Blvd., (386) 734-0088* Another airport eatery located right at the Skydive DeLand building. The view of the divers coming down just feet away from the restaurant makes some interesting entertainment while you eat. The menu is mostly burgers and sandwiches but they do have a full bar with Tiki decor and an outdoor patio. $$

Santorini's Greek Cuisine *210 N Woodland Blvd., DeLand, FL 32720 (386) 736-7726* For something beyond burgers, you can get some authentic gyros with homemade tzatziki sauce, fish stuffed with feta or even vegetarian mousaka. It's on a busy street so you can have your food out on the patio and do some DeLand people-watching. Closed on Sundays, they're otherwise open for lunch and dinner the rest of the week. $$

Where to Stay

Comfort Inn *400 E Intl Speedway Blvd., DeLand, FL 32724* The closest accommodation to the airport is the Comfort Inn, which would be just over a half hour on foot (or a 5 minute drive). It's on the main highway that passes the airport. It's your usual Comfort Inn, with complimentary hot breakfast and Wi-Fi and there is a swimming pool too. Some of the king rooms have jacuzzi hot tubs if you think you might need to unwind. $$

DeLand Country Inn *228 W Howry Avenue, DeLand, FL 32720* The DeLand Country Inn is near the center of the city, where highways 15 and 44 cross. All five guestrooms are decorated in vintage English style, and your hosts go the extra mile to make sure you're comfortable during your stay. The big covered porch is perfect for sitting around in the evenings, and their gourmet breakfasts are worth getting up for in the morning. Though the place is quite historic, it's nicely modernized with air-conditioning and free Wi-Fi. $$

Hontoon Landing Resort & Marina *2317 River Ridge Rd., DeLand, FL 32720 (800) 248-2474* If the Hontoon Island State Park interests you, you can stay at the Hontoon Landing Resort & Marina for a full range of nature sights and boating activities. Stay in a standard room, or get some added space and privacy with a guest cottage. The marina is a busy spot and you can rent boats for touring the river on your own, book a tour with Blue Heron tours, or get a boat to do some fishing (you're likely to catch bass and crappie). $$

DeLand Municipal-Taylor

KDED

UNICOM ©**123.075**

Airport Manager Phone
[386] 740-6955

AWOS-3 119.575 [386] 740-5811

DAYTONA App/Dep ®125.35

Elevation	Traffic Pattern	Flight Service Station
80' MSL	1080' MSL (1000' AGL)	800-WX-BRIEF

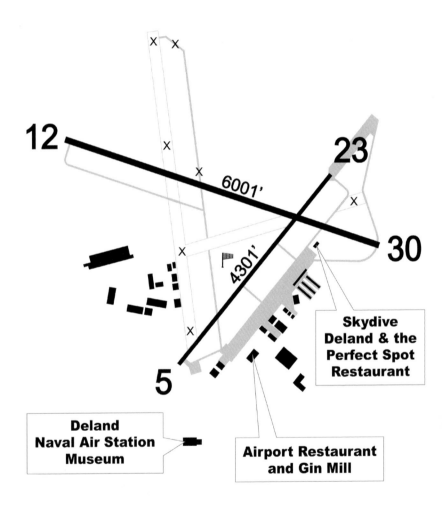

Skydive Deland & the Perfect Spot Restaurant

Deland Naval Air Station Museum

Airport Restaurant and Gin Mill

Destin/Fort Walton

Destin/Ft. Walton is a very attractive destination with a very convenient airport that's just a three minute drive to beautiful beaches. Destin airport is also located within and near unusual and complex airspace. Don't let that put you off, but do prepare for your flight.

For beaches in the panhandle, you won't find a better place to visit. For local sights, the Air Force's museum is a big attraction for many pilots.

Fort Walton Beach and Destin are two busy beach towns that are joined together by the Okaloosa Island, and a roadway that links them all together.

Destin, founded by Connecticut sea captain Leonard Destin, has always been a fishing town. The waters are very rich in fish due to a 100 foot drop in the sea bed about 10 miles offshore. Marlin, amberjack and tarpon are frequent catches. Since more billfish are caught in Destin than the rest of the Emerald Coast combined, Destin calls itself the "world's luckiest fishing village."

Author John Grisham and TV chef Emeril Lagasse are a few of the local celebrities who have homes in Destin.

Destin Beach

Flying There

Destin is just six miles south of Eglin Air Force Base. The result is that Eglin/Destin are in FAR Part 93 airspace, which is relatively rare. It shows up as a white area on the sectional chart with North/South and East/West corridors.

The easiest way to remember the operating requirements here is to think of the North-South Corridor with its solid blue arrows as similar to Class B Airspace in that you need a clearance. You need to establish two-way radio communications with ATC (usually Eglin Approach) and get a clearance and a discrete transponder code prior to entering.

The East-West Corridor with its open arrows is similar to Class C Airspace in that you need to establish two-way radio communications with ATC (usually Eglin Approach) and have a discrete transponder code prior to entering.

Since Destin is not a towered airport (as of this writing), on arrival, Eglin Approach will turn you over to the Destin CTAF at an appropriate time, where you will make the usual non-towered radio calls for active runway, and declare your position and intentions. **NOTE: A new tower is scheduled to go in operation early**

Part 93 Airspace

to mid-2017. Check the NO-TAMs for the change.

It is a good practice to check the Destin ASOS (133.92) before getting into Eglin's busy airspace. You can generally pick up Destin's ASOS 50 or more miles from the airport.

Another interesting potential conflict when you enter the Destin pattern is the large number of banner tow airplanes that are working along the beach much of the year. Banner tow pilots are very good about making radio calls announcing their position on UNICOM (123.07) when they are near Destin. When they are eastbound along the beach they will be at 500 feet and below and when they are westbound they will be at 1,000 feet, traffic pattern altitude, and will generally pass over the southern end of the runway. They are slow moving and the banner is easy to see if you are looking for it, so they are quite easy to avoid

On departure, whether you are **VFR or IFR, you must contact Eglin Clearance Delivery (121.6) on the ground at Destin prior to takeoff** and get departure instructions and a discrete transponder code.

The easiest way to prepare for your first visit to KDTS is to take the free FAA Safety Knowledge course. Do an online search for "Destin/Eglin AFB FL Part 93 Operations" to find it.

Since northwest Florida has one of the densest populations of aircraft in the U.S. and is almost entirely covered in MOAs and Restricted airspace, using VFR Flight Following or filing IFR is highly recommended.

Destin Jet is the FBO *(850) 424-6890*.

Walking Distance Activities

There is nothing across from the airport, but if you want to walk about 20 minutes to the south, it will bring you to Route 98 and the strip malls, beachfront condos and resorts you would expect, but that section of town is not a charming place to wander around.

Getting Around

Destin and the airport are connected to the rest of Fort Walton Beach via the Miracle Strip Parkway that crosses over Okaloosa Island. It's about a 20 minute drive, so a vehicle will be necessary if you want

to explore both towns.

There is public bus service courtesy of the **Okaloosa County Transit** *(850) 833-9168* and fares are $1.50. Route 32 has a stop near the airport and will take you around Destin as well as back toward Fort Walton Beach. You'll have a 20 minute walk south on Airport Road to Route 98, where you can pick up a bus going east or west. The buses run every half hour.

For a car rental, Destin Jet has luxury car rental company GoRental on site. In addition to luxury cars, they have some regular cars for rent too. Destin Jet also has a courtesy van if you just need a lift to town.

For a taxi, call **Advantage Airport Shuttle** *(850) 420-7807* to get you anywhere in Destin or over in Fort Walton Beach.

What to See and Do

Air Force Armament Museum *100 Museum Dr., Eglin Air Force Base, Fort Walton Beach, FL 32542 (850) 822-4062* The perfect attraction for the aviation enthusiast. This historical museum of the Air Force focuses on planes and military weaponry. It's a little

Destin Harbor

farther out of the way, about a half hour from the airport, past Fort Walton Beach but the admission is free and you'll get to see exhibits from early WWI up to the present. Full aircraft are on display outside, with the SR-71 Blackbird being their pride and joy though there are 24 other aircraft in their collection. Inside, there are exhibits on bombs, missiles, rockets and more. Open six days a week, closed on Sundays.

Indian Temple Mound Museum *139 Miracle Strip Pkwy SE, Fort Walton Beach, FL 32548 (850) 833-9595* It's not all about the beaches around Destin and Fort Walton. The Indian Temple site is a very popular historical monument that combines ancient burial mounds with a re-created vil-

Destin Pass

lage. There is a school house, a post office and several other small buildings that all hold their own displays with local history. Overall, they have more than 1,000 artifacts on display that cover more than 12,000 years of Native history. The museum is closed on Sundays, and tickets are $5 for adults.

Okaloosa Island This long narrow island sits between Destin and Fort Walton Beach, and the entire place is lined with gorgeous beaches. There are lots of shops and restaurants in the center of the island, where the bridge connects it to Fort Walton Beach. If you keep on going to the west, it gets more and more remote if you prefer to get away from the crowds. The popular fishing pier is also here.

Beaches

Henderson Beach State Park *17000 Emerald Coast Pkwy, Destin, FL 32541 (850) 837-7550* Though there are more beaches all along Okaloosa Island, the Henderson Beach State Park is too close to the airport to ignore. Not only are there miles of smooth white sands, but also you can see more of the park through the nature trails, and boardwalks too. As a state park, there is a fee for admission. A vehicle with up to 8 people is $6 and you can get in for just $2 if you're on foot.

Crab Island. This is where the locals hang out. It is not really a beach or an island, it is a sandbar on the north side of the Destin Bridge. Many vacationers call their visit to Crab Island the highlight of their trip. The only way to get to Crab Island is via boat, kayak, paddleboard, or other watercraft which you can rent. People anchor out and wade the sand bar. There are a couple of places to buy food, drink, and ice cream, but they only take cash. Or bring your own food and beverages.

Boating and Fishing

Destin has the largest fishing charter fleet in Florida, so serious fishermen have plenty of options to find the captain that is right for them. One popular choice is **Gulf Angler Fishing Charters** *(850) 428-0118.* They are very customer focused and have two inshore and one offshore capable boat.

Okaloosa Island Pier *1030 Miracle Strip Parkway East, Fort Walton Beach, FL 32548 (850) 244-1023* The Pier goes 1/4 mile out into the Gulf. $2 fee to walk the pier. People see dolphins, turtles, stingrays and more. $7.50 fishing fee and if you need to rent fishing gear you can. People catch everything from small fish to sharks and tarpon.

Crab Island Watersports *1198 Miracle Strip Pky, Fort Walton Beach, FL 32548 (850) 243-2722* has pontoon boats for rent for a leisurely tour along the coast, as well as jet skis if you want a little more speed in your afternoon. You can also book a dolphin tour with them to see some local wildlife.

Golfing

The 27-hole championship course at **Indian Bayou Golf**

Club *1 Country Club Drive East, Destin, FL 32541 (850) 837-6191* is adjacent to the airport if you're craving a round of golf on one of Northwest Florida's finest courses. Rates start from as low as $35 for 9 holes.

Where to Eat

Louisiana Lagniappe *775 Gulf Shore Dr., Destin, FL 32541 (850) 837-0881* Some of the finest dining in the area is just five minutes outside the airport by car. Louisiana Lagniappe has a menu of classic Southern-styled seafood and you should consider the grouper, soft-shelled crab or stuffed shrimp if you want to sample one of the crowd favorites. Take a seat outside on the patio for perfect waterfront views over the marina. They're only open for dinners until 9 p.m. $$$

Capriccio Cafe Shoreline Mall, *810 Hwy 98 E, Destin, FL 32541 (850) 460-7050* For a more casual bite to eat, but just as close to the airport, stop in at the Capriccio Cafe. This is a quaint little Italian sandwich shop, opened by an Italian transplant from Milan. You can get a fresh cup of coffee in any style you like (latte, espresso, you name it) and they have a menu bursting with tasty pastries, sandwiches and more. They're open early enough for breakfast (7 a.m.) so you can start your day here. $

Sealand Restaurant *47 Miracle Strip Pkwy SE., Fort Walton Beach, FL 32548 (850) 244-0044* If you're heading over the island to Fort Walton Beach, the Sealand Restaurant is just on the other side of the bridge and very close to the

Temple Mound Museum. Grouper and triggerfish are big on the menu but don't forget to ask about the catch-of-the-day. They have a lovely outdoor patio, and they are only open for dinners (except on Sundays when they open early for lunch). $$

Asiago's Skillet *110 Amberjack Dr., Fort Walton Beach, FL 32548 (850) 586-7998* On Okaloosa Island, near the bridge over to Fort Walton Beach, is the best breakfast joint in town. French toast, eggs Benedict, classic bacon and eggs, hash browns and crab-cakes are served all morning long if you want to fill up for a day on the beach. $

Where to Stay

Sandestin Golf and Beach Resort *9300 Emerald Coast Pkwy West, Sandestin, FL 32550 (877) 620-3642* If you are looking to do it all in one place, you can do it here. 2400 acres and 1,250 rentals in different villages, can give you any kind of vacation experience, especially if you have kids with you. Activities include miles of beach, 19 swimming pools, 72 holes of golf, tennis, fishing, boating, ice skating, zip lines, a bungy jump, free bike rental and much more. There is also a 598 room **Hilton** in the resort. *(850) 267-1816.* $$$

Best Western Fort Walton Beachfront *380 Santa Rosa Blvd., Fort Walton Beach, FL 32548 (877) 722-3422* Want to stay right on the beach? The local Best Western is down on Okaloosa Island, right between Destin and Fort Walton Beach. Great free amenities like beach umbrellas and chairs, Wi-Fi that reaches to the beach,

breakfast, parking, and cable. It's a good choice to get a beach front room without the high beach resort prices. $$

Aunt Martha's Bed and Breakfast *315 Shell Avenue, SE, Fort Walton Beach, FL (850) 243-6702* For a more intimate and personal stay, try Aunt Martha's. The inn itself is a lovely old Victorian home and the rooms are beautifully decorated with views over the

Fun at the beach

water. Located on the south shore of Fort Walton Beach, you are within walking distance of many town shops and services, or you can cross over the bridge and spend some time at the beaches. $$

Henderson Park Inn *2700 Scenic Hwy 98, Destin, FL 32541 (866) 398-4432* If you're heading to Henderson Park, you can stay in luxury at the Henderson Park Inn. You'll have access to their private beach, and both breakfast and lunch is included in your room price. The resort is adults only, so you can expect some peace and quiet as you wander the beach or just lie in the sun. $$$

Destin Executive

KDTS

CTAF/UNICOM ©123.075

Airport Manager Phone
[850] 651-7160

NOTE: New tower opening in mid 2017. Check to see if in operation and for tower frequency.

ASOS 133.925 [850] 654–7128

ELGIN App/Dep ®132.1

EGLIN CLNC DEL 121.6, 127.7

NOTE: All aircraft (VFR and IFR) must contact Clearance Delivery before takeoff

Elevation 22' MSL	Traffic Pattern 1080' MSL [978'] AGL	Flight Service Station 800-WX-BRIEF

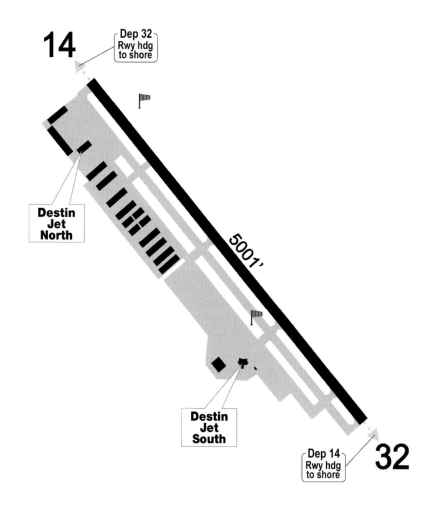

14
Dep 32
Rwy hdg
to shore

Destin
Jet
North

5001'

Destin
Jet
South

Dep 14
Rwy hdg
to shore

32

Dunedin

This is a beautifully picturesque historical town with boutiques, restaurants, clubs, cafes, and the best beach in America. Its Scottish heritage is highlighted by a Highland Games festival held in the Spring. Baseball Spring Training is another feature of this small town.

The town gets its name from the Gaelic name for **Edinburgh** (Dun Eideann), and there are many places in Dunedin where you can see its Scottish heritage even today.

Just north of Clearwater, Dunedin (pronounced DO-NE-EE-DIN) feels a little like a small town within the bigger city of Tampa.

The Scottish influences in Dunedin date back to the town's founding in 1870, when **John I. Branch** opened his store to supply passing ships. Soon several Scottish families joined him.

This Scottish heritage is celebrated every year in March or April with the **Dunedin Highland Games and Festival.** In November they have the **Celtic Music and Craft Beer Festival.** They also host a not so Scottish annual **Mardi Gras Celebration** in February with an outrageous parade down Main Street.

Dunedin's streets are lined with quaint buildings plus

Caladesi Island State Park

quirky and unique shops. You'll quickly notice the absence of the usual "big box stores," a fact that Dunedin is quite proud of.

During spring, the **Toronto Blue Jays** baseball team comes to Dunedin to train for the upcoming MLB season. They often host the **New York Yankees** and **Boston Red Sox.**

If you enjoy spending time in more natural settings, there are two wonderful island parks just off the coast. A short drive along the causeway and you can wander the beaches of **Hon-**

eymoon Island State Park, and from there you can enjoy a ferry ride to **Caladesi Island State Park.** This year Caladesi Island took the coveted #1 spot for the best beach in America according to Dr. Beach.

Flying There

Clearwater Air Park is a tidy, uncontrolled airport that was named the 2014 **General Aviation Airport of the Year** by Florida DOT. KCLW is located under the 3000 foot shelf of Tampa's airspace and is barely a mile northwest of St

Dunedin Highland

Pete-Clearwater International's (KPIE) controlled space. Flying in from the north or south on the coast line, you can scoot in without much of a problem. Note, if you are flying just off the coast, there is the **Caladesi Island Special State Conservation** area where pilots are requested to avoid overflights below 2,000 feet. Flying from the east, your best bet is call Tampa Approach on 125.3

The **Clearwater Airpark** FBO is a friendly place with no landing fees and a crew car. *(727) 443-3433* or UNICOM 123.00.

Walking Distance Activities

The **Clearwater Air Park** is surrounded mainly by business and residential neighborhoods, but there are a few places you can easily walk to for a meal.

Expo Restaurant *1185 North Hercules Avenue, Clearwater, FL 33765* is just across the street from the Air Park and will take you less than four minutes to get there. It serves casual diner food, with big breakfasts and cheeseburgers. Their fried fish is very popular.

Kelli's Corner, *1400 N*

Hercules Ave., Clearwater, FL 33765 is a small but popular sandwich shop featuring a great Gyro. It is a six minute walk north of the FBO.

There is also a golf course adjacent to the runway if golf is your thing. **The Landings Golf Club of Clearwater** *(1875 Airport Drive, Clearwater, FL 33765 (727) 447-5272)* is a public 18-hole, par 63 course and has a clubhouse where you can enjoy a drink or a meal.

Getting Around

You can easily access public transit from the airport to visit the rest of Dunedin.

The **Pinellas Suncoast Transit Authority** (PSTA), have a good network of buses across the area. A single cash fare is $2, or you can get an all-day pass for $4.50. Route 67 goes right past the Airpark, and it will take you to the Westfield Countryside Mall where you can connect to most other bus routes. If you don't want to wait for buses, then call the **Dunedin Taxi Network** *(727) 484-2381.*

There is no car rental on site, but there are two differ-

ent **Enterprise Rent-A-Car** *(727) 796-3442* locations within three miles as well as an **AVIS** *(727) 447-1295* and **Hertz** *(727) 723-8661.*

Driving to the historic downtown will take less than 15 minutes. Taking the bus downtown will take about 40 minutes.

What to See and Do

Honeymoon Island State Park *1 Causeway Blvd., Dunedin, FL 34698 (727) 469-5942* Get to Honeymoon Island State Park from the mainland via Causeway Blvd, a drive that takes around 20 minutes from the Airpark. There is an admission fee to enter the park, which is around $8 for a vehicle (with up to 8 passengers). The island has many great natural areas to explore, like the beaches, mangrove swamps and inland pine forests. Collecting seashells is a popular pastime in the park as the beach is always filled with them.

Caladesi Island State Park *1 Causeway Blvd., Dunedin, FL 34698 (727) 469-5918* You'll need to take the ferry across from **Honeymoon Island State Park** to get to this island as there isn't a ferry directly from the mainland. It's a virtually undisturbed and natural barrier island, where you can go to do some hiking (either along the coast or through the interior), have a picnic, go fishing or check out the sandy beaches.

Dunedin Fine Art Center *1143 Michigan Blvd., Dunedin FL 34698 (727) 298-DFAC* This is Dunedin's jewel for arts and arts education. They were voted "Best Museum" in a recent Visit St. Petersburg/Clearwater survey. The museum features a series of open galleries where you can browse through the local artist exhibits.

The Fine Art Center also has an ongoing schedule of live performances if you enjoy an evening at the theatre. There is a lovely little coffee shop and a gift shop too.

Clearwater Marine Aquarium *249 Windward Passage, Clearwater, FL 33767 (727) 441-1790* Though technically the aquarium is in Clearwater, it's very close to Dunedin. Located on a barrier island that's accessed via a causeway, the aquarium is approximately a 15-minute drive from the Airpark. It's a large aquatic facility with tanks and exhibits filled with all kinds of sea life. The sharks and sting rays are a particularly exotic sight. The dolphin adventure is a new addition, and it's included in the main ticket price.

Downtown Dunedin

Downtown Dunedin has a quaint and individual feel that makes this a lovely place to explore antique shops and artist's galleries.

The vibrant center of town includes bars and pubs as well. **Dunedin Brewery** *937 Douglas Ave., Dunedin, 34698 (727) 736-0606* is Florida's oldest craft brewery. Also look out for the Friday and Saturday morning downtown market each fall.

Check out the **Dunedin Historical Museum,** *Dunedin, FL 34697 (727) 736-1176* Right in the center of eclectic Dunedin in the old railroad station. It is a fun little museum that doesn't take long to see. Great permanent and rotating exhibits. There is a suggested $2 donation to enter, and the tone is always fun and hands-on. Open Tues.-Sat.

Right around the corner from the Dunedin Brewery is **7venth Sun Brewing** *1012 Broadway, Dunedin, FL 34698 (727) 733-3013* If you're looking for a no frills tap room with great beer, look no further. 7venth Sun has lighter, fruity beers than Dunedin Brewery which are perfect on a hot day. This is a brewery, not a brewpub so there's no food menu. There's a chalk board on the wall with the various available drafts listed. The customer area is small with very limited seating inside and out.

Strachan's Homemade Ice Cream and Desserts *310 Main Street, Dunedin, FL (727) 733-3603* This cute little family-run ice cream parlor at the

Dunedin Brewery

end of Main Street is filled with all sorts of tempting ice cream, cakes, chocolate covered key lime pie on a stick and more. The long lines will tell you how popular this place is. A tip if you go: don't wait in the long line inside, go to the outside window on the side of the building and you will probably be served faster.

Boat Tours

With so many little interesting islands off the west coast of Dunedin, you can always find something to see if you take a boat tour. Many charters offer the chance to get out on the waves for a little ocean sight-seeing. **Tropical Exposure Charters** *51 Main Street, Dunedin, FL 34698 (727) 742-1636* is one choice with private tours on a 21 foot cabin cruiser. **By Request Charters** *(727) 587-0714* is also at the same marina location, and they offer various boat tours as well as opportunities to go sport fishing, snorkeling or even go watching for dolphins.

For the more do-it-yourself type of boater, you can rent kayaks, sailboats and paddle boards at **Sail Honeymoon** *61 Causeway Blvd., Dunedin, FL 34698 (727) 734-0392* and see some of the sights on your own terms.

Where to Eat

There are many choices in the main street area from pubs to martini bars and fine restaurants.

Welcome to Dunedin

The Black Pearl *315 Main Street, Dunedin, FL 34698 (727) 734-3463* You can find a fine-dining mix of American and French food at the Black Pearl, perfect for celebrating a special occasion. Start off with some butternut ravioli, and then maybe try some shrimp scampi or glazed roast duck. The Black Pearl is centrally located right in downtown Dunedin, so you shouldn't have any trouble finding it. $$$

Kelley's *319 Main St., Dunedin, FL 34698 (727) 736-5284* Coincidentally, this casual eatery is right next door to the Black Pearl. Open for breakfast, and then on until well after dark, this is a comfortable spot for all sorts of seafood with a Mediterranean flair. There is a patio out back if you enjoy open-air dining. After the dinner hour has passed, the Chic-a-Boom Room Martini Bar is the place for some Dunedin nightlife. $$

The Living Room on Main *487 Main Street, Dunedin, FL 34698 (727) 736-5202* Also in the downtown area of Dunedin, the Living Room on Main has a mixed menu that is mostly snacks and tapas (small appetizer-sized portions). Try a dozen different tastes during your meal, all accompanied by some fine wine of course. Everything is served with style, and the cuisines are a mix from around the world. You can have simple calamari, or try something more exotic like mango and brie quesadillas. Their menu does include larger meal portions too, and you can stay on for the live music. $$

Delco's Original Steaks and Hoagies *1701 Main Street, Dunedin, FL 34698* Want to indulge in some fast food? If you want a huge sandwich that will fill you up, get a cheese steak at Delco's. They're big, fresh and loaded with cheese and onions. Just like they make them in Philly. They don't take any credit cards, so plan on having cash handy. Add a Tasty Kake to your order, and you're all set. $

Where to Stay

La Quinta Inn Clearwater Central *21338 US Hwy 19 North, Clearwater, FL 33765* If you want some accommodations near the airport, this might fit the bill. It's a modern hotel chain, and the rooms are updated and have free Internet access. Breakfast is com- plimentary, and most rooms are equipped with a microwave and a mini-fridge. If you stay often, you can collect loyalty points towards a free night with La Quinta. $$

Palm Court Motel *2090 Bayshore Blvd., Dunedin, FL 34698* If you plan on visiting the island nature parks, the Palm Court Motel is close to downtown as well as to the causeway bridge over to Honeymoon Island. Cozy and with a retro feel this motel is set around the swimming pool and you can park right outside your door. It's simple, clean and the staff are always super-friendly. Ranked as one of the top hotels in Dunedin based on customer reviews. $$

Amberlee Motel *1035 Broadway, Dunedin, FL 34698* This cute little motel has a real 70s feel to it, but the personal service, attention to detail and very clean rooms at a low price more than make up for the dated interior. It's just off Main Street, so it would be very suitable if you plan on spending time in the downtown area and don't want to worry about driving. Not a lot of amenities, though some units do have kitchenettes and there is a pool. $

Best Western Plus Yacht Harbor Inn *150 Marine Plaza, Dunedin, FL 34698* For location and views out to the water this Best Western cannot be beat. The hotel extends out into the water and is a perfect place to see the sunset or to see the boats come and go from the marina. Just a block into town for the restaurants and bars or stay and enjoy a meal at the on-site restaurant overlooking the water. $$

Clearwater Air Park

KCLW

UNICOM ©**123.0**

AWOS–3P 119.225 [727] 449–2184

Airport Manager Phone
[727] 462-6954

TAMPA App/Dep ®125.3

Elevation 71' MSL	Traffic Pattern 1071' MSL (1000'AGL)	Flight Service Station 800-WX-BRIEF

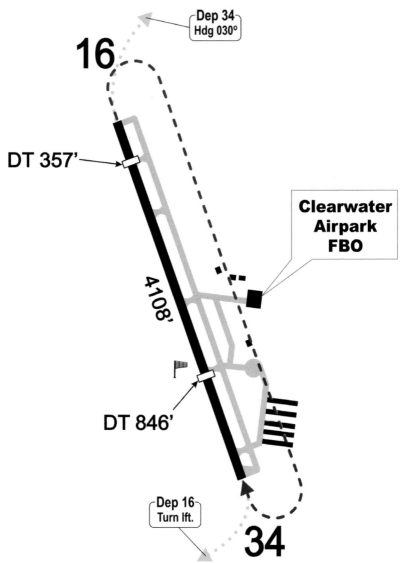

16

Dep 34
Hdg 030°

DT 357'

Clearwater
Airpark
FBO

4108'

DT 846'

Dep 16
Turn lft.

34

Everglades City

If you're looking to explore the vast wilderness of the Everglades, this is the place where you should begin your adventure. When you land at the first airport chartered in Flordia (X01) you're only minutes away from getting started.

Everglades City Airport

Everglades City is not a huge place; fewer than 200 families live here full-time but it is real Old Florida. The town is geared towards tourism because it's the gateway to the **Everglades** so you will find everything you need as a traveler passing through.

Surrounded on all sides by the wilds of various wetland expanses, the area hasn't much in the way of development over the years. Its major growth came when Baron Collier established it to house workers for the **Tamiami Trail** which was constructed across the state in the early 1900s. The Trail finally gave Everglades City an overland connection with the rest of Florida.

Featured in the 2011 documentary **Square Grouper,** Everglades city was a hotbed of marijuana smuggling in the 1970s due to the National Park Service phasing out commercial fishing combined with the labyrinth of mangroves, called the 10,000 islands, that only the local residents knew how to navigate.

Despite its small population the city's annual **Everglades Seafood Festival** draws more than 50,000 visitors a year. Held the first full weekend in February, there is plenty of food, music and crafts.

In the winter, pilots are welcome at a monthly pancake breakfast hosted by Chuck Gretzke of Wings Aero Tours.

Flying There

Everglades Airpark is located right on the the Gulf of Mexico's Chokoloskee Bay with no controlled airspace nearby. Since there is no automated weather on the field, your best bet is to check Marco Island's AWOS on 120.075 or call (239) 394–8187.

The runway is the second shortest paved runway of Florida's public airports at 2,400 feet long. It has a 50 asphalt center with 5 feet of turf on each side. If you don't touch down in the first 1/3 of the runway, *go around.*

Crosswinds are common, as are up or down drafts because you are making your approaches over water. The friendly FBO has fuel prices that are generally a dollar or two less than other airports in the Keys. There is limited parking on the pavement, but plenty of well-maintained turf to park on.

Getting Around

Bicycles are available at the airport, but no rental cars.

Most of the town is accessible on foot, and you can walk to the downtown area of Everglades City in approximately 20 minutes from the airport. **Lee Taxi** *(239) 687-3555* will happily shuttle you around the city if you prefer.

A phone call to any restaurant will get you picked up and returned to the airport.

Walking Distance Activities

As mentioned above, you can walk to just about anything in town. The airport is in the southwest corner of the city with the closest restaurant being the **Oyster House Restaurant,** *(239) 695-2073* about a 15 minute walk to the south. It is one of the oldest fish restaurants in the area, and serves everything from grouper, and stone crab to gator tail. A 75-foot **observation tower** gives you a great view of **The 10,000 islands.** You'll find the **Glades Haven Cozy Cabins** *(888) 956-6251* at the same location for some very handy accommodations. The cabins, in true Florida eccentric fashion, were built from log cabin kits by owner Bob Miller!

Walk north into the city for access to more restaurants and places to stay.

Jungle Erv's Airboat Tour

What to See and Do

Museum of the Everglades *105 West Broadway, Everglades City, FL (239) 695-0008* If you're planning to head into the Everglades, this museum is a good place to visit beforehand to learn more about the Everglades area. The culture and history of the area is displayed, and there is also a small art gallery and gift shop. The building is on the U.S. National Register of Historic Places and was once the Everglades Laundry. It is one of several historic buildings in the city, including the Bank of Everglades Building and the Old Collier County Courthouse. The museum is open six days a week, closed on Sundays.

Gulf Coast Visitor Center *815 Oyster Bar Lane, Everglades City, FL 34139 (239) 695-3311* Just a few minutes walk from the airport is the Gulf Coast Visitor Center. Here they can help you understand the various options for seeing the Everglades parks, how to book boats, and get any backcountry permits you might need. You can also rent a boat here if you prefer to head

out on your own without an organized tour. Open daily.

Everglades National Park and **Big Cypress National Preserve** The two parks are pretty much continuous with each other though the landscapes and wilderness of both can be noticeably different. Most of your tour options will take you through areas in both parks, so you generally don't need to differentiate. Either way, you're going to get to explore vast stretches of marsh, mangrove forests and open swampland.

Generally, the best way to see the Everglades is with a tour rather than just heading out and wandering around on your own. Airboats are the most popular way of seeing the park, and the thrill of the speed boat is a one-of-a-kind experience. **Captain Jack's Airboat Tours,** *200 Collier Ave, Everglades, FL 34139* launches right from the east side of Everglades City. **Jungle Erv's** *(877) 695-2820* also runs airboat charter tours right from the city that will take you through the famous mangrove tunnels on a short one-hour trip, perfect if you're

Everglades National Park

pushed for time.

Want something a little more peaceful? There are places you can go for canoe or kayak tours instead. You'll have to drive up to the **Everglades Area Welcome Center** north of town for some eco-friendly tour options by kayak. **Everglades Area Tours,** *32016 Tamiami Trail East, (239) 695-3633* can take you out into the park in a kayak. The pace is far slower than the airboats, but it can be better to really see the landscape.

Not all tours are by boat either. **Captain Steve's Swamp Buggy Adventures** *(877) 871-5386* will take you through the (mostly) dry land areas of Big Cypress in their unique big-wheeled swamp jeeps. By traveling on land, you get to see more of the mammals that live in the swamps and you get the chance to stretch your legs and have a walk too.

Fishing Charters

Sport fishing is a huge activity in the area, and you can take your pick from many charter choices. **Captain Glenn of Fishing the Everglades** *875 S. Copeland Ave., Everglades City,* *FL 34139 (239) 280-9085* can take you out in search of redfish, tarpon and snook. To fish out in the 1000 Islands as well as in the Everglades Park area, **Outgoing Charters** *(239) 825-6283* can take you where the trophy fish are hiding.

Out towards **Chokoloskee Island,** you can fish for tarpon, snapper, tripletail and more with **Captain Rapps** *(239) 571-1756.* They offer fishing tours through the 1000 Islands as well as all the way to the Florida Keys.

Where to Eat

Camellia Street Grill *202 Camellia St., Everglades City, FL 34139 (239) 695-2003* One of the best rated restaurants in Everglades City, this friendly place has a menu filled with seafood and Mediterranean cuisine. It's really casual, and there are plenty of patio tables outside for fresh-air dining while you watch the boats at the nearby marina. They're open for lunch and dinner. $$

Triad Seafood Inc. *401 School Dr W., Everglades City, FL 34139 (239) 695-2662* Towards the north end of town and a little off the main road.

Though they are best known for their stone crabs, you can try all kinds of seafood dishes. Clams, shrimp, grouper, oysters, conch, you name it. Try the gator basket! The atmosphere is that of a simple diner but the staff are friendly and helpful. You can't miss the bright pink building and there is a screened-in deck for outdoor dining by the water. $$

Sweet Mayberry's Cafe *207 W Broadway Ave., Everglades City, FL 34139 (239) 695-0092* This cute little cafe offers a range of coffee and espresso drinks, gelato and locally-made sweet treats. It's also a gift shop so you can get some Everglades souvenirs after you've had your refreshments. It's a family-owned place, and you can feel that homey atmosphere as soon as you walk in the door. $

City Seafood *702 Begonia Street, Everglades City, FL 34139 (239) 695-4700* Considering all the fishing that goes on here, it's no surprise that the best restaurants serve seafood. Looking like an old crab shack outside, City Seafood has a huge menu that includes stone crab, scallops, Cajun-style blackened fish, and lots of shrimp. You can even try some gator nuggets. Covered picnic tables keep the style casual, and they do serve fried chicken or hamburgers if you aren't in the mood for seafood. In either case you can eat next to the water watching birds, airboat and hopefully dolphins. $$

Where to Stay

The Ivey House Bed and Breakfast *107 Camelia St., Everglades City, FL 34139 (239)*

695-3299 It's not the closest hotel to the airport (30 minute walk or 5 minute drive), but it's one of the nicest places to stay in the city. You can choose from a private cottage, a standard room, or save a little money with the simpler lodge (with shared bathrooms). **Speedy's Airboat Tours** is right next door, and Ivey House offers their own kayak tours too. $$

Everglades City Motel *310 Collier Ave., Everglades City, FL 34139 (239) 695-4224* There is a little thatched gazebo outside for some shade when you want to sit out, but the rest of the motel has a very classic 1950s look to it. The rooms are large and clean, and there is free Wi-Fi. $$

Captain's Table Lodge and Villas *102 East Broadway, Everglades City, FL 34139 (239) 695-4211* Near the center of town, the Captain's Table Lodge and Villas has bright clean rooms, and the upstairs rooms have screened in balconies. It's a great budget spot but the amenities are minimal, so don't expect Wi-Fi. They do have air-conditioning and a pool though. And though the name may imply a restaurant, there isn't one. If you have your own rental boat, you can moor it at the Captain's Table during your stay. $$

Glades Haven Cozy Cabins *875 S Copeland Ave, Everglades, FL 34114 (239) 695-2082* Part of the Miller's World Resort, you can rent your own private cabin that has all the comforts of home. There is a marina with boat rentals, and the **Oyster House** restaurant is also on the premises so you can find everything you need for your stay in just a few minutes walk from the airport. $$

The Rod and Gun Club *200 Riverside Dr., Everglades City, FL 34139 (239) 695-2101* The Everglades Rod and Gun Club could feature in our attractions, places to eat, and where to stay sections as it has a little of all these things. A beautiful historic landmark it offers a glimpse into days gone by whether you're here for a drink, a meal, or to stay the night. The Club has hosted Presidents and other notable guests and features a swimming pool and vintage charm. These days visitors report an inconsistent experience in both the restaurant and the lodgings. Perhaps the safest approach is to stop by for a drink and enjoy the surroundings. **Bring cash.** (no credit cards) Ask for a refrigerator if you need one. $$

The Sitting Room off the Lobby at the Rod and Gun Club is like Being in a Time Warp

Everglades Airpark

X01

CTAF/UNICOM ©**123.075**

Airport Manager Phone
[239] 695-2778

ACTIVATE MIRL Rwy 15–33–CTAF

**High density bird population on
and around airport.**

Elevation 5' MSL	Traffic Pattern 1000' MSL (995')AGL)	Flight Service Station MIAMI 126.7

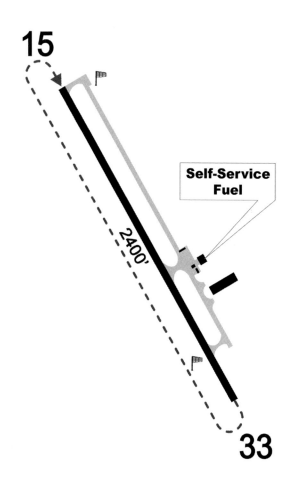

15

Self-Service Fuel

2400'

33

Flagler Beach

Pilots fly here for the on-field restaurant, High Jacker's. If you want more than a meal, it's the ideal quiet beach town where you can swim with dolphins, surf, walk and hang out with the local crowds to get away from the big city.

Flagler Beach is a small beach town spread out over several miles along the coast. The attitude is thoroughly laid back, and you don't get the hard-partying spring breakers here. Take your time to enjoy the beaches, the fishing and the various natural spots around town.

The town was named after Henry Morrison Flagler who helped build the city with the railway. Various industries, from lumber to sugar to citrus helped the town stay alive and grow. Though even today there are fewer than 5,000 people living in Flagler Beach. It's a true small town destination.

You can spend your day out on the water, or walking along the unique rust-colored sand of Flagler Beach. The tint comes from tiny bits of coquina stone. Don't worry, it's still super smooth and lovely for sunbathing or just walking barefoot through the sand. Be sure to check out the many interesting shops and one-of-a-kind cafes along the way.

Nature areas like the Betty

Marineland Dolphin Adventure

Steflik Preserve or the larger Graham Swamp Conservation Area can take you off the beaten path to see some of the regions untouched wetlands. Both of these parks have boardwalks so you can tour the marshes without getting your feet wet.

Flying There

Arriving from the north, down the coast, is straightforward with no obstacles or airspace south of St. Augustine. From the south, filing a flight plan for V 3 to the Ormond Beach VOR (OMN) will help the Daytona Beach approach controllers assist your arrival through their busy airspace.

From the west, consider routing via Gainesville and then flying east to avoid the Palatka 2 Military Operations Area and R-2906 Restricted Area. Also be alert for a tower 7 nm northwest of FIN that rises to 1,248 feet MSL.

Southwestern arrivals should be prepared to navigate complex airspace in the Orlando/Sanford area.

Flagler County's Class D airspace is in effect while the tower is staffed from 6 a.m. to 8 p.m. every day. Runway 6 is the designated calm-wind runway, and runway 11 has a right-hand traffic pattern. Be alert for seaplanes using the water runway on Gore Lake at the southwest corner of the field.

Flagler County Airport's *(386) 437-0401* FBO is operated by the county and is located on the north side of the field. Full service is available while they're open from 7 a.m. to 6 p.m. Monday-Saturday and 8 a.m. to 3 p.m. on Sunday. Self-serve 100LL is available 24/7 with credit card. Advance arrangements are required for fuel at the seaplane dock.

Getting Around

You can rent a car from **Enterprise** *(386) 437-0350* right from the airport, or call **Anytime Taxi** *(386) 597-0960* for a ride from the airport into town. Of course, you can get a taxi anytime you need to travel around the city when you're sightseeing too. There aren't any public bus services in Flagler Beach though.

Walking Distance Activities

The airport is well outside of town, and it's a 10 minute drive by car. You can get a quick bite to eat right at the airport, at High Jacker's (see below for more information).

What to See and Do

Marineland Dolphin Adventure *9600 Ocean Shore Blvd., Marineland, FL 32080 (904) 460-1275 (http://www. marineland.net/index.html)* The

world's first oceanarium has been around over 75 years. A 30 minute drive from the airport, it is located right on the ocean. They don't do dolphin "shows" anymore, but they offer experiences from just walking around and looking at a turtle, shark and dolphins (general admission $12.95) to behind the scenes tours ($23) and a feed the dolphin experience ($33). For a chance to swim with the dolphins, budget about $225.

Flagler Beach Historical Museum *207 S. Central Ave., Flagler Beach, FL (386) 517-2025* This little local museum is right in the center of town, at the end of the highway you take coming in from the airport. It's worth a stop if you want to learn more about Flagler Beach's history, from the stone-age to the space era (like how the city flag was in orbit aboard the space shuttle). Artifacts and photos fill the rooms and you can always hear all the best stories from the museum volunteers. The museum is open seven days a week until 4 p.m. Admission is by donation.

Bulow Plantation Ruins Historic Park *3501 Old Kings Road, Flagler Beach, FL 32136 (386) 517-2084* Once you've seen the museum, you can head out and see an example of local history at the Bulow Plantation ruins. Destroyed in 1836, during the Second Seminole War, these ruins represent one of the early sugar plantations that helped the area thrive. Old wells, foundations and the tall smoke stacks of the mill are still in place, and signs around the site tell you the story. There are also nature

trails through the 150 acre park and picnic facilities. Like most national parks, the fee is $4 per vehicle (have the right change though, as it's paid through an honor box). You can access the park Thursday through Monday during daylight hours.

Betty Steflik Preserve *815 Moody Lane, Flagler Beach, FL 32136 (386) 313-4020* Just across the river on the way into town is the Betty Steflick Preserve, where you can walk along the raised boardwalk to see the wetland scenery. There are some great shore fishing spots, and you can also bring some food to have a picnic. The park opens up when the sun comes up, and stays open until 11 p.m. so you could take a walk after dark and see the park in a whole different light.

Fishing

If you don't feel like walking through a nature park to find some fishing, there are a few other spots where you can cast out your line. The **Flagler Beach Municipal Pier** *215 S. Oceanshore Blvd., Flagler Beach, FL 32136* extends out over the waves and you can get some fresh bait at the shop there. For an afternoon of casual fishing, you can even grab a bite to eat at the nearby **Funky Pelican.** Tickets to access the pier are $1.50 each. There is a beach to either side of the pier but the water can be rough for swimming. To get farther out on the water, book a fishing charter with **Osprey Fishing** *(386) 439-2636.* Captain Ron will take you out on his 17 ft. Action Craft in search of trout, snook or redfish.

Water Sports

Boating and other water sports are pretty popular around Flagler, and you can take your pick from whatever activity interests you. **Flagler Surf Lessons Inc.** *5000 John Anderson Hwy., Flagler Beach, FL 32136 (386) 449-9353* Lessons are offered year 'round in Flagler Beach as long as it is safe and surfable. Lisa Tanner, owner/operator grew up surfing in Flagler Beach and she makes the lessons fun for kids and adults.

Tropical Kayaks *(386) 445-0506* operate a little farther north in Palm Coast, but they're happy to come to Flagler Beach to drop off a rental kayak for you. They arrange eco-tours too if you prefer to head out in a larger group.

Where to Eat

High Jacker's *202 Airport Rd., Bunnell, FL 32110 (386) 586-6078* Right at the airport, you can get a casual mix of seafood dishes served with their house specialty: crisp homemade potato chips. Watch planes on the airfield, or chat with other pilots. If you can't linger at the airport because you have a busy day ahead of you, get your burger or blackened mahi-mahi to go. $$

Oceanside Beach Bar & Grill *1848 S Oceanshore Blvd., Flagler Beach, FL 32136 (386) 439-6345* The name probably gave it away, but this great eatery is right on the beach and the outside deck has wide-ranging views over the water. Inside, it's a lovely spot with an elegant dining room. They're open early enough for breakfast, and late enough for drinks after dinner, so stop in whenever you're in the neighborhood. The menu is definitely a mix of "bar & grill" goodies, like burgers, fish & chips, pizza and grilled chicken. $$

Kokomo's Cafe *202 S Central Ave., Flagler Beach, FL 32136 (386) 693-4912* It's that beach cafe you always hear about in summer songs, with friendly staff, cute decor and a sunny location. Big portions of classic breakfast dishes, or huge lunch sandwiches are on the menu. Open early for breakfast but they close up at 4 p.m., so it's a fine spot for a late lunch but not dinner (closed on Tuesdays). It's about 10 minutes from the airport, right in the center of town. $

High Jacker's Restaurant on the Field

Where to Stay

Si Como No Inn *2480 N Oceanshore Blvd, Flagler Beach, FL 32136 (386) 864-1430* This cute inn might be the most colorful place you've ever stayed. Decorated in a bright, whimsical beach style, you'll feel right at home at the Si Como No Inn. The beach is steps away, or you can relax outside your room in one of their big string hammocks and take advantage of the free Wi-Fi. There are only eight rooms, so it's quite private though the other guests often hang out at the Tiki Hut for drinks. The inn is about 15 minutes from the airport, and very handy if you plan on visiting the Graham Swamp Park. $$

Hilton Garden Inn Palm Coast *55 Town Center Boulevard, Palm Coast, FL 32164 (855) 277-5057* Between the airport and town, you can find a comfortable stay at the Hilton Garden Inn. If you don't feel like driving out to the coast to eat, there is a full service Great American Grill onsite for any meal of the day, or the Pavilion Lounge for drinks and snacks. Other amenities include a large swimming pool, fitness center and business facilities if you need to get any work done while you're there. The Hilton is just off the main road leading into town, so it's very easy to get to. $$

The White Orchid Inn and Spa *1104 S Hwy A1A, Flagler Beach, FL 32136 (386) 439-4944* If you want a little pampering during your stay, then you have to book a room at the White Orchid Inn and Spa. The accommodations are B&B style, and there is a full-service spa on the premises. Rooms include a full breakfast every morning, as well as free Wi-Fi. The heated mineral pool is a favorite way to unwind after spending a day around Flagler Beach. $$

Flagler County Airport · KFIN

FLAGLER TOWER ©**118.95**
[0700-2100]

GROUND CONTROL 121.75

Airport Manager Phone
[386] 437-0401

AWOS–3 128.325 [386] 437-7334

ATIS 128.325

®DAYTONA App/Dep 125.8

CLNC DEL 121.75

Elevation 33' MSL	Traffic Pattern 1000' MSL [1033'AGL]	Flight Service Station 800-WX-BRIEF

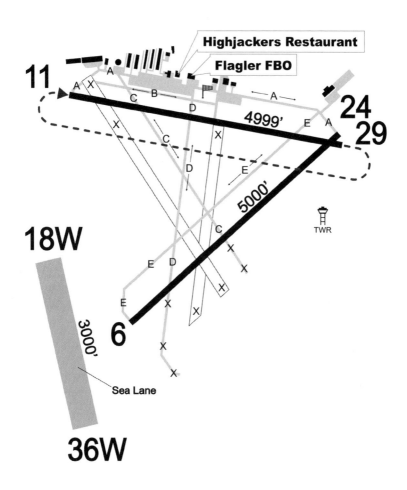

Highjackers Restaurant

Flagler FBO

Fort Lauderdale

While you can do just about anything in Ft. Lauderdale, the two best reasons for pilots to fly here are the Jet Runway Café and the Banyan Pilot Shop. It is also a popular spot to begin a trip to the Bahamas and to clear customs when coming back.

Fort Lauderdale is full of water-based activities and fun, from its canals to the river to the ocean. Known for its vibrant, party atmosphere, this could be the place to come for beaches and nightlife or to experience something a little different from the norm. If you're looking for beaches, there are many here but try those at Lauderdale by the Sea if you prefer them quieter. So why else would you come to Fort Lauderdale?

Well if you'd like to eat somewhere different you'd be hard pushed to beat the choice of over 4,000 restaurants in Greater Fort Lauderdale. There are 12 shopping malls if shopping is your thing, and over 60 golf courses if you're looking for time on the fairways. Yachting is really big here, and there's no shortage of marinas housing something like 45,000 resident yachts. The fact is, you can do just about anything in Fort Lauderdale so here are some suggestions for things you might not have thought of.

Fort Lauderdale

Flying There

Lying just inside the 30 nm Mode C veil for Miami International's Class B airspace, and below the shelf of Fort Lauderdale/Hollywood International's Class C, FXE is a Class D airport with 24/7 control tower staffing. Regardless of where you're coming from, or what time of day, contact Miami Approach 119.7 for assistance with your arrival.

The surrounding area is noise-sensitive. At night, it's preferred to land on runway 9 and depart on 27, to minimize overflight of residential areas to the east.

FXE is a popular jet base for the northern Miami metropolitan area, and light general aviation aircraft benefit greatly from the excellent facilities and services offered at the airport. The U.S. Customs and Border Protection facility is open daily, 8 a.m. to 9 p.m.

Banyan Air Service is located midfield, just west of the midpoint of runway 13/31, and offers 24/7 FBO services. Additionally, Banyan provides survival equipment rental/sales for overwater flights, and has a cafe and pilot shop on site. Radio 130.80 or call (954) 491-3170.

Sano Jet Center sits next to the customs ramp on the east side of the field. They provide full FBO services from 6 a.m. to 10 p.m. and have Hertz car rental available at their pet-friendly facility. Radio 131.275 or call *(954) 351-2003.*

World Jet is another 24-hour FBO, situated on the far northeastern corner of FXE. Enterprise car rentals available. Radio 129.375 or call *(954) 772-7444.*

W Aviation provides FBO services from 6 a.m. to 10 p.m. from their location on the northwestern corner of the airport. Enterprise car rentals available. Radio 131.95 or call *(954) 938-1962.*

Getting Around

Being such a large city there are plenty of options for getting around. Public buses are operated by **Broward County Transit** *(954) 357-8400* and there is a route passing right by the airport, although you might have to hunt around to find the bus stop. For taxi service call **Yellow Cab Broward** *(954) 777-7777* or rent a car from **Hertz** *(954) 489-0837* right from the airport for the ultimate in convenience. If

you'd like to get around the city in something a little more stylish, try renting a Jeep from **SoBeJeeps** *2530 West Commercial Blvd, Ft. Lauderdale, FL 33309 (855) MIA-JEEP* They offer free delivery to the airport if you're renting for multiple days.

Walking Distance Activities

You don't have to walk far to get a good meal and shop for all your pilots accessories as you'll find both right at the FBO. The **Jet Runway Café** is a pilot favorite for breakfast and lunch (read more in the Where to Eat section), and **Banyan Pilot Shop** *(954) 493-8615* is renowned for its size and number of items in stock. You can buy just about anything you need from here.

Off the airport you need to walk just a couple of minutes for more dining options; take your pick of everything from **Dunkin' Donuts** to independent eateries.

What to See and Do

Banyan Pilot Shop *(954) 493-8615* This 5,000+ square foot store located in Hangar 63 at Fort Lauderdale Executive Airport is one of the largest in the country. It is packed with everything aviation related, from electronics, a nice selection of headsets and charts, to cleaning supplies, clothing and toys. Jump in the cockpit of the Gulfstream II fuselage and fly the Microsoft Flight Simulator X!

Chef Jean-Pierre Cooking School *1436 N Federal Hwy, Ft. Lauderdale, FL 33304 (954) 563-2700* Looking for a different way to spend an evening? Chef Jean-Pierre Cooking School is both fun and educational and is run by French-born chef Jean-Pierre who is a regular guest chef on the Today Show. Spend the evening learning from a professional how to prepare and cook a selection of dishes, depending on what night you come. The menus vary every night and are often themed according to the season. You can bring your

Banyan Pilot Shop with a Gulfstream Cockpit on the Floor

favorite bottle of wine (they provide the glasses), and yes, you do get to eat the food that is prepared! Be sure to reserve your place in advance as many classes fill quickly.

Segway Fort Lauderdale *300 SW 1st Ave., Ft. Lauderdale, FL 33301 (954) 304-5746* A great way to get around Fort Lauderdale without having to rely on a car or walking power is on a Segway. Segway tours are fun, don't require much energy to ride on, and they're easy to master after just a quick lesson from the pros. Take a 1 or 2 hour guided tour in which you'll soar through the heart of downtown and see celebrity mansions and yachts. The 1 hour tour covers 5 miles while on the 2-hour tour you'll also cover 10 miles and travel over the 17th Street Causeway Bridge in addition to the above.

Boating

Dozens of boat charters and captains are always ready to take you out on the waters around Fort Lauderdale. Whether you're looking for a leisurely cruise or you want to find the best spots for sport fishing, there are ample options to choose from. **Tropical Sailing** *801 Seabreeze Blvd, Ft. Lauderdale, FL 33316 (954) 579-8181* will take you out on their catamaran, or contact **Captain Ron Yacht Charters** *(954) 401-9278* for a memorable personalized yacht cruise.

Las Olas Gondolier Tours *(800) 277-1390* Here is something a little different from the regular fishing charters and yachts. Take advantage of the inland canals and waterways on a gondolier tour, just like

they do in Venice, Italy. Slowly floating along Ft. Lauderdale's canals is the perfect way to spend a romantic evening or a special occasion. Guides point out interesting landmarks and play music while you sit back and enjoy a glass of wine.

Where to Eat

Jet Runway Café *5540 NW 21st Terrace, Ft. Lauderdale, FL 33309 (954) 958-9900* This is a famous spot among pilots

Jet Runway Café at Banyan Air Service

for breakfast or lunch. Located at the airport, taxi your plane right up to the restaurant at Banyan Air Service. Inside you can sit and watch the airplanes taking off and landing while you eat. This modern and sleek establishment has a lively atmosphere and is often full. Breakfast has the usual choices including Eggs Benedict, as well as some unusual choices like brioche almond french toast. For lunch there are tasty choices including Mexican favorites, burgers,

sandwiches, steaks, salads and pizza. The Grilled Three Cheese & Tomato Bisque is consistently popular. Hours: Mon - Fri 7:30 a.m. - 3 p.m. Sat 7:30 a.m. - 2 p.m. $$

Anthony's Runway 84 *330 W State Rd 84, Ft. Lauderdale, FL 33315 (954) 467-8484* This very good old school Italian restaurant gets a mention here because the rooms are decked out like airline cabins. Big menu of authentic Italian food and a Piano Bar. Go with the idea of having a good time and a different experience. $$$

La Dolce Vita *3331 NE 33rd Street, Ft. Lauderdale, FL 33308 (954) 565-5707* La Dolce Vita is perfect if you're in downtown Fort Lauderdale and looking for an upscale place to dine. Open for dinner (no lunches) every day from 5 p.m., this Italian restaurant is among the best in the city. Great service, food and atmosphere that is raved over by everyone who visits, just expect to pay more for such quality. Everything is homemade and authentic, so if you've ever wanted a real taste of Italy this is the place to come. $$$

Aruba Beach Café *1 Commercial Blvd, Lauderdale by the Sea, FL 33308 (954) 776-0001* About a ten minute drive directly east from the airport. You'll get to Lauderdale by the Sea and the Aruba Beach Café. Quieter than in Fort Lauderdale itself, Lauderdale by the Sea has a nice beachy "islands" atmosphere, and this popular café is right on the beach. They serve fresh seafood, steaks, burgers, pasta, and salads and are open seven days a week for breakfast, lunch and dinner. There's live island music every day to keep you entertained. $$

Where to Stay

Holiday Inn Express *1500 W Commercial Blvd, Ft. Lauderdale, FL 33309 (954) 772-*
3032 The closest hotel to the airport, Holiday Inn Express is just a quick walk from the FBO so you can be checked in in no time. The hotel offers everything you'd expect from the Holiday Inn Express brand including hot savory complimentary breakfast, an outdoor pool, business center, Wi-Fi and comfortable, modern rooms. $$

Windjammer Resort *4244 El Mar Drive, Lauderdale by the Sea, FL 33308 (954) 776-4232* When craving an oceanside setting that's not too far from the airport, the Windjammer Resort hits the mark. Just a block down to the beach from the Aruba Beach Café the Windjammer has a beautiful location right on the beach and is only around a ten minute drive from the airport. Suites overlooking the ocean offer all the ingredients for a romantic getaway. Being suites rather than simple
hotel rooms you get a lot more space to stretch out, with the amenities to cook (full kitchen) if you want to. The resort has two pools, free parking, and access to the uncrowded beach. $$

Breakaway Inn *4457 Poinciana Street, Lauderdale by the Sea, FL 33308 (954) 772-4910* For more of a motel experience and the affordable prices that go with it, try the Breakaway Inn. It too is located in Lauderdale by the Sea, just a block back from the beach. The motel is always clean, and you'll receive far more personal service than you might in larger national chain hotels. There's a nice swimming pool and well maintained grounds and the building has a Southern beach style. Free Wi-Fi, free tennis and shuffleboard, and free parking are just a few more reasons to stay here. $

Table in the Bar of Anthony's Runway 84 puts you on Board a Flight

Fort Lauderdale Executive KFXE

EXECUTIVE TOWER ©120.9

GROUND CONTROL 121.75

Control Tower Phone
(954) 776-1046

Airport Manager Phone
(954) 828-4955

ASOS (954) 772–2537

ATIS 119.85

MIAMI App/Dep ®119.7 (Usable 4000 and below)

CLNC DEL 127.95

UNICOM 122.95

Elevation 13' MSL	Traffic Pattern 1013' MSL (1000'AGL)	Flight Service Station 800-WX-BRIEF

W Aviation

U.S. Customs

Executive Jet Center

World Jet

Sano Jet Center

Jet Runway Café

Sheltair

Banyan Air Service

Fort Myers

The Edison & Ford winter estates along with the Red Sox and Minnesota Twins spring training are the best reasons to make this a fly-in destination. Of course fishing and beach activities are also available.

Fort Myers

Fort Myers is known as the winter home of Thomas Edison, Henry Ford and Harvey Firestone who all spent their winters there. The three of them knew one another and actually worked together at the workshops known today as the Edison Ford Winter Estate. It's one of the main attractions in town.

A stop in Fort Myers can bring all sorts of activities, ranging from beaches and nature parks to unique historical sites and artistic venues. There is something for everyone in the City of Palms. Zombie movie fans might be interested to know that several scenes from George Romero's "Day of the Dead" were filmed at the Edison Theatre in Fort Myers.

Flying There

Fort Myers Class D airspace underlies the shelf of Southwest Florida International's (KRSW) Class C. Frequencies for Fort Myers Approach depend on direction of arrival and are clearly marked on VFR sectionals. If Fort Myers Approach is closed, contact Miami Center on 134.75.

The airport fits snugly in a fairly dense suburban area. Be alert for roads and fences close to the ends of all runways. Even with several displaced thresholds, all runways are large enough to comfortably accommodate light general aviation aircraft. Runway 5 is the calm wind runway. See flylcpa.com/fmy for additional information including noise abatement.

Base Operations at Page Field provides FBO services from 7 a.m. to 11 p.m. on the west ramp. Self-serve 100LL and Mogas are available 24/7 with credit card. Courtesy cars are available. Air-to-FBO radio frequency is 130.55 or telephone (239) 590-6600.

Getting Around

You'll need a vehicle to get downtown. You can get a rental at FBO **Base Operations** *(239) 590-6600.* Or call a cab with **Bluebird** *(239) 348-2378* or **A Better Taxi** *(239) 288-5587.*

There are public buses operated by **LeeTran** *(239) LEE-*

TRAN, and Route 140 goes right by the airport and will take you directly downtown. The closest bus stop is at the Edison Mall to the north, which is about a 25-minute walk. Cash fares are $1.25 and an all-day pass is $3.50.

Walking Distance Activities

Page Field airport is located right within Fort Myers, but the major sights and attractions are not within walking distance. Inside FBO **Base Operations,** there is a great little gift shop that sells snacks, souvenirs, pilot charts and gear, and other aviation goodies. They're open seven days a week.

What to See and Do

Edison and Ford Winter Estates *2350 McGregor Boulevard, Fort Myers, FL 33901 (239) 334-7419* History and science collide at the estate with 20 acres of restored buildings where famed inventors Thomas Edison and Henry Ford once worked together. This is a fascinating walk back in time. Outside there are extensive groomed gardens, and inside you can see the main house as well as their botanical laboratory, workshop and other cottages around the property. The view of the Caloosahatchee River is breath-taking. The buildings are filled with artifacts and inventions from these two great scientists. It's particularly beautiful at Christmastime, when it's open at night and decorated with thousands of white lights. The estate is open seven days a week, and admission starts at $12 for adults (depending on the tour you choose). There

Edison Home

is a great little cafe there too if you want to stop for lunch.

JetBlue Park, *11500 Fenway South Drive, Fort Myers, FL 33913* The spring training home of the **Boston Red Sox,** JetBlue Park seats about 10,000. Don't be fooled by the five-digit capacity as it routinely sells out for spring games. The park is a 20-minute drive from the airport. The ballpark's field has exactly the same dimensions as Fenway Park in Boston. A number of the characteristics of the ballpark are taken from Fenway Park,

including a "Green Monster" and a manual scoreboard. Other features from the ballpark in Boston that are present in the spring training stadium are Pesky's Pole, the triangle and the Lone Red Seat that marks the longest home run hit in Fenway's history. Spring training takes place in March. In addition to serving as the home field for Red Sox spring training games, JetBlue Park is the home field for the Gulf Coast League Red Sox, who play during the summer.

Hammond Stadium *14100*

Hammond Stadium

JetBlue Park

Six Mile Cypress, Fort Myers, FL 33912 **The Minnesota Twins** have their spring training camp in this newly renovated 9,300 seat stadium just 15 minutes south of the airport. After spring training season, baseball continues being played here. The stadium is also the home of two Twins' minor league affiliates, housing both the **Ft. Myers Miracle** of the Single-A Florida State League and the Rookie level **Gulf Coast League Twins.**

Southwest Florida Museum of History *2031 Jackson Street, Fort Myers, FL 33901 (239) 321-7430* This local museum located in a restored railroad depot holds historical exhibits for the area dating back to the time of the dinosaurs, with some pretty impressive skeletons and fossils. Artifacts and photos illustrate the times of the Native American as well as the arrival of Spanish explorers. Larger exhibits show off a 1920s fire pumper, a luxury rail car and a single room "cracker" house. They're closed Sundays and Mondays. An adult admission is $10.

Six Mile Cypress Slough Reserve *7791 Penzance Blvd, Fort Myers, FL 33966 (239) 533-7550* A 10-minute drive from the airport and you could be walking along the boardwalk among alligators, otters, wild boar, herons and more bird species than you knew existed. The place is peaceful and beautiful. The Six Mile Cypress Slough Reserve is a nearby section of the Everglades ecosystem, and it's pretty easy to get to. If you don't have time to head out into the deep wilderness, this is a great option. Free, except for a nominal parking fee.

Four Mile Cove Ecological Preserve *East End of SE 23 Terrace, Cape Coral, FL Park Office (239) 549-4606* Technically, this park is across the river in Cape Coral, but the nearby Mudpoint Bridge gives you easy access by car. Just like the Cypress Slough Reserve mentioned above, you can be there in about 10 minutes from the airport. The boardwalks through the mangroves make you feel like you are embarking on a secret walk through nature. You come out onto a pier on the river. Kayak rental available in season if you want to see some of the landscapes by water.

Fort Myers River District. Downtown Fort Myers has everything you could ask for — restaurants, shops, boutiques, more restaurants, art, historic buildings, great sunsets, and convenient parking. The old buildings are beautifully painted and restored and parking is easy to find. Lots of downtown weekend action. Check out the River District's Music Walk, Art Walk and other Friday Night River District street parties. Go to fortmyersriverdistrictalliance.com for schedules.

Evening Artistic Entertainment

The arts and culture scene is very active in Fort Myers and if you are tired of nature parks, you'll find several great options for a night out on the town. The **Southwest Florida Symphony** *(239) 418-0996* is the only professional orchestra in the county, and they have regular performances through the winter and spring months. For theatrical performances, the **Florida Repertory Theatre** *2267 1st Street, Fort Myers, Florida 33901 (239) 332-4488* is right down on the harbor in a beautiful old building. They put on regular performances with rave reviews. Comedies, dramas, and musicals make up their usual repertoire. For something more interactive, try the **Seminole Gulf Railway Murder Mystery Dinner Train** *2805 Colonial Blvd, Colonial Station, Fort Myers, FL 33916 (239) 275-8487* A five-course dinner is served during your train ride while you watch and participate in the onboard murder mystery performance. It's a fun and unique night out!

Where to Eat

Cibo *12901 Mcgregor Blvd, Ste 17, Fort Myers, FL 33919 (239) 454-3700* Immerse yourself in fine Italian cuisine at Cibo, only 15 minutes away from the airport to the south of the city. It's easy to miss because it's located in a rather unassuming strip mall, but the regulars have learned that it's a hidden culinary gem. The menu has an array of truly traditional Italian dishes along with an extensive wine list. There is no outdoor patio, but the indoor dining room has a great atmosphere. $$$

Taqueria San Julian *11601 S Cleveland Ave., Fort Myers, FL 33907 (239) 936-0037* Just a few blocks south of the airport is a popular taco joint that has tasty Mexican food at a low price. Though it's usually described as a dive or a hole-in-the-wall, don't let that scare you off. The delicious food and large portions make up for the lack of atmosphere. $

Farmer's Market Restau-rant *2736 Edison Ave., Fort Myers, FL 33916 (239) 334-1687* The Farmer's Market is practically a landmark in Fort Myers, as it's been a favorite restaurant in town for more than 50 years. It's all about Southern comfort food, and you'll always go away feeling very full. Grits, okra, fried chicken and corn bread are the dishes that get the best reviews. $$

Love Boat Homemade Ice Cream *16229 San Carols Blvd, Fort Myers, FL (239) 466-7707* For a sweet treat, this is a must-visit. Everything is rich, creamy and freshly homemade. There are dozens of flavors to choose from, like blueberry cheesecake, coconut and salted caramel. It may even be the best ice cream in the state. Open seven days a week from noon until 10 p.m. $

Where to Stay

Legacy Harbor Hotel & Suites *2038 West First Street, Fort Myers, FL 33901 (239)*

Fishermen Wading in Ft. Myers Beach

332-2048 For accommodations in downtown Fort Myers rather than near the airport, the Legacy Harbor is a fine choice. Its located right on the harbor next door to Joe's Crab Shack. The rooms are large and nicely decorated and the prices are great. You'll get free Wi-Fi, access to the pool and fitness center, and there is a tiki bar open for drinks on the weekends. $$

Hibiscus House B&B *2135 McGregor Blvd., Fort Myers, FL 33901 (239) 332-2651* The Hibiscus House is a lovely little B&B near the harbor and the Edison Ford Winter Estate. All of the rooms are tastefully done, have large bright windows and the staff always make guests feel welcome. $$

Hampton Inn & Suites *4350 Executive Circle, Fort Myers, FL 33916 (239) 931-5300* If you prefer to stay closer to the airport, you can get to the Hampton Inn & Suites in under 10 minutes by car. Parking is free and so is the Wi-Fi and breakfast. There is a swimming pool, business center and also a gym. $$

Mango Street Inn *126 Mango St, Fort Myers Beach, FL 33931 (239) 233-8542* If you are looking for a place to stay and love B&Bs then Mango Street Inn is for you. The owners, Dan and Tree, are friendly and accommodating. The rooms are spacious and clean. A gourmet-inspired breakfast is served 6 days a week. You are a half mile from Time Square and all the restaurants are a short walk down the road. The beach is across the street. Beach chairs, bicycles and umbrellas are provided for guests.

Page Field; *Fort Myers*   KFMY

PAGE TOWER ©**119.0**
(0700-2300)

Ground Control **121.7**

Control Tower Phone
(239) 936-7867

Airport Manager Phone
(239) 590-6601

ASOS (239) 936–2318

ATIS 123.725

FT MYERS App/Dep ®126.8 (0700-2300)

MIAMI App/Dep ®134.75 (2300-0700)

CLNC DEL 121.7

Elevation 17' MSL	Traffic Pattern 800' MSL (783' AGL)	Flight Service Station 121.1R 122.65 122.2 122.1 MIAMI

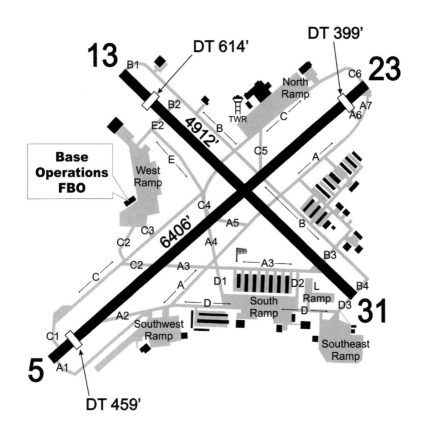

Fort Pierce

Primarily known by pilots as a place to clear customs when returning from the Bahamas, or to get a $100 hamburger, another great reason to fly here is the Navy Seal Museum.

Northbound pilots coming from the Bahamas clear customs in Ft. Pierce because the FARs require pilots flying at low altitudes to clear customs at an airport nearest their entry into Florida, and KFPR is the most northerly acceptable airport.

The airport also features the popular **Airport Tiki** restaurant which was once written up in the *Wall Street Journal.*

An 11 minute ride from the airport brings you to the excellent **Navy Seal Museum.** It is located by the beaches where the first volunteers for Naval Combat Demolition Units and Underwater Demolition Teams (UDT) trained. These were the forefathers of today's SEALs.

The Navy Seal Museum

Flying There

Pilots flying into FPR must consider the Class D airports of Vero Beach to the north and Witham (Stuart) to the south. Avoid loitering in the vicinity of the nuclear power plant, marked "plant" on the VFR sectional, approximately 10 miles south of Fort Pierce along the beach.

Fort Pierce and Vero Beach are home to large flight schools and training activity in the area is heavy, particularly to the west of the airports. Runway 10L/28R at FPR is a dedicated VFR training runway and is not connected to the rest of the airport by taxiways.

APP Jet Center operates the FBO, conveniently located right next to the Customs office. They're open from 7 a.m. to 9 p.m. daily. Life vests and raft rentals are available for overwater flights. They have

courtesy cars and Hertz rentals. The Airport Tiki restaurant is in the FBO and open 7 a.m. to 4 p.m. Full-service 100LL and Jet A are available during business hours, and self-serve 100LL is also available. Radio 129.025 or call *(772) 489-2285.*

Walking Distance Activities

Other than the Airport Tiki restaurant, you are too far away from everything to walk around.

Getting Around

APP has a crew car and also handles Hertz rentals.

What to See and Do

Navy Seal Museum *3300 N. Rte. A1A, Fort Pierce, FL 34949 (772) 595-5845* This is a wonderful museum full of historic memorabilia, art work and interactive displays. Newly expanded and updated, it is a visual, tactile and auditory museum that both adults and children will enjoy. There are displays both inside and outside. You'll find lots of history and hands-on equipment. Sit in an actual Blackhawk helicopter, pick up some of the mock weaponry to gauge the weight of those carried by SEALS, view the actual *Maersk Alabama* life boat from the 2009 pirate attack (i.e Captain Phillips), try your hand at the obstacle training course on the grounds and view a myriad of memorials, photos and artifacts. $10. Tuesday-Saturday, 10 a.m. to 4 p.m., Sunday, 12-4 p.m. and closed on Mondays.

South Jetty Park and Seaway Drive. The park is right at the tip of the Ft. Pierce inlet. Recently refurbished and upgraded, you get great views of the Atlantic Ocean and the inlet. Perfect place to catch a sunrise. The jetty extends 1,200 feet into the Atlantic which makes it a good place to fish. The park has restrooms as well as restaurants across the street, including the original **Hurricane Grill and Wings** restaurant (there are now 80 across the country). The south side of the jetty is one of the best windsurfing spots in the state. Seaway Drive, which runs parallel to the inlet, is home to many small hotels, restaurants and bars making this a place vacationers like to hang out.

Downtown Fort Pierce. The historic downtown has been renovated over last 20 years. Fort Pierce has lots of shops, restaurants, museums and art galleries. The **1st Friday** of every month there is a street party and food fest that is fun. The **fresh market** is every Wednesday and on Saturdays the market expands to include arts and crafts and lots of creative and interesting hand-made product stands. There is a popular **Manatee Observation & Education Center** *(772) 466-1600 ext. 3333* and the Fort Pierce City marina has fishing charters available.

Beach Tours on Horseback *Frederick Douglas Memorial Park, 3600 South Ocean Dr., Fort Pierce, FL 34949 (772) 468-0101* Great way to spend an hour or so soaking up the sun and the beautiful view via horseback! The pristine beaches make it a one of a kind ride along the ocean. They adjust the riding to your skill level, so you don't even need to know how to ride to enjoy this experience. Tours are available on Saturdays and Sundays.

Where to Eat

The Airport Tiki *2982 Curtis King Blvd, Fort Pierce, FL 32946 (772) 489-2285* Located in the **APP Jet Center** this restaurant with a thatched roof entranceway is well known to pilots. It has been around for years and was mentioned in a 2001 *Wall Street Journal* article. Renovated in 2013, you can see the field through its glass atrium, while you eat your meal. If you have just cleared customs, you can walk the 100 yards over to the Tiki and they will tow your airplane to the restaurant. Unlike many airport restaurants that get most of their customers from off field, the Tiki seems to get the majority of their diners from people involved with aviation. $

12A Buoy 22 Fisherman's Wharf, *Seaway Drive and Indian River Drive, Fort Pierce, FL 34950 (772) 672-4524* After an eight minute drive from the airport, your first view of this

Riding Horses on the Beach

Riverwalk

restaurant will have you judging it as typical bar/dive, but don't be fooled. The food is fabulous and beautifully presented at this seafood restaurant. Their lobster roll is better than any you will find in New England. Dine early for daily specials. They buy fresh daily and run out occasionally, but the food is always fresh and almost always locally sourced. In season it can get crowded. You can eat outside on the deck or inside. Beer and wine only. $$

Hurricane Grill and Wings *2017 Seaway Drive, Fort Pierce, FL 34949 (772) 595-9051* If you are a wings fan, just for fun you have to visit this place. It is the original location for the chain of the same name started by then 22-year-old Chris Russo. He long since sold this location to a franchisee (and sold the company too), but the original restaurant still stands overlooking Ft. Pierce inlet. Apparently it hasn't lost any of the founder's magic because people say this location's food surpasses the chain's other locations. Sit inside or out; enjoy the comfort, beauty and relaxation of the nearby ocean; people watch; and soak in the uniquely 'beachy' atmosphere. $

Where to Stay

Hutchinson Island Plaza Hotel and Suites *1230 Seaway Drive, Fort Pierce, FL 34949 (772) 879-5651* Nice refurbished hotel on the inlet with a friendly, competent staff. It is a short walk to a couple of good restaurants and relaxing bars. Many of the rooms have views of the inlet, which is a constant source of entertainment with boats, Coast Guard activity, and marine life. The pool also overlooks the inlet. They have a private pier that you can fish off. $$

Mellon Patch Inn *3601 North A1A, North Hutchinson Island, Fort Pierce, FL 34949 (772) 413-0200* This B&B is built in Old Florida style and has a beach across the street. In the back there is a spacious terrace with grounds that lead down to the Indian River and a private dock. The whole place has a friendly relaxed feel to it and they serve an excellent breakfast. The Inn is a one minute drive from the Navy Seal Museum. $$

Fort Pierce Inlet with the Fishing Jetty on Beach on the Right

St Lucie Co Intl; *Fort Pierce* KFPR

FT PIERCE TOWER ©**128.2**
[0700-2100]

Ground Control **119.55**

Control Tower Phone
[772] 465-0761

Airport Manager Phone
[772] 462-1727

ASOS 772-489-4281

ATIS 134.825

PALM BEACH App/Dep
123.625 [North]
125.925 [South]

Elevation 22' MSL	Traffic Pattern 1000' MSL [978' AGL]	Flight Service Station MIAMI 122.55 800-WX-BRIEF

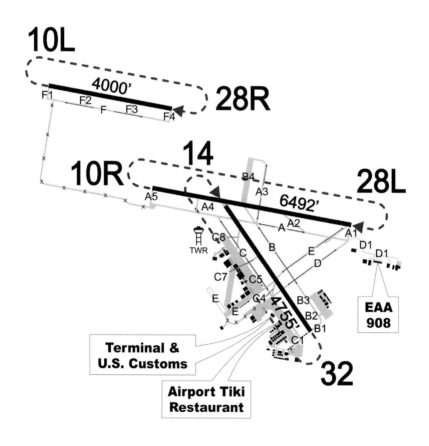

Terminal & U.S. Customs

Airport Tiki Restaurant

EAA 908

TWR

KEYW

Key West

Key West's quirky atmosphere has been attracting interesting characters for decades. It's a hip and happening bohemian kind of place where anything goes, and usually does! Downtown is a 10 minute taxi ride from the airport. Or just fly in for a meal at the Conch Flyer.

Key West is the most southerly city in the United States, sitting at the end of the long string of islands known as the Florida Keys. The city is famous for many reasons besides its geography. Ernest Hemingway lived here for many years, and it was the site of the winter White House during President Truman's term. The island is also a key military position and the home of Key West Naval Air Station.

In 1982, in response to heavy-handed border patrol stops on the highway, Key West declared independence from the USA and renamed itself the Conch Republic. It was only a symbolic gesture and not actually official, though they do celebrate their independence day every April 23, and this is just one example of the eccentric Key West spirit.

Go for the beaches and scuba diving, or spend more time on land and see the various historical and cultural sites around town. The best place

Key West

to find all that free-spirited personality that Key West is so famous for? The streets of Old Town.

Flying There

Key West is a small island, and all flights should be considered "over water" unless you choose to fly over the island chain from the east. Although

the southwestern part of the Florida peninsula is charted as land, it is essentially a giant swamp offering no dry landing areas. In the event of an emergency, make sure you have proper, current, water survival equipment within reach, and your passengers know how to use them.

Several Victor Airways offer

direct overwater routing from points northward. These airways (except Victor 157) penetrate the Contiguous U.S. Air Defense Identification Zone. Pilots crossing the ADIZ must be on an active IFR clearance or an active Defense VFR (DVFR) flight plan. Review 14 CFR §99 for ADIZ crossing procedures.

Approaching Key West from the east, pilots are requested to maintain at least 2,000 feet when flying over the Great White Heron National Wildlife Refuge north of the islands and west of Marathon Key. Restricted Area R-2916 contains an unmarked tethered balloon extending to 14,000 feet and must be avoided.

If you are flying down the east coast of Florida, and you don't want to file IFR or request Flight Following through the Palm Beach to Miami stretch, check out the VFR Flyway Planning Chart printed on the reverse side of the Miami Terminal Area Chart. It shows a pathway to the west of that congested airspace. If you don't have a copy of the chart, you can find it on the SkyVector website.

Flying to the Florida Keys from the east or northeast, consider navigating to VFR waypoint VPRLN (Ranger Station) just south of Homestead General (X-51) and then flying a heading of 150° to intersect the Keys just west of the US 1 bridge connecting the mainland to the Keys.

Key West Naval Air Station hosts extensive military jet activity. Contact Key West Approach on 124.025 for help avoiding the fast-movers and safely crossing the NAS's Class

D airspace on the way into EYW. If Key West Approach is closed, contact Miami Center on 133.50.

Signature Flight Support is the current FBO in Key West. They're open from 7 a.m. to 9 p.m. and other times by prior arrangement. *(305) 296-5422.* Fees can be high for larger planes. Call ahead for pricing.

Getting Around

If you are staying in Key West, you don't need a car, nor do you want one because parking in Key West can be horrible. Take the 10 minute cab ride from the airport. The FBO front desk will be happy to call a cab for you.

If you really want to, you can rent a bicycle, scooter or golf cart from one of the many rental shops in Key West. Head into downtown and you'll come across one of them in no time.

If you are exploring the upper and middle keys, you will need a rental car, which can be rented at the airport. **Avis** *(305) 296-8744;* **Dollar** *(305) 296-9921;* **Budget** *(305) 294-8868* and **Enterprise** *(305) 292-0220.*

There is public bus service around town, as well as to other islands up through the Keys to Marathon. Around Key West, fares are $2 (or $4.00 if you plan on taking the bus to the other Keys). There are no day passes, but a 7-day pass is just $8. The Blue and Green routes have a stop just outside the airport. The Blue Route goes west from the airport, so it gives the shortest ride downtown, about 20 minutes. Coming back the Green goes east and is the best choice. You can access the route

Key West Harbor

map, including a real-time look at when the next bus will be at your stop from their mobile phone friendly site: kwtransit.com.

Walking Distance Activities

Right at the airport is the the **Conch Flyer Restaurant** run by former DC-3 pilot John Richmond. The walls are covered with photos and posters depicting the history of the airport. Behind the bar and above the door are replica 1927 rotary engines. Carefully crafted model airplanes are also part of the decor.

Walk six minutes to the east from the FBO, and you will come to a **Benihana** Japanese steakhouse, and **La Tratoria** serving excellent Italian food and featuring ocean views.

If you are in tourist mode, the **Fort East Martello Museum** is right outside the airport grounds and **Smathers Beach** is across the street from the airport.

What to See and Do

Key West Butterfly Conservatory *1316 Duval Street,*

Key West, FL 33040 (305) 296-2988 Walk through the enclosed glass conservatory, among clouds of colorful butterflies that fly freely among the trees and the visitors. Around 50 different butterfly species are loose in the building, along with a mix of exotic birds. It's a very unique experience to see so many butterflies up close, and the perfect example of Key West whimsy. They're open seven days a week until 5 p.m., and tickets are $12 for adults (discounts for seniors and military).

The Southernmost Point

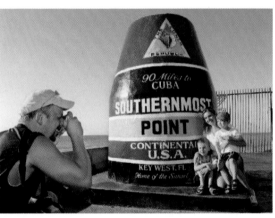

Southernmost Point in the Continental USA

in the USA is at the end of White Street near Harvey Rest Beach Park. While not a particularly exciting site, it's a unique point that should at least be photographed while in Key West. There is a big red marker right at the southern edge of the island that indicates the southernmost point of the USA. If you enjoy searching out the one-of-a-kind places in Florida, this is definitely a good one. The Old Town Trolley tour will take you to the

marker, so it's not hard to find.

Old Town Trolley Tours *1 Whitehead St, Key West, FL 33040 (305) 296-6688* If you're pushed for time and want to see the best that Key West has to offer, these trolley tours are the perfect option. With 13 hop-on / hop-off stops you can stay on the trolley for a quick tour, or opt to get off when something piques your interest. Stops include Mallory Square, the Historic Waterfront and Simonton Row. This is a great way to sample the historic flavor of the island with a tour through the Old Town. Travel past the wonderfully old buildings and see Key West the way Hemingway did. With parking so tricky in Old Town, this is the best way to see it all. Regular adult price is $30.45 though you'll get to ride the second consecutive day for free. Buy your tickets online for additional savings.

Ernest Hemingway Home and Museum *907 Whitehead St., Key West, FL 33040 (305) 294-1575* Famed literary author Ernest Hemingway lived

and wrote in this Key West home for more than 10 years. You can see where he lived, and explore memorabilia from his life and work on display throughout the house. Even if you're not familiar with his writing, the house is a very nice example of Key West history. The house has a large population of six-toed cats, all said to be descendants of Hemingway's own cat. Open seven days a week, and tickets are $13 each. There are guided tours available too.

Fort East Martello Museum *3501 South Roosevelt Boulevard, Key West, FL 33040 (305) 296-3913* As you are leaving the airport, the Fort East Martello Museum will be the very first thing you see. The old fort is still in pretty good shape, and you can wander around the fortification and see displays about its history and other local military history as well. The main attraction at the museum isn't the building itself, but the haunted doll named "Robert" that is on display. Unless you want bad luck following you home, you should be polite to Robert and ask permission before taking any photos (seriously). Entrance to the museum is $9 and they're open daily.

Dry Tortugas National Park *PO Box 6208 Key West FL 33041 (305) 242-7700* About 70 miles to the west is the Dry Tortugas National Park. The main island of the park was completely enclosed by the 19th century Fort Jefferson, making it a spot equally as interesting for its natural sights as its historical ones. There are sandy beaches, boardwalks and opportunities to go snorkeling in extremely clear waters. The

Ernest Hemingway Home and Museum

fort is open year-round, and access to the park is only $5. The ferry, **The Yankee Freedom** *(800) 634-0939,* costs $175 per adult, round trip and takes just over 2 hours to get there. As a pilot, you might like to take the seaplane, **Key West Seaplane Adventures** *(305) 293-9300,* which takes about 40 minutes to get there. $317 per adult for a half day round trip.

Key West Nightlife

One of the great things about Key West is the personality of the city, and you can see that in many different neighborhoods. No other place captures this like **Mallory Square** at sunset. Everyone gathers by the pier at the west end of the island, and the party gets started as the sun goes down. Jugglers, musicians, clowns, psychic readers, and lots of food vendors keep things hopping. If you want a drink, there is a fancy beverage cart run by the

Westin Hotel. Their signature drink is the **"Green Thing"** which people rave about. This frozen concoction is made of Bacardi, KeKe Beach Liqueur, Rose's lime juice, and Kiwi Passion Fruit juice.

Mallory Square may be the party spot at sunset, but **Duval Street** is busy all through the day. It's in the Old Town quarter, and the street is lined with boutiques, restaurants and unusual art galleries. After dark, the activity just keeps going.

Where to Eat

La Trattoria Oceanside *3591 S Roosevelt Blvd., Key West, FL 33040 (305) 295-6789* One of the nicest restaurants on the island just happens to also be one of the closest to the airport. You can be dining in luxury in just minutes after you have your plane settled in. Italian cuisine is on the menu, with dishes like lobster bisque, gorgonzola gnocci, grilled hogfish and chicken picatta. Don't

forget canolis or tiramisu for dessert. They have an exceptional wine list but no outdoor patio, and you might want to make reservations. Their cocktail lounge, Virgilios, has jazz until 2 a.m. $$$

Hogfish Bar & Grill *6810 Front St., Key West, FL 33040 (305) 293-4041* If you're planning on checking out nearby Stock Island, then you should be eating at the Hogfish Bar & Grill. Only eight minutes from the airport, it's actually closer than many other points on Key West itself. Conch fritters, shrimp poor boys and grilled hogfish are a few of their seafood delicacies. If you bring in your own fresh catch, they'll actually cook it for you. Casual and very rustic, they're open late for great food or just for drinks. $$

Garbo's Grill *409 Caroline Street, Key West, FL 33040. (305) 304-3004* Garbo's Grill is a little **food cart** off Duval Street that was featured on the Diners, Drive-In's and Dives TV show. Rated as the #1 restaurant in Key West on TripAdvisor, it is a nice break from the usual Duval street fare. Set behind Grunts bar, you can grab a drink and enjoy a beautiful little patio while you eat. There are three people in the cart, one taking the orders, one cooking the meat and one putting the orders together. You can wait in the bar in the building in front of them, where you can get drinks. After waiting in line to order, you get a pager and it takes them 15-20 minutes to prepare the orders. Standout dishes that people rave about include the Korean BBQ short rib burrito, Cayo fish tacos, umami burger and mango dog. Open Monday through Saturday for lunch and dinner. $

Santiago's Bodega *207 Petronia St., Key West, FL 33040-7305 (305) 296-7691* This sexy little tapas place is a few short blocks away from Duval Street in the Bahama Village neighborhood. If you are looking for something different from the usual Key West restaurants, Santiago's is the place. It's got a very hip, laid back feel with lots of art. The food is great and the tapas style menu gives you a huge variety of choices. If you are concerned that a "tapas" restaurant won't fill your appetite, you'll be happy to know the food is plentiful and delicious. Although not on the main drag, this is a popular place and fills up quickly, so make a reservation. $$$

Blue Heaven *729 Thomas St., Key West, FL 33040 (305) 296-8666* The infamous Blue Heaven is located in the Bahama Village, just two blocks from Ernest Hemingway's home and museum. Run by hippies, this is a popular place to come for breakfast, lunch or dinner. In many ways a visit here is more about the history

and the atmosphere than the food! Among the bizarre things that Hemingway did in Key West was refereeing boxing matches right in this building, and like at Hemingway's home there are cats (and chickens!) freely roaming around this outdoor restaurant. Come here for the quintessential Key West outdoor dining experience. $$

Better Than Sex - A Dessert Restaurant *926 Simonton St., Key West, FL 33040-7412 (305) 296-8102* Dark, romantic, dessert restaurant with only 15 small tables. This adult restaurant has sexy pictures on the walls and decadent desserts with wine and coffee pairing to match. Sultry servers, mood music, dark lighting and red and gold walls create an ambiance of intimacy. The iPad menus are a great idea and you can't help but smile at the over-sexualized descriptions of the dishes. Don't miss the drinks in the glasses drizzled with chocolate and caramel. Really different and fabulous desserts and a true guilty pleasure. Reservations strongly suggested. $$

Where to Stay

Mallory Square

Hyatt Windward Point *3675 S Roosevelt Blvd., Key West, FL 33040 (305) 293-5050* Looking for a place that is just steps from the airport? The Hyatt Windward Point is about a four minute walk, which is about as convenient as is possible. All the rooms are spacious suites, with free Wi-Fi and a swimming pool. There is a shuttle that can take you into the main part of the city for $5 (which is cheaper than a taxi). You get great views of the ocean from most of the rooms. $$

Amsterdam's Curry Mansion Inn *511 Caroline St., Key West, FL 33040 (305) 294-5349* The Inn is a crisp white Southern mansion that was originally built in the 1800s. Though completely updated several times since then, the style and charm of the period is still evident in the decor and the collections of antiques throughout the home. It's an elegant place to stay and the staff are all very friendly and personable. Located on a quiet street, you're still within easy walking distance to all the downtown spots in Key West. Amenities include a swimming pool with hot tub, Wi-Fi and computer access, and complimentary cocktail hour. $$$

Eden House *1015 Fleming St., Key West, FL 33040 (800) 533-5397* Another quaint B&B that is a little more budget-friendly is the Eden House. The grounds are so heavily planted with trees and lush foliage that it looks positively tropical. You can walk to the busy Duval street neighborhood or spend a quiet afternoon in the Inn's gazebo and hot tub. $$

Key West International   KEYW

TOWER ©**118.2**
[0700-2300]

Ground Control **121.9**

Control Tower Phone
[305] 294-2549

Airport Manager Phone
[305] 809-5200

ASOS 119.65 [305] 292–4046

ATIS 119.675

®NAVY KEY WEST App/Dep 124.025
[0700–2200]

®MIAMI CENTER App/Dep 133.5
[2200–0700]

CLNC DEL: 121.9

UNICOM 122.95

Elevation	Traffic Pattern	Flight Service Station
3' MSL	800' MSL [797'AGL]	800-WX-BRIEF

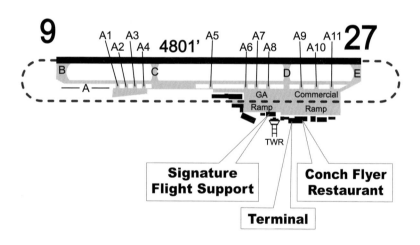

Kissimmee and Orlando

Kissimmee is the closest airport to Walt Disney World and all the other theme parks. One KISM based company will have you flying a real AT-6 Texan. Another one will put you in the pilot's seat of a P-51 Mustang or an L-39 jet. There is also a small air museum for those that just want to look.

The name Kissimmee means "heaven's place" in the language of the Calusa Indians, which is appropriate for a location that is both an airport and the home of **Warbird Adventures** and **Stallion 51.**

For pilots, Kissimmee is the gateway to Disney and the other Orlando theme parks. But there are also things to see right in Kissimmee, like **Old Town,** which has classic car cruise-ins four nights a week. There are also several popular dinner shows in Kissimmee including the **Manor Professional Wresting Dinner Theatre!**

There are so many things to do in Orlando. Here are a few suggestions of some interesting places to visit.

Flying There

Kissimmee Gateway is a tower-controlled airport that is partially within, and completely below, the Orlando Class

Disney Springs

B airspace. While it's possible to come in under the Class B from the west, making contact with Orlando Approach early on will increase safety and situational awareness for everyone involved. The north-south orientation of Orlando's

busy runways means you can expect vectors to remain low and to the west to stay out of the way.

ISM is only a few miles southeast of the **Walt Disney World** attractions, where a **Temporary Flight Restriction** up to 3,000 feet AGL appears to be permanently established. Close proximity to the TFR is another great reason to remain in contact with approach control.

The tower is open from 7 a.m. to 10 p.m., and the airport is very hospitable to general aviation with ample runways and three good FBOs to choose from.

Signature Flight Support on the north ramp provides the usual jet center amenities from 7 a.m. to 10 p.m., and even has a taxi-through sheltered overhang in front of their facility. National rental cars available. Radio 122.775 or UNICOM 122.95, call *(407) 846-6128,* or email ism@signatureflight.com.

Quantem operates an FBO on the west ramp. Normal business hours are 7 a.m. to 10 p.m. Crew cars, as well as Enterprise and Hertz rentals, are available. Radio 128.9 or call *(407) 846-8001.*

Kissimmee Jet Center on the east ramp offers fewer amenities, but lower fuel prices and five days of free parking with a 10-gallon fuel purchase. They're pet-friendly and can arrange rental cars. Open 7 a.m. to 9:30 p.m. with fuel service starting at 7:30 a.m. Radio 122.875 or call *(407) 847-9095.*

Getting Around

Walt Disney World Resort is a 25 minute drive from the airport.

Instead of renting a car, how about renting a classic motorcycle instead? Find out more in the "What to See and Do" section.

LYNX is the name of the

Stallion 51 Planes

bus system and it costs just $2 for a single ride, one-way. You can take a bus pretty much anywhere in the Orlando area. You can even take the bus to **Walt Disney World.** If you parked at the **Kissimmee Jet Center** you will walk east on Patrick Street for about 4 blocks and then North on N Thacker Ave about 8 blocks to the intersection of N Thacker Ave and West Vine Street to pick up the Route 55 bus at the stop in front of the **Race-Track** gas station. It is about a 30 minute walk if you can't get a lift. Plan a little over an hour to get to WDW on the bus.

Walking Distance Activities

Warbird Adventures and Kissimmee Air Museum *233 North Hoagland Boulevard, Kissimmee, FL 34741 (407) 870-7366* Located right on the field, the museum has a nice collection of airworthy warbirds, aircraft waiting for restoration, and "Precious Metal" a P-51 Mustang fighter turned air racer. But the amazing part for pilots is that you can fly the North American T-6 Texan! Priced from $250 for a

15 minute flight you can book flights up to an hour. You can also buy a video of your flight. Adult museum admission $10. Kids $5.

Stallion 51 *3951 Merlin Drive, Kissimmee, FL 34741 (407) 846-4400* Also located on the field, **Stallion 51** conducts flight operations in two rare dual control P-51 Mustangs which costs $2,350 for a half hour flight. Their T-6 Texan is a bargain at $700 per hour. They also do upset training in an Aero Vodochody L-39 Albatros jet. The full two day VFR/IFR program costs $7500, while the VFR only portion is $4,500.

There are no other interesting walking distance destinations from the airport.

What to See and Do

Right in Kissimmee, one of the most popular attractions is **Old Town,** *5770 West Highway 192, Kissimmee, FL 34746 (407) 396-4888* This is a street/mall/park with old west inspired architecture that has shopping, restaurants, haunted house, go cart track, magic hall and more. They have different themed car cruises every

Wednesday through Sunday evening, and several annual car shows.

Dinner theater

Kissimmee is home to several dinnershow theaters.

Medieval Times Dinner & Tournament *4510 W. Vine Street (US Highway 192), Kissimmee, FL 34746 (888) WE-JOUST* You sit at ringside, grouped in one of the six contender's teams and then have the fun of cheering for your contender during the live jousting tournament. All the while you'll be eating dinner medieval style with your hands (no spoon or fork). Reports are that the food is surprisingly good.

Capone's Dinner and Show *4740 West US Highway 192, (W. Irlo Bronson Hwy), Kissimmee, FL 34746 (800) 220-8428* A smaller scale dinner show set in a prohibition era speakeasy and cabaret. The show is funny, cute and eye catching with good voices. Buffet dinner price also includes unlimited drinks (beer included) and dessert. Adults $65.98. Consider paying extra for VIP tickets. You get better seats, priority seating and eating and two premium drinks before the show.

Orlando

Walt Disney World *World Drive, Orlando, FL 32830 (407) 934-7639* Opened in 1971 with the **Magic Kingdom,** the Disney resort has been added to substantially. There are now four theme parks here including the **Magic Kingdom,** plus **Animal Kingdom, Epcot** and **Disney's Hollywood Studios** in addition to two water parks, four golf courses, a camping resort, and 27 themed resort hotels. **Disney Springs** and **Disney's Boardwalk** also offer nightlife, restaurants, shopping and attractions without having to go into the theme parks themselves. You could spend weeks exploring everything there is at Disney World, and ticket prices vary considerably. It is about a 25 minute drive from KISM

Universal Orlando Resort *6000 Universal Boulevard, Orlando, FL 32819 (407) 363-8000* The Universal Orlando Resort started with the opening of **Universal Studios** and it's now a vast entertainment complex with two theme parks, hotels, nightlife and restaurants. It's a place that you could spend just one day in, but you really need several days to even begin to appreciate everything that's here. From heart-pounding roller coasters to the backlot studio tour, this huge resort area has something for everyone. **The Wizarding World of Harry Potter** is the current hot spot. The two worlds of Harry Potter are spread across two parks so remember you'll now need a dual park ticket to make the most of HP World. **The Hogwarts™ Express** carries you between parks which is why you need a two park ticket. Ticket prices vary hugely depending on what you want to do and how long you want to stay. The resort is about a 30 minute drive from the airport.

Hot Air Balloon Rides

You may be used to flying, but have you ever flown in a hot air balloon?! Here in Orlando this is a popular activity and there are several companies who can get you floating above

Universal Studios

the streets of Orlando. **Orlando Balloon Rides** *44294 US Highway 27 Davenport, FL 33897-4504 (GPS address 2400 Access Road, Davenport)* offer 3 to 4 hour adventures that take off one hour before sunrise from one of their 25 departure locations in the Disney area. Follow your ride with a complimentary champagne toast. **Bob's Balloons** *8293 Champions Gate Blvd, Orlando, FL (407) 466-6380* is another option and is a half hour drive from KISM.

Modern Classic Motorcycle Rental *12500 Belrose Avenue, Orlando, FL 32837 (407) 583-6988* They have four different classic Triumphs for rent, and if you arrange it in advance they will happily meet you at the airport with your bike, making this incredibly easy. All you need is to be at least 21 years of age and have a motorcycle endorsement on your driver's license. Rentals can include comprehensive insurance, delivery and pickup, unlimited miles and a helmet.

Tantalizing Tastes and Tours *1929 S Kirkman Rd, Orlando, FL 32811 (407) 739-3292* Part city tour, part dining experience, Tantalizing Tastes and Tours offer food tours of many different restaurants giving you the opportunity to try cuisines you may not have tried before, all while seeing the city of Orlando. The company actually offers three different tours: **Taste of Orlando** takes in five local eateries over a three hour lunch tour and includes one of the best Latin restaurants in the city. **The Fun Dinner Dining Tour** is an evening tour taking in four of the finest restaurants in Orlando, and

Hot Air Balloons

finally the **Pub-N-Grub Beer Tour** which combines good beer with good food in four different locations. All tours are guided and are perfect for couples and groups.

Downtown Orlando

Downtown Orlando has benefited from plenty of revitalization over the past few decades to become a popular and vibrant nightlife destination. The area between South Street and the 526, just to the west of Lake Eola, is the most happening neighborhood in the city, home to many nightclubs, bars and restaurants. **Church Street Station** *127 West Church Street, Orlando, FL 32801 (321) 202-5855* has long been attracting visitors with its heritage buildings, dining and nightlife and is a nice place to spend an evening.

The biggest venue in downtown Orlando is the **Amway Center** *400 West Church Street #200, Orlando, FL 32801 (407) 440-7000,* just minutes from Church Street Station. The arena is home to the NBA's **Orlando Magic** and hosts

many big name performers including Billy Joel, Fleetwood Mac and more. Check their schedule to see who's playing when you're in town.

Titanic: The Experience *7324 International Drive, Orlando, FL 32819 (407) 248-1166* You don't need to have a huge obsession with the Titanic to enjoy this interesting attraction. Wander around the exhibits on your own time so you can focus on the ones that interest you most, but be sure to join one of the guided tours as these are fun and entertaining, and are led by costumed characters who have a great deal of knowledge about the ship and the exhibits. There are actual artifacts from the Titanic that have been brought up from the icy depths of the ocean. The re-created grand staircase is very impressive. For an extra special visit buy tickets for the Friday or Saturday night **Titanic Gala Dinner** that includes three courses and champagne in the company of some of the ship's legends. Dinner tickets cost $69 while general admission is $21.95.

Where to Eat

There are 2,919 restaurants in the Orlando/Kissimmee area, but here are three curated suggestions:

Victoria & Albert's at Disney's Grand Floridian Resort & Spa, *Walt Disney World, Orlando, FL 32830 (407) 939-3463* If you are looking for fine dining, you probably aren't thinking of eating at Disney World. But this is the highest rated restaurant in the Orlando area and was recently rated the #2 restaurant in the USA by TripAdvisor. It is a wonderful place to spend a special occasion. You don't have to be staying in Walt Disney World to be able to enjoy this spectacularly luxurious restaurant. Prices are high (all-in with wine, plan $700 to $1000 per couple) but then this is very much a fine dining restaurant on par with the finest in New York. You will spend 3 to 4 hours enjoying the experience. The food, the service and the atmosphere are all impeccable – this is not a Disney themed restaurant! NOTE: Reservations need to be booked months in advance. $$$$$

Harp and Celt Irish Pub and Restaurant *25 South Magnolia Avenue, Orlando, FL 32801 (407) 481-2928* There are countless restaurants that you could choose from right in the heart of downtown Orlando but this one stands out for its atmosphere and value, and for the variety of meals on the menu. You can try some traditional Irish cuisine like the cream of potato leek soup or the Irish stew, or opt for more American-styled food such as burgers and a variety of salads. Of all the places former

President Obama could have chosen in Orlando, he came here for a pint of Guinness! $$

Cafe Tu Tu Tango *8625 International Dr, Orlando, FL 32819-9334 407-248-222.* If you find yourself in the International Drive area it is worth checking out this restaurant. It is vibrant, lively and unique in a sea of boring chain restaurants. The atmosphere alone is fun, with painters, dancers, jewelry making, music, and vibrantly colored walls. The food is interesting and different in a wonderful way. Mexican, Korean, Moroccan and eclectic foods meld into a great small plate menu. $$

Where to Stay

If you want to head over to Disney there are many places within the resort to stay but for a cheaper option Kissimmee is known for having some less expensive hotels available.

Gaylord Palms Resort & Convention Center *6000 W. Osceola Pkwy., Kissimmee, FL 34746 (407) 586-0000* An impressive installation featuring a lovely atrium that covers a replica of the Castillo de San Marcos from St. Augustine. It is landscaped with lush plants and waterfalls complete with crocodiles, turtles and koi pond. There is a water park area with water slides, a play area, a shallow sunbathing area, basketball hoops, and a separate adult only pool. Free shuttle to Disney. Daily resort fee in addition to room charge. $$$

Eo Inn *227 N Eola Drive, Orlando, FL 32801 (407) 481-8485* Located away from the theme parks, The Eo Inn is a boutique hotel that's set right by Lake Eola and the

park, yet just a couple blocks from the action and nightlife of downtown Orlando. Here you get the best of both worlds with this quiet though central location. The building dates from the 1930s although has been recently restored and updated. Some of the rooms and bathrooms are on the small side though comfortable and cozy. Choose a room with a balcony to enjoy the views over the park. Enjoy a spa treatment after a day of sightseeing. $$

Grand Bohemian Hotel *325 South Orange Avenue, Orlando, FL 32801 (407) 313-9000* The Grand Bohemian Hotel also enjoys a central downtown location close to all the restaurants and nightlife, plus this large hotel has a luxurious feel and offers plenty of leisure activities such as the heated outdoor pool and fitness center. Rooms are spacious and if you ask for one on a higher floor you'll enjoy a great view of downtown. Great restaurant. $$$

The Courtyard at Lake Lucerne *211 N Lucerne Circle E, Orlando, FL 32801 (407) 648-5188* The Courtyard at Lake Lucerne is a charming historic B&B. Set within beautiful private gardens you feel like you are a million miles from the hustle and bustle of Orlando. In reality it is set just across the street from Lake Lucerne and it is less than 10 minutes walk to the restaurants and bars. This is the perfect place for a romantic getaway, featuring quaint Victorian rooms or larger suites with all the mod-cons, and a hearty complimentary continental breakfast each morning. $$

Kissimmee Gateway | KISM

KISSIMMEE TOWER ©**124.45**
(0700-2200)

Ground Control **121.7**

Control Tower Phone
(407) 847-2932

Airport Manager Phone
(407) 847-4600

AWOS-3 128.775 (407) 847-0533
ATIS 128.775

®ORLANDO App/Dep 119.4 Clearance
Del 121.7

CLNC DEL 119.95 (when twr clsd)
UNICOM 122.95

Elevation	Traffic Pattern	Flight Service Station
82' MSL	1000' MSL (918'AGL)	800-WX-BRIEF

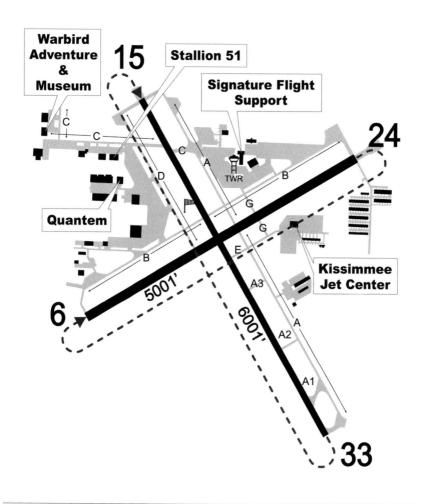

Lake City

Lake City calls itself the "Gateway to Florida" since it sits near the northern edge of the state. For many pilots, the restaurant directly across from the terminal might be the biggest draw. Experienced adventurers might like to kayak the largest white-water rapids in the state. History buffs will come for the Civil War history.

One of the largest Civil War battles in the state took place just outside of Lake City, and there is a lot of interest in Civil War history in town. In more recent times, the forestry industry is what kept the town going when the railway came in. Today, the Lake City Historic Commercial District is a registered historical neighborhood, with several buildings still looking exactly as they did more than 100 years ago.

The big **Civil War Festival** is an annual event that draws people from across the country to the **Olustee Battlegrounds** (more on that below). Another big annual event is the **Alligator Warrior Festival,** commemorating the Native American history of the town, particularly the life and accomplishments of the Alligator Warrior of the Seminoles. This is a newer event but it's been growing in popularity every year since starting.

Olustee Battlefield

It's not only history buffs that enjoy coming to Lake City though. There are several really good natural parks in the area, like the Osceola National Forest. Pack your hiking boots and see the backwoods of northern Florida.

Flying There

Lake City is one of the very few airports in the United States with a control tower but no Class D airspace. However, the operating procedures are basically the same as if the surrounding airspace were Class D. Communications with the tower must be established prior to 4 nm, up to and including 2,500 feet AGL. (See 14 CFR §91.126(d))

The tower is generally operational from 8 a.m. to 4:30 p.m., Monday through Friday, but may be open at other times as well. Monitor the CTAF/tower frequency on 119.2.

Pilots flying to Lake City should use caution when crossing the charted Military Training Routes north and south of the field, as well as the Live Oak Military Operations Area to the west. Contact Gainesville Radio on 122.2 to determine the status of the MOA.

The **Lake City Gateway FBO** is municipally owned and operated. Full-service fuel, courtesy cars, and car rentals are available. Call *(386) 752-1066* for rates and operating hours.

Getting Around

There isn't any public transportation in Lake City. The **USA Taxi & Airport Shuttle** *(386) 755-1711* has good service and comfortable cars to get to town from the airport or to see the sights. **Hertz** *(386) 754-3774* and **Enterprise** *(386) 755-4005* both operate in Lake City if you want a rental car. It's probably the best idea for getting around Lake City since several of the attractions are at least a 20 minute drive.

Walking Distance Activities

The airport is on the eastern outskirts of town so nothing is nearby except a small homey restaurant. Directly across from the Lake City's terminal is **The Landings Restaurant,** *3445 E Us Highway 90, Lake City, FL 32055 (386) 243-8077* Open for breakfast and lunch, this is a family-run business and everything is fresh. Menu changes daily with seafood on Friday. The breakfast buffet is great. Prices are very reasonable, and the wait staff is very friendly.

You might want to spend a little time looking around the airport itself. The facility is used by TIMCO, a company that modifies and rehabs large military aircraft. You might see some unusual planes if you keep your eyes open.

What to Do and See

Webb's Antique Mall *245 SW Webbs Glen, Lake City, FL (386) 758-5564* Plan to spend several hours wandering through the past at Webb's Antique Mall. Hundreds of vendors are all under one roof, and the vintage goodies seem to go on forever. It's a 20-minute drive from downtown, but it's right on the highway for an easy drive.

Lake City Columbia County Historical Museum *157 SE Hernando Ave., Lake City, FL 32025 (386) 755-9096* The best way to get to know a new town is to visit the local museum. It's right downtown and a very short drive from the airport. Located in a beautifully restored 1870s home, their collection of memorabilia covers the local Native American era, settlement of Lake City, the Civil War and contemporary times. They're only open Thursdays and Saturdays (10 a.m. to 1 p.m.) so you'll have to plan your visit.

Olustee Battlefield and Museum *5815 Battlefield Trail Road, Olustee, FL 32087 (386) 758-0400* Located within the Osceola National Forest, this smaller park marks the site of the largest Civil War battle in Florida. You can take a walk around the battlefield site, or check out the museum building for information on the battle and a good collection of local Civil War artifacts. The park is

free to enter, and the museum is open daily until 5 p.m.

If the Civil War really peaks your interest, try to come to Lake City on President's Day weekend in February. There is a huge historical battle re-enactment at the park, along with dozens of other historical demonstrations, games and a parade. It's one of the biggest events of the year.

Lake DeSoto Farmer's Market *778 NE Lake DeSoto Circle, Lake City, FL 32055 (386) 719-5766* If you want the full small-town experience, spend some time checking out the local farmer's market. It's on the banks of Lake DeSoto, right in town, and open every Saturday morning. There are tables of homegrown produce and well as handicrafts if you're looking for a souvenir. While you're there, follow the footpath to see some of the town as you circle the lake.

Nature Areas

The **Osceola National Forest** *(386) 752-2577* is minutes from the airport and is a mix of deep woodland and more open marshes. You can go hiking, swimming, fishing or hunting throughout the park. Ocean Pond is a particularly nice spot for the sandy beach and picnic areas. Most of the park is free to use, though you may need to purchase a day-use permit for areas like Ocean Pond.

Head north a little ways from town, and you can see a whole new landscape at **Big Shoals State Park** *11330 SE County Road 135, White Springs FL 32096 (386) 397-4331.* They have the largest whitewater rapids in the state and some amazing river views along 28 miles of marked nature trails. Viewing the rapids from dry land is what most visitors do. There are no rafting companies offering tours, but if you're an experienced kayaker you may be able to ride the rapids.

Finally, if you don't want to head far, check out **Lake De Soto** right by downtown. This small lake is a nice relaxing spot for a casual walk, and the road – with pedestrian walkway – encircles the entire lake.

Where to Eat

The Landings across from the terminal (see above).

Marion Street Bistro & Brew House *281 N Marion Ave, Lake City, FL 32055 (386) 487-6194* Marion Street offers a different dining experience from all the "chain" restaurants in Lake City. Set in a charming, renovated 100 year old building you'll enjoy selections such as upscale artisan pizza's, great appetizers, steaks, sandwiches, and more. The quality of the food and service definitely sets itself above the rest. Open for lunch and dinner. $$

Longhorn Steakhouse *3092 W US Hwy 90, Lake City, FL 32055 (386) 752-1881* Open for lunch or dinner, you can get a surprisingly good grilled steak or a burger

platter at this chain restaurant. The dining room is comfortable and casual but there is no outside seating. You'll have to head across town from the airport, but you're still only looking at a 20 minute drive. $$

Ray's Deli & Grill *419 SW State Rd 247 Lake City, FL 32025 (386) 438-8592* Ray's is where all the locals go when they want huge portions of comfort foods. Burgers and a whole range of big fresh sandwiches are on the menu, and the prices are really good. If you're there early enough, it's a good choice for a hearty breakfast too. Next door is a fun old-fashioned candy shop where you can pick up a few extra sweets. $

Ole Times Country Buffet *2469 W Us Hwy 90, Suite 106, Lake City, FL 32055 (386) 752-1670* Load up your plate with any number of Southern classic dishes like fried chicken, okra, dumplings and more. The Ole Times Country Buffet is an all-you-can-eat place that features friendly staff and a really big selection of hot choices. Great Southern cooking, excellent service and a decent price. It's really casual and they're open for lunch too. $

Yamato *1115 W Us Hwy 90, Lake City, FL 32055 (386) 754-*

8839 Though steak and burgers are pretty popular in Lake City, you can get a change of pace with excellent Japanese cuisine at Yamato. You may not expect to find a good Asian restaurant in a small town like Lake City, but you can enjoy teriyaki, miso soup and fresh sushi. $$

Where to Stay

Hampton Inn & Suites *450 SW Florida Gateway Dr., Lake City, FL 32024 (386) 487-0580* You'll have to head past the main part of Lake City to get to the Hampton Inn, but most of the accommodations in town are on Hwy 75 anyway. The rooms have Wi-Fi, hot tubs, and a hot continental breakfast is also included. Everything is stylishly decorated and very up-to-date. $$

Country Inn & Suites *350 SW Florida Gateway Dr., Lake City, FL 32024 1-800-596-2375* This is one of the best ranked hotels in town, and the prices are low enough to fit any travel budget. Also located across town near the Interstate, you'll find a fitness center, free breakfast, Wi-Fi, outdoor swimming pool and very large suites are available. The staff are friendly and are always ready to help you when you need anything, or want to know more about the sights around town. $

Comfort Suites Lake City *3690 W. US Hwy 90, Lake City, FL 32024 (855) 849-1513* Another chain hotel in Lake City where you can count on the quality and service. Breakfast is on the house, and you can use the gym 24 hours a day. There is also a business center if you need to get any work done while you're in Lake City. $$

Ole Times Country Buffet

Lake City Gateway

KLCQ

LAKE CITY TOWER ©**119.2**
[0800-1800]

GROUND CONTROL 121.9

Control Tower Phone
[386] 754-0484

Airport Manager Phone
[386] 752-1066

AWOS–3 120.675 [386] 754–9366

®JACKSONVILLE App/Dep 125.375

UNICOM 122.95

NOTE: Tower may be open at other than published hours, monitor CTAF at all times.

Elevation 201' MSL	Traffic Pattern 1000' MSL [799'AGL]	Flight Service Station GAINESVILLE 122.6

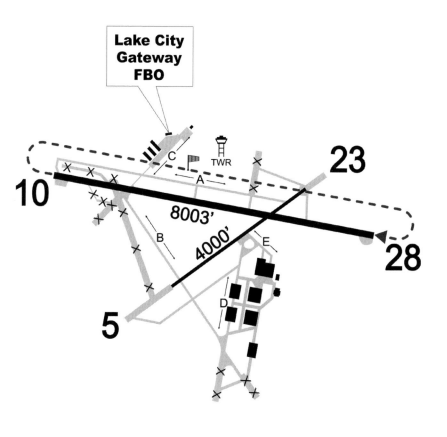

Lakeland

Home to the SUN 'n FUN air expo there is actually more to see in Lakeland. From natural parks, historic buildings and local museums to baseball spring training. Plus you can fly in for lunch at Hallback's Bar and Grill. And check out the Pilot Mall aviation superstore.

Lakeland is aptly named as there are more than thirty lakes within the city limits, giving great water views from most points downtown. Many of the lakes are home to several flocks of swans, all descendents of two swans given to the town by Queen Elizabeth.

The area was first settled in the 1870s and began to really thrive during the Spanish-American War. Thousands of troops were stationed here. A construction boom took over and many of the buildings from that era can still be seen around town today. Speaking of architecture, there is a large collection of Frank Lloyd Wright buildings at **Florida Southern College.**

In the spring, the **Detroit Tigers** train just 16 minutes from the airport.

For aviation enthusiasts, Lakeland is well-known for the huge annual **SUN 'n FUN International Fly-in Expo.** If you are planning on visiting Lakeland, coinciding your trip

SUN 'n FUN

this festival could be the best time to come. Then again, you might be so busy with the air show that you don't have time to do any other sightseeing!

Besides the aviation attractions, there are many natural areas in and around the city that are perfect for hiking, birdwatching and wildlife spotting.

Flying There

Lakeland's Class D airspace lies immediately east of the Tampa Class B. To the east,

Bartow also has Class D. Pilots coming in from the east should be alert for traffic around Bartow and Winter Haven, including seaplanes and gliders.

The narrow path between the Orlando Class B airspace and the R-2901 B, E, and M Restricted Areas generates lots of traffic from VFR aircraft avoiding the restricted airspaces. Keeping a sharp watch for other aircraft is advised.

Other than potentially high traffic in the area, arrival into Lakeland poses no special challenges. The control tower's published operating hours are 6 a.m. to 10 p.m. Tower frequency 124.5 doubles as the CTAF after hours.

During events at **SUN 'n FUN,** check the NOTAMS and the SUN 'n FUN website for special procedures.

Sheltair is located on the north ramp and provides full FBO services from 6 a.m. to 10 p.m. Courtesy cars are available, and the FBO is adjacent to a restaurant. Self-serve 100LL is available 24/7. Contact via UNICOM 122.95 or call *(863) 647-3911.*

Getting Around

There are public buses that serve the entire Lakeland area, and Route 57 can be picked up right outside the airport. They will take you downtown for a fare of $1.50. You can also get day passes for $3.00. **Hertz Rent-a-Car** *(863) 644-0839* operates out of the airport if you prefer to have your own vehicle for your stay.

Several taxi companies serve Lakeland, and you can call **Sunset Limo & Airport Shuttle** *(863) 226-5444* or **Angel Yellow Cab** *(863) 533-6999* to get you around town when you need a ride. There is also a shuttle service from the airport into town, with **H&H Transport** *(863) 712-3775.*

Walking Distance Activities

Definitely a few things to see and do within easy walking distance of the Lakeland Linder regional airport. Have some lunch at **Hallback's Bar & Grill** in the terminal and then taxi over to the **Florida Air Museum. Pilot Mall,**

the online retailer, has a very nice retail store at the SUN 'n FUN Campus *(863) 226-1106.* **F.A.A. Safety Center** is also located at the Sun 'n Fun campus. They do safety seminars all the time. You can learn something and get WINGS credits too.

Walking right into town isn't feasible, but it's about a 20 minute drive by car. Once you're downtown, you'll be able to walk around to many of the shops and restaurants.

What to See and Do

Florida Air Museum *4175 Medulla Road, Lakeland, FL 33807 (863) 644-0741* Located on the Sun 'n Fun campus, they have a large indoor facility filled with planes and equipment from many different eras, with a focus on WWI and WWII, as well as featuring many of the people who made an impact on the aviation world. In addition to their main collection of restored aircraft, they have a fine exhibit of unique Howard Hughes aviation memorabilia as well. The large **Buehler Center** is adjacent to the museum, and it's a workshop for aircraft res-

toration that you can also visit to see what they're working on. They're open seven days a week until 4 p.m., and admission is $12 (free for active military).

Sun 'n Fun International Fly-in Expo takes place every April, and there are five days of aviation events and activities to take in. Airshow performances, air racing, a hot air balloon showcase, special museum exhibits, workshops and a parts exchange are all on the agenda each year. Admission for the entire week is $150, or $37 for single day passes.

Not going to be around in April? In November, the **When Pigs Fly South BBQ** is another event you might be interested in. It's a two-day BBQ festival with airplane displays, an airshow and the Warbirds Flyover Team. Admission is free.

Polk Museum of Art *800 East Palmetto St., Lakeland, FL 33801 (863) 688-7743* For something a little less aviation oriented, a visit to the Polk Museum of Art can be a very pleasant way to spend the afternoon. Fun pieces of modern art are mixed in with the more classical works to keep

Pilot Mall

things interesting. Many pieces have historical importance and include one very good exhibit of pre-Columbian artwork. Located just one block over from Lake Morton, it's one of the downtown sights you should visit. Admission is $5, with a discount for seniors.

Safari Wilderness Ranch *10850 Moore Rd, Lakeland, FL 33809 (813) 382-2120* Take a Jeep tour through more than 200 acres of wildlife refuge, to see zebra, gazelle, camels, big-horned sheep and water buffalo out in an all-natural setting. Hand-feeding the lemurs is always a fun point of the trip. They are open from Wednesday through Sunday, but you have to book your tour ahead of time. It's outside of town to the north, about a half hour from the airport.

Hollis Garden *702 E.*

Hollis Garden

sculpture. The park is a popular place for locals and visitors to unwind without having to leave downtown.

Circle B Bar Reserve *4399 Winter Lake Road, Lakeland, FL 33803 (863) 668-4673* If you don't mind getting out of town a bit more, you can see over 1,000 acres of wetland preserve at the Circle B Bar Reserve. It's just on the outskirts of Lakeland, and about 15 minutes from the airport by car. There are many hiking trails through woods, wetlands and along the river, as well as places to go fishing. If you are around Lake Hancock, watch out for alligators. The reserve is free to the public.

Detroit Tigers. The Tigers have been training in Lakeland since 1934 at Joker Marchant Stadium. *Al Kaline Dr., 2301 Lake Hills Blvd., Lakeland, FL*

remaining runway behind the outfield wall. Fly to Lakeland (KLAL). It is a 16 minute drive to the stadium.

Where to Eat

Hallback's Bar & Grill *3900 Don Emerson Dr., Ste 201, Lakeland, FL 33811 (863) 937-8900* For convenience, you can't beat Hallback's Bar & Grill since it's right at the airport. You can watch over the airport while you have some of their famous BBQ pulled pork, chicken parmigiana or a crab cake BLT. It's not your usual airport diner. Open for lunch all week long. Saturday and Sunday they also open for breakfast at 8 a.m. and stay open for dinner. $$

Bay Street Bistro *211 E Bay St., Lakeland, FL 33801 (863) 683-4229* Right downtown and near the farmer's market, the Bay Street Bistro serves a mix of fine dining dishes like filet mignon, blackened salmon and portabella mushrooms with crab. Dine in the bright elegant dining room, or do some people-watching from the sidewalk patio. Open only for dinner, except for Saturdays when they have a lunch sitting too. Closed Mondays. $$$

Black & Brew *205 E Main St., Lakeland, FL 33801 (863) 682-1210* When you're in downtown Lakeland and not looking for anything fancy, stop by Black & Brew for a good sandwich. Their baristas can also make you the perfect coffee or espresso drink for when you're on the go. You can even place your order online so it's ready for you when you arrive. $

Cafe Zuppina *4417 S Florida Ave., Lakeland, FL 33813*

Orange Street, Lakeland, FL 33801 (863) 834-6035 Sitting between Lake Mirror and Lake Morton, the Hollis Garden boasts a lovely landscape of groomed flower gardens, fountains, lake views and several pieces of outdoor

33805. Called **Tiger Town,** the stadium was built on the site of a World War II flight school, the **Lodwick School of Aeronautics.** Between 1940 and 1945 more than 8,000 trained on that spot. The 2004 renovation removed the

Tiger Town

(863) 644-5144 For something out of the ordinary, try a little authentic Turkish cuisine while you're in Lakeland. Their signature dish is chicken zuppina with rice, but they have moussaka, kabobs, and feta rolls too. It's a friendly little place with a bright and cheerful interior (no patio though), and it's one of the top rated restaurants in Lakeland. Unfortunately, they're closed Saturday and Sunday so hopefully you'll be in town during the week. $$

Where to Stay

Hilton Garden Inn Lakeland *3839 Don Emerson Drive, Lakeland, FL 33811 (855) 277-5057* If your visit to Lakeland is going to center on the airport, then book a room at the Hilton Garden Inn. It's located on the edge of the airport grounds just across the street from the main airport building so you can be checked in within minutes of landing. There is a restaurant, pool, bar, and fitness center on the premises and you'll get free Wi-Fi in your room. $

Lakeland Terrace Hotel *329 E. Main St., Lakeland, FL 33801 1-888-644-8400* The Terrace is a very centrally-located place to stay, right on the banks of Lake Mirror in the heart of Lakeland. They offer a full restaurant and bar, fitness center, and they have a free continental breakfast each morning. The building is a gorgeous old classic with high vaulted ceilings and spacious rooms. It's convenient as well as comfortable. $$

Shaw House B&B *605 E Orange St., Lakeland, FL 33801 (863) 686-0888* Literally next door to Hollis Gardens, this B&B is a cozy place that is within walking distance of many Lakeland sights and shops. The house is a restored 100-year-old residence with wrap-around verandas on both floors. Breakfasts are always lavish, and they have a complimentary cocktail hour every evening at 5 p.m. $$

The Pfeiffer Chapel at Florida Southern College, designed by Frank Lloyd Wright

Lakeland Linder

LAKELAND TOWER ©**124.5**
[0600-2200]

Ground Control **121.4**

Control Tower Phone
[863] 648-3305

Airport Manager Phone
[863] 834-3298

AWO-3 118.025
[863] 834-2030

ATIS 118.025

®TAMPA App/Dep 120.65 119.9

UNICOM 122.95

Elevation 142' MSL	Traffic Pattern 1000' MSL [858' AGL]	Flight Service Station ST PETERSBURG 122.1R 116.0T

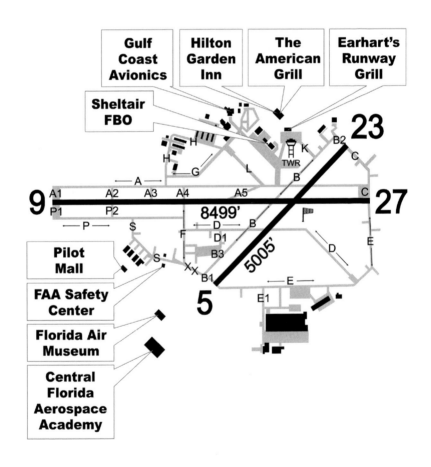

Gulf Coast Avionics

Hilton Garden Inn

The American Grill

Earhart's Runway Grill

Sheltair FBO

Pilot Mall

FAA Safety Center

Florida Air Museum

Central Florida Aerospace Academy

Marathon

Known as the "Heart of the Keys," this small island city is home to all the great sights you would expect from the Florida Keys. Boating, scuba diving and casual beach living are what Marathon is all about. Plus there is an on-airport EAA airplane museum.

Marathon isn't a very big city, and much of it is within walking distance. It's popular with fishermen, divers and boaters due to the high number of marinas all around the Keys. At one time, Bruce Willis and Demi Moore lived in Marathon, though it's not as big a draw for celebrities as some of the other keys.

Most of Marathon is urban, so at first glance it lacks charm. But most people come to Marathon for the boating and island atmosphere. Once on the water or at the beach, it has all the attractions of the Keys.

Seven Mile Bridge

Flying There

Flying here can be a beautiful experience. The easiest, and probably the prettiest way to navigate to Marathon is to come from Miami airspace following U.S. 1. You and your passengers will see beautiful water, lovely beaches, boats sprinkled everywhere and the homes of the rich and famous. Be sure to stay over or to the north of the highway, as Military Training Route IR53 is just south of the Keys running all the way to Key West.

From the east coast of Florida, if you don't want to file IFR or request Flight Following through the Palm Beach to Miami stretch, check out the VFR Flyway Planning Chart printed on the reverse side of the Miami Terminal Area Chart. It shows a pathway to the west of that congested airspace. If you don't have a copy of the chart, you can find it on the SkyVector website.

From the west coast of Florida, flying is more complicated and risky. Flying over the Gulf crosses the ADIZ which will require filing IFR or a Defense Visual Flight Rules plan. And if you are flying down the western coast or the middle of the state, you will be over the Everglades for at least 70NM with no landing areas. The safest route is to navigate to VFR waypoint VPRLN (Ranger Station) just south of Homestead General (X-51) and fly at 150° to intersect the Keys just west

EAA Museum

of the US 1 bridge connecting the mainland to the Keys.

There are two FBOs at the airport. Jets and Turbines should head for the Marathon Jet Center to the west of the terminal. Marathon General Aviation is east of the terminal and does an excellent job of taking care of everyone else.

Getting Around

If you are just flying in for the $100 hamburger, there are several places you can walk to in 10 minutes or less.

It may be easier to get around in your own car (unless you plan on walking). There is an **Enterprise** *(305) 289-7630* location right in the airport, for hassle-free pick up. The Jet Center also has a crew car that might be available.

Bicycle Rentals

Sometimes it's nice to explore a place by bicycle, and Marathon is no exception. There are several places in Marathon where you can rent a bike by the day or week, depending on how long you're staying. The closest supplier to the airport is **Wheels-2-Go** *5994 Overseas Hwy., Marathon, FL 33050 (305) 289-4279* They will deliver bikes to the airport. They rent beach cruisers if you want to look the part and provide helmets and locks free of charge. Rates start at $10.

Walking Distance Activities

You can do some sightseeing without even leaving the airport, by stopping at the **EAA Air Museum.** It's not a big facility but it is a popular one for visiting pilots. They have a hangar with several vintage planes, informational displays and volunteers who can impart many great stories about the aircraft. They even have a DC-3 that Grace Kelly once flew in.

Directly across from Marathon General Aviation is a very average **Pizza Hut,** so if you are looking for cheap and okay food, you'll do fine.

Take a ten minute walk up Route 1 to the east, and you'll find several small eateries. On the right side of the road is **King Seafood Market & Restaurant,** *10925 Overseas Highway, Marathon, FL 33050 (305) 735-4132* with excellent seafood for lunch and dinner. A few steps farther on the left and you'll come to one of the most popular dessert destinations in Marathon: **Sweet Savannah's,** an ice cream cafe and cupcake bakery!

If it is a nice day and you want to take a 15 minute walk, go west on the Overseas Highway, and you'll come to **Stout's Restaurant,** which has been across from the airport since 1964. This retro place is open M-F 6 a.m. to 2 p.m., but on weekends they only do breakfast. Walk another five minutes and you'll find another good eatery: **Lulu's Garden Grill** open every day for breakfast through dinner.

Other than that, several shops, restaurants, resorts and marinas are within a 30 minute walk.

What to See and Do

The Turtle Hospital *2396 Overseas Hwy, Marathon, FL 33050-2232 (305) 743-2552* Take a guided educational tour of the hospital facilities and the sea turtle rehabilitation area. The hospital has its own turtle ambulance, surgery center and large tanks to view the turtles. Making a reservation is a good idea as the number of guests on the 90 minute experience is limited. Adults $18. Children $9. Under 4, free.

Dolphin Center *58901 Overseas Highway, Marathon, FL 33050 (305) 289-1121*

This research facility lets you learn all about dolphins and get up close and personal with the resident group. You can swim and interact with them, or just stay on the boardwalks and watch these graceful animals. There are many places in Florida where you can go on dolphin tours to glimpse them in the wild, but this is a rare opportunity to see them close at hand. By car, they are about 12 minutes away from the airport. The center is open seven days a week, and tickets are $25.

Seven Mile Bridge Contrary to the name, the old bridge is only two miles long but it still gives you a fantastic view over the water if you take a walk along the whole length. Getting two miles away from shore gives you a very special opportunity to see wildlife and sea creatures you don't see from the beach. Watch the water for dolphins, manatees, manta rays, sharks, turtles and more. The bridge extends westward from the tip of the island, and

Turtle Hospital

you can walk to Pigeon Key.

Pigeon Key *1 Knights Key Boulevard, Marathon, FL 33050 (305) 743-5999* The tiny island of Pigeon Key is an important part of the local history, as the workers who were building the railway bridges lived here. There are several old buildings you can explore, and it makes a picturesque spot to stop when walking along the Seven Mile Bridge. You'll have to take the ferry if you don't want to walk the bridge. The ferry will cost you $12.

Scuba Diving

If the Seven Mile Bridge didn't quench your thirst for ocean sights, then plan to do some diving. There are many great dive sites around Marathon, and you can get a little training when you arrange a dive so don't worry about being a novice.

Captain Hook's Marina and Dive Center *11833 Overseas Hwy., Marathon, FL 33050 (800) 278-4665* is a good place to start since it's minutes from the airport. They specialize in taking divers out to the coral, and they do fishing charters too. The captains at **Tilden's Scuba Center** *(305) 743-7255* have about 30 different sites on their roster so you can really explore the ocean when you dive with them.

Paddleboard Tours

If you're craving more water-based activities, how about trying something different to the norm? A paddleboard tour with **Gnarly Harley Paddle** *Sombrero Beach Rd, Marathon, FL 33050 (239) 682-3319* is a unique and fun way to explore the waters by private guided

tour through the Florida mangroves. They have three different tours that range between two and three hours including one with the opportunity to snorkel and shell at a secluded island. Their adventures start at $55.

Where to Eat

King Seafood *10925 Overseas Hwy., Marathon, FL 33050 (305) 735-4132* Not planning on straying far from the airport? Then King Seafood is roughly a 10 minute walk away and they're well-known for their great food. The menu is loaded with seafood, all done in a variety of Caribbean styles. Cajun blackened snapper, thick Cuban sandwiches, conch fritters and huge lobster platters are a few of your choices. They don't have a patio but there are a couple of picnic tables outside. $$

Brutus Seafood Market & Eatery *6950 Overseas Hwy, Marathon, FL 33050 305-743-9181* From ethnic to Keys cuisine this fish market/deli/restaurant delivers. Featuring local fish and seafood. Outstanding food quality. Great pies. Open Monday — Saturday 11:00 a.m. - 9:00 p.m.

Stout's Restaurant *8349 Overseas Hwy., Marathon, FL 33050 (305) 743-6437* Another great place for breakfast, plus a good lunch spot if you're visiting during the week. Stout's has been here for fifty years and is still a firm favorite with locals and tourists. You'll find home-cooked breakfasts and service with a smile. No credit cards accepted so be sure to bring cash. $

Lulu's Garden Grille *7537 Overseas Hwy., Marathon, FL*

Dolphin Center

33050 (305) 289-2220 Just across the highway from the runway (but a 20 minute walk to the west from the terminal) Lulu's Garden Grille offers a slightly more up-market setting. Serving breakfast, lunch and dinner, so you can choose when to come, though the atmosphere livens up from lunch onwards when the Tiki Bar opens. On Wednesday through Saturday nights there's live entertainment, and the gardens surrounding the Tiki Bar provide a nice, tropical feel. $$

Barracuda Grill *4290 Overseas Hwy., Marathon, FL 33050 (305) 743-3314* There aren't that many fine dining places in Marathon so when you do want a restaurant for that special night, try the Barracuda Grill. Right in the main part of Marathon, you can enjoy shrimp scampi, grilled grouper, rack of lamb or roast duck. Top the meal off with just the right wine, and your evening is complete. $$$

Juice Paradise Cuban Cafe *2603 Overseas Hwy., Marathon, FL 33050 (305) 735-4051* Fresh juice is served all day long, and they have a good menu of casual Cuban dishes too. Stop for breakfast or when you need a snack on the go. It's a popular local hang-out, so don't let the outside dissuade you from entering. $

Burdine's Waterfront Chiki Tiki *1200 Oceanview Ave., Marathon, FL 33050 (303) 743-9204* Once you've worked your way down to the tip of the island, Burdine's is waiting for you. It's not fancy, and you might want to label it as a bit of a dive. But that's the charm. The food is great and it's actually pretty nice inside. Have your dinner out on the patio and watch the sun set over the water. It doesn't get much better than that for ambiance. $$

Where to Stay

Seascape Motel and Marina *1275 76th Street Ocean East, Marathon, FL 33050 (305) 743-6212* Just a five minute drive from the airport and you're right on the coast at the Seascape Motel and Marina. There won't be any big crowds at this small resort because there are only eight rooms. It's small and private yet still has lots of amenities to make your stay memorable. Grab a free kayak and explore the shore, or take advantage

of their boat ramp. There is a stretch of private beach as well as a swimming pool. $$

Holiday Inn Express *13201 Overseas Highway, MM 54, Marathon, FL 33050 (305) 289-0222* Clean, newer hotel (rare in Marathon) with a friendly helpful staff. Free breakfast and Wi-Fi. Nice pool and and a bar that is on the water. Not the best sound insulation, so try to get a room on the third floor. $$

Sea Dell Motel *5000 Overseas Highway, Marathon, FL 33050 (305) 743-5161* Head farther down through the island and you can get a room at the Sea Dell Motel, where you'll be a little more central to all the action. It's a pretty simple place that's clean and within walking distance of several marinas and beaches. There aren't a lot of extras, but they do have a pool and free Wi-Fi. $$

Tranquility Bay Beach House Resort *2600 Overseas Hwy, Marathon, FL 33050 (844) 900-0597* Tranquility Bay is a four-star resort right in the middle of Marathon on the northern coast of the main key island. You can rent boats and jet-skis from their marina to get out on the water, but they also have three swimming pools. Diving equipment and instruction is also available if you want to do some scuba diving off the shore. Enjoy the private beach, with access from all the beach house rooms. There is a spa, fitness room, and the Butterfly Cafe serves dinner in the evenings. $$$

The Florida Keys Marathon — KMTH

CTAF/UNICOM ©**122.8**

ASOS 135.525 [305] 743-8373

Airport Manager Phone
[305] 289-6060

®MIAMI App/Dep 133.5

Elevation	Traffic Pattern	Flight Service Station
5' MSL	1000' MSL [995'] AGL	100.0 122.6 MIAMI

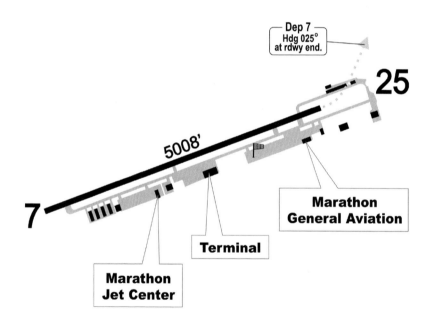

Dep 7
Hdg 025°
at rdwy end.

25

5008'

7

Marathon
General Aviation

Terminal

Marathon
Jet Center

Mount Dora

This hidden gem is packed with amazing food and festivals. Voted Florida's friendliest small town, Mount Dora really has a small town New England atmosphere that you generally won't find elsewhere in Florida. Mt. Dora's canopy trees, rolling hills and gorgeous lakes make this the perfect location for a romantic escape.

The town's first hotel still stands today. The **Lakeside Inn** and enjoys a scenic lakeside setting. The Lakeside Inn played host to many important people including Henry Ford, Thomas Edison and two American presidents: Eisenhower and Coolidge.

Today Mount Dora's historic buildings, lakeside setting, antique stores and nice restaurants keep the tourists coming back. There are probably more interesting and varied antique dealers per square foot than any other city in Florida.

Downtown Mount Dora

Festivals

To keep things interesting, Mt. Dora has a festival every few weeks. They include the Mt Dora Florida Highwayman Art Show; Annual Health and Fitness Expo; a dog show; Music festival with Grammy Winners, Spring Collectibles and Craft Show; Antique Boat Festival; Blueberry Festival; three-day Bikefest; Paddle Fest; Seafood Festival; Bicycle Festival; Scottish Highland Festival; Christmas celebration and more. For more information on any of these events contact **Visit Mount Dora, Inc.** at *(352) 735-1191.*

Flying There

There are two airports within close proximity of Mount Dora: Umatilla Municipal Airport (X23) and Mid Florida Air Service (X55). X55 is closer (about 6 miles from Mount Dora) though X23 is a more substantial airport (about 10 miles from Mount Dora).

X55 Mid-Florida

Mid-Florida is a rare public-use grass airfield lying under the edge of the shelf of Orlando's Class B airspace. Leesburg has Class D airspace 9 nm to the west, and pilots must be alert for traffic at numerous uncontrolled airports within a few miles, including glider and seaplane traffic.

Leesburg's ASOS (134.325) is the closest source of broadcast weather information.

Restricted Areas R-2910B and C block access from the north, and arrivals from the northeast should be alert for a pair of 1,700-foot towers in the Deltona area north of Sanford's Class C.

The 3,200-foot turf runway has a full-length parallel taxiway and will easily accommodate light general aviation aircraft, but it's still a good idea to call ahead to check on runway condition, especially if there has been rain in the area.

Mid-Florida Air Service manages the airport. Fuel is not available. Call *(352) 589-0767* to speak with the owner if you're considering a visit.

X23 Umatilla

Pilots operating at Umatilla must avoid the R-2910B and C Restricted Areas immediately north and east of the airport. Leesburg's Class D airspace is 9 nm southwest, and the outer shelves of the Orlando Class B are not far south. South of Umatilla, be alert for traffic at numerous small, non-towered airports.

The 2,500-foot runway is short but well-kept, with a paved parallel taxiway on the northern half.

Umatilla Aero operates from a small building on the northwest side of the airport from the hours of 8 a.m. to 1 p.m. Tuesday through Saturday. For service at other times call *(352) 669-2290* (office), *(352) 748-9578* (home), or *(352) 603-2188* (mobile). Self-serve 100LL is available 24/7 with credit card.

Getting Around

Neither airport has car rental desks, though **Enterprise** *(352) 735-0470* has an office just outside Mount Dora and may be able to meet you with a car at X55. A taxi cab would be another option if you want to get into Mount Dora for the weekend. **Eutco** *(352) 357-5270* is the closest option.

Once you've arrived at Mount Dora the best way to explore is on foot. The compact historic center makes walking around a breeze, as everything is within easy reach.

What to See and Do

Downtown Mount Dora

Strolling around the attractive streets of downtown Mount Dora is enough to keep many visitors to the city occupied. Full of antique stores and specialty stores where you can pick up some really unique and special gifts or souvenirs, the downtown area has history and charm and some great places to eat too. Look out for some of the historic landmarks, including the striking Queen Anne style **Donnelly House** on Donnelly Street and the historic railroad station that's now home to the city's Chamber of Commerce.

Segway Tours of Mt. Dora *430 Alexander Street, Mt. Dora, Florida 32757 (352) 383-9900* If you want to get the lay of the land, take a Segway tour of Mount Dora. The hour tour takes you along the waterfront to the lighthouse, then through nature paths, the historic neighborhoods, past the Historic Lakeside Inn and back to town. Tours are every day at 9:30 a.m., 11:30 a.m. and

1:30 p.m. $55

Orange Blossom Cannonball *305 E Ruby Street, Tavares, FL 32778 (352) 742-7200* If you've never heard of the Orange Blossom Cannonball you're probably wondering what on earth it is! The fact is, this historic steam train ride is one of the most popular attractions in Mount Dora. Running between Mount Dora and the neighboring city of Tavares the train travels alongside the lake before heading slightly inland at Tavares. You'll have a little time to stop there before the train returns. Take a walk in **Wooton Park** or just sit and admire the lake views. Check the schedule in advance as rides times and dates vary depending on the season.

Mount Dora Museum of Speed *206 North Highland Street, Mt. Dora, FL 32757 (352) 385-0049* is on the edge of downtown, about an 18 minute walk from the Lakeside Inn. While this isn't the largest automobile museum what they have is very good – antique cars and plenty of auto and related memorabilia plus the museum is always acquiring more for its exhibits. Open Monday to Friday from 10 a.m. to 5 p.m. and admission is $12. Sometimes open Saturdays but call ahead to check.

Mount Dora Ghost Walk *100 N. Alexander Street, Lakeside Inn, Mt. Dora, FL 32757 (352) 630-2553* Always a unique way to see a city and hear about its history, ghost walks are also fun and entertaining and this one in Mount Dora is no exception. The tour begins with an introduction then a 60-minute lantern-led walking tour of Old Mount

Dora. The tour is suitable for all ages with its unique blend of humor and macabre.

Modernism Museum *145 E 4th Ave, Mount Dora, FL 32757 352-385-0034* For a cozy town, this museum is an unexpected find. If you are a fan of modernism you will be blown away by this amazing collection. Make sure you watch the video on the two main artists (Esherick and Nakashima). Don't miss the lovely gift shop across the street.

The Mount Dora History Museum *450 Royellou, Mt. Dora, FL 32757 (352) 383-0006* is downtown, located within the city's first fire station and the city jail. It makes for an interesting visit if you'd like to learn more about the history of the city from the 1880s to the 1930s. The museum is open Tuesday through Sunday from 1 p.m, to 4 p.m. and admission is just $2.

Boat Tours

You can't visit Lake County without spending some time on the water. There are numerous lakes in the area surrounding Mount Dora as well as the scenic Dora Canal that connects Lake Dora to Eustis Lake. This stretch of water has been described as the most beautiful mile of waterway in the world, so it really must be experienced while in town.

Rusty Anchor Boat Tours *400 W. 4th Avenue, Mt. Dora, FL 32757 (352) 383-3933* has three different tour options to choose from including their two hour Dora Canal Tour, a one hour sunset cruise, and a one hour shoreline cruise.

Premier Boat Tours *100 N. Alexander Street, Mt. Dora,* *FL 32778 (352) 434-8040* has similar tours, departing from the Lakeside Inn. Most days they will offer two hour Dora Canal Tours and a one hour sunset tour, plus they have special cruises at holiday times too.

Where to Eat

The Goblin Market *330 Dora Drawdy Lane, Mt. Dora, FL 32757 (352) 735-0059* If you can get past the name – no this restaurant doesn't have goblins on the menu – you'll discover a great little eatery on a narrow lane right in the heart of Mount Dora. Small and quaint, The Goblin Market offers both inside and outside seating and an eclectic menu that blends American and International cuisine. Dishes include the raved-over tempura-dipped artichoke hearts, New Zealand rack of lamb, and pistachio-dusted chicken breast. Although on the pricey side, the quality of food and service is worthy. $$$

Pisces Rising *239 W 4th Avenue, Mt. Dora, FL 32757 (352) 385-2669* For a meal closer to the lake and great sunset views, try Pisces Rising. Specializing in seafood and steaks, this popular restaurant has some of the best views in town both from inside and outside on the patio. Order from an extensive array of fish and seafood including Cuban Snapper, jambalaya, seafood paella and Caribbean crab cakes as well as steaks, chicken and lamb. $$$

Cupcake Delights *122 E. 4th Avenue, Mt. Dora, FL 32757 (352) 383-2200* For a sweet treat while you're wandering around Mount Dora, visit Cupcake Delights. Their cupcakes are delicious, and with the choice of 18 different flavors, there should be something for everyone. Have yours with a cup of fresh coffee. $

Frog & Monkey Restaurant and Pub *411 N Donnelly Street, Mt. Dora, FL 32757 (352) 383-1936* For great atmosphere, excellent burgers and pub-style food, and a wide selection of beer and other beverages, you can't go wrong with the Frog Monkey. Set in the basement of the Renaissance Building, you wouldn't come here for the views, but the whimsical decorative touches inside are fun. There's often live music so don't plan on a quiet dinner, expect a more lively night out at this place. $$

Where to Stay

Grandview Bed and Breakfast *442 E. 3rd Avenue, Mt. Dora, FL 32757 (352) 383-4440* Considering this is a bed and breakfast, the amenities are really very good – a large salt-water swimming pool, personal concierge service, full breakfast, free Wi-Fi, and TVs in each room. They provide more facilities than many motels do, and this historic house has plenty of charm too. Built in 1906 there is even a windmill on site and it's just a brief walk to the center of town. The rooms are beautifully furnished with period charm, and all have private bathrooms. Choose the Windmill Cottage for extra space and privacy. $$

Adora Inn *610 North Tremain Street, Mt. Dora, FL 32757 (352) 735-3110* The Adora Inn is set within a 1916 Arts and Craft style home that has been completely renovat-

106 | **Florida Flying Guide**
Not for navigation or inflight use | © 2017 Adventus Media LLC

ed to modern standards while retaining the heritage of the architecture. Friendly and welcoming hosts provide the warm and personal service you expect from a B&B, and it's located just a few minutes walk from the heart of historic downtown. They serve a gourmet breakfast and can even arrange a custom-made candlelight dinner on the front porch. They will happily prepare lunches to eat in or to go. $$

Lakeside Inn *100 N. Alexander Street, Mt. Dora, FL 32757 (352) 383-4101* For the historical value and beautiful lakeside setting, you cannot beat the Lakeside Inn. If you take the hotel as a heritage building and don't expect everything to be quite up to modern standards, you'll enjoy your stay. $$

Umatilla Municipal — X23

CTAF/UNICOM ©122.9

Airport Manager Phone
(352) 669-3125

ASOS at LEE (9.5 W) 134.325
(352) 787-1565

®ORLANDO App/Dep 121.1

Elevation	Traffic Pattern	Flight Service Station
107' MSL	1100' MSL (893'AGL)	800-WX-BRIEF

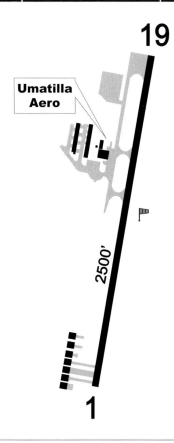

19

Umatilla
Aero

2500'

1

Mid Florida Air Service; Eustis · X55

CTAF/UNICOM ©122.8

Airport Manager Phone
(352) 558-2588

ASOS at LEE (9.5 W) 134.325
(352) 787-1565

®ORLANDO App/Dep 121.1

Elevation	Traffic Pattern	Flight Service Station
167' MSL	1100' MSL (933'AGL)	800-WX-BRIEF

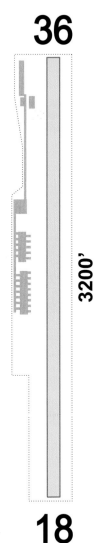

36

3200'

18

Naples

Naples has beaches, shopping, golf, a high-class atmosphere, and a booming tourist industry. Shop at the downtown boutiques, enjoy the Gulf scenery, or explore the local wine country. Pilots will appreciate the on-airport Pilot Shop and three restaurants within a five to eight minute walk.

Naples is one of the wealthiest cities in the country, and you can find several notable residents in the area. Bill Gates, Tom Cruise, Buzz Aldrin and author Robin Cook all have homes in Naples (though they don't all live here permanently). And with all that money around, it's no surprise that Naples is home to more than 80 golf courses and has a high-end feel.

The bay has so many man-made channels that boating and fishing is a very popular pastime in Naples, and there is direct boat access to many parts of the city. Many of the resorts will have their own marinas and offer boat-rentals if you want to hit the waves on your own.

The population of this small city is about 20,000, and it is surrounded by natural areas like the Picayune Strand State Forest and the Corkscrew Swamp Wetlands Sanctuary. To the north, Fort Myers offers a larger metropolitan city area. The arts and culture scene is

Naples Pier

vibrant in Naples, with several theatre companies, an opera house and the Naples Philharmonic all bringing their own artistic experiences to the city.

Flying There

Arriving in Naples is fairly straightforward. To the east, the Everglades have wide-open airspace, but are inhospitable in the event of a forced landing. Pilots are requested to avoid flight below 2,000 feet AGL in the Big Cypress National Preserve.

Coming down the west coast, flight following with Fort Myers Approach will establish radar contact and facilitate a smooth handoff to Naples Tower. The tower operates from 6 a.m. to 10 p.m. **Naples Municipal Airport** operates a full-service FBO on the east ramp. Self-serve 100LL is also available. **Avis, Hertz,** and **Enterprise** car rentals are available. Open 6 a.m. to 10 p.m. Radio 128.825 or telephone *(239) 643-0404* or *(239) 643-0733*.

Naples Jet Center is located on the north ramp and is open weekdays 7:30 a.m. to 7 p.m. and weekends 8 a.m. to 6 p.m. Rental and courtesy cars are available. Fuel service is provided by the airport authority. Radio 130.875 or call *(239) 649-7900*.

Getting Around

Collier Area Transit (CAT) handles the public transportation for Naples, and Route 12 runs right alongside the airport grounds. Fares are $1.50, or get a day-long pass for $4.00. Car rental services at the airport include **Avis** *(239) 643-4013* and **Hertz** *(239) 643-1515*. You can call a cab from **Naples Taxi Services** *(239) 300-6575*, or plan ahead and make a taxi reservation so they're waiting for you when you arrive.

Walking Distance Activities

If you need any gear, the **Airport Pilot Shop** is a full service pilot supply shop. They have extensive inventory, because they also sell by mail order. It's right at the airport and carries headsets, GPS units, simulators, charts and a lot more. Open Monday through Friday: 8 a.m. to 5:30 p.m., Saturday: 8 a.m. to 3 p.m. Sunday: Closed *(239) 263-9121*

Michelbob's Restaurant, *371 Airport Pulling Road North, Naples, FL, 34104* (239) 643-2877 is an eight minute walk from the GA terminal. Sometimes you can get a lift from the staff at the airport. The grand-daddy of rib joints in Naples, this place is rustic

Naples City Dock

and cute decorated with old-style coke machines. Ribs, pulled pork, and excellent onion rings. Hours change with the season, but typically are 11 a.m. to 8 p.m. weekdays. Saturdays dinner only. Closed Sunday. $$

Naples Rain Forest Cafe *3400 Radio Rd, #110, Naples, FL 34104 239-825-6303* If you want the option for something different than the usual airport food, this might be it. Cute place across from the airport; about a five-minute walk. In addition to regular breakfast and lunch items, they offer a few selections with a central American twist.

Good Times Diner, *325 Airport Pulling Rd N, Naples, FL 34104-3519* (239) 434-8778 A very average diner serving breakfast from 5 a.m. to 2 p.m. and lunch from mid morning to 5 p.m. The big plus is that it is a six minute walk from the GA terminal. $

The Museum of Military Memorabilia is located in the commercial terminal of the airport which is a 20 minute walk from the GA terminal. This museum room at the airport is not large (900 square feet)

and displays just a fraction of the 10,000 artifacts they have available so the displays rotate. The museum displays photos, medals, flight jackets, uniforms, and newspaper clippings. The exhibits are well-documented, clean and properly lighted. Be sure to call ahead to check open times. *(941) 575-0401*

What to See and Do

Naples Trolley Tours, *1010 6th Avenue South, Naples, FL 34102 (Old Naples), (800) 595-0840 or (239) 262-1914* A great and fairly cheap way to get a good perspective of Naples is to take this tour. It lasts almost two hours and stops at 21 locations. The guides have interesting stories and a good sense of humor. You can get off and on as many times as you want for free once you pay for your initial pass, so it is an excellent way to get around without renting a car or using a car service. Since they stop at several hotels (including the Bayfront Inn, LaPlaya Beach Resort, Vanderbilt Beach Resort, The Ritz-Carlton, Waldorf Astoria Naples, Inn of Naples and Naples Beach Hotel & Golf Club), you wouldn't need another mode of transportation once you checked in to your hotel. Trolley runs 9:30 a.m. until 5:30 p.m. seven days a week. $25. Two day passes are also available.

The Naples Fishing Pier is one of the most popular attractions in Naples. Originally built in 1888 as a freight and passenger dock, the Pier is a Naples icon. It is situated on a beautiful public beach area, and there is ample parking. Sunset is a popular time, but the Pier is worth a daytime visit too. Dolphins seem to play around the Pier much of the time. You can fish without a license. There are washrooms and a concession stand on the Pier.

Naples Depot Museum *1051 5th Ave S., Naples, FL 34102 (239) 262-6525* For transportation buffs, the Naples Depot Museum will take you on a trip through rail and automotive history. There are a mix of old vehicles and rail cars, all restored and on display. Next door is the Naples Train Museum where you can see some elaborate model train layouts in action, though be aware the Train Museum is open only Thursday, Friday and Saturday.

Segway Tours of Naples *1010 6th Avenue South, Naples, FL 34102 (239) 262-3006.* If you'd prefer something different than the Trolley Tour, the Segway Tour will fit the bill. A tour guide takes you through historic downtown Naples while narrating using wireless headsets. The tour passes Naples Pier, Palm Cottage, City Dock, Crayton Cove, Fifth Avenue South, and other points of interest. Tours include a brief training session in which the guide will train you how to ride the Segway. Three tours daily, 9 a.m., 12 p.m., and 2:30 p.m. Call *(239) 262-3006* for reservations. $75

Sweet Liberty *880 12th Avenue South, Crayton Cove, Naples, FL 34102 (239) 793-3525* This is a catamaran sailing and boat tour company that is most notable for their shelling trips to Key Island, where there are seven miles of remote beaches with an abundance of sea shells. The three-hour trip in

the morning leaves Naples City Dock. You might even have a few dolphin and manatee sightings during the voyage. They also do sightseeing and sunset cruises. Adults $40.

Captain CJ's JetPack Adventures *1345 Fifth Avenue South, Naples, FL 34102 (239) 389-9JET* Experience a different way to fly with a water-propelled jet pack. The instruction and flight lasts up to 30 minutes in a most spectacular setting on the Naples waterfront. Have your own James Bond moment if you are 14 or older and between 100 and 350 pounds. They will even shoot a video for you. Not cheap but coupons tend to be available. Call ahead to make reservations.

Silverspot Cinema

Naples Zoo at Caribbean Gardens *1590 Goodlette Rd Naples, FL 34102 (239) 262-5409* Their wildlife collection spans the globe, with an emphasis on the world's big cats. Enjoy the animals in natural habitat enclosures, including many rare animals that aren't

found in many other zoos (have you ever seen a fosa?). Adult tickets for the zoo are $19.95, with discounts for kids and seniors. They're open seven days a week, all year long (except Thanksgiving and Christmas). By car, the zoo is only a 10 minute drive from the airport.

Coral Cay Adventure Golf *2205 Tamiami Trail East, Naples, FL 34112 (239) 793-4999* Only a seven minute drive from the airport. If you are looking for a cheap and cheerful distraction, this is one of the nicest mini golf courses around. Great activity for couples (if you like that kind of thing) as well as kids. They have two 18 hole courses; one with a cave and one with waterfalls.

Silverspot Cinema *9118 Strada Place, Suite 8205, Naples, FL 34108 (Old Naples) (239) 592-0300* If you are staying overnight, this is a movie theater for adults. Huge comfortable leather seats (some are loveseats for two), a full bar and good snacks. Order wine and cheese for a different movie snack. There is also a very good restaurant inside. There are many other bars and restaurants in the area if you want something else before or after the movies. In addition to first run movies, they often show live performances from Lincoln Center in New York City.

Naples Botanical Garden *4820 Bayshore Drive Naples, FL 34112 (239) 643-7275* For an experience in beauty, peace and tranquility, spend some time at the Botanical Gardens in Naples. Themed garden areas show you the flora from Asia, Brazil, the Caribbean as well as local Floridian plants. A new 90-acre reserve gives you the chance to see less-groomed areas in their natural states. For dining in the garden, there's the new Fogg Cafe, offering a lovely outdoor patio and a menu focusing on local produce. Walk around on your own or take a guided tour. Entry is $14.95 for adults and parking is free.

Corkscrew Swamp Sanctuary *375 Sanctuary Road West, Naples, FL 34120 (239) 348-9151* A 40-minute drive from the airport will take you outside of Naples to the Corkscrew Swamp Sanctuary, where you can explore a huge wilderness area of old cypress swamps. Don't worry about getting your feet wet. There are more than two miles of raised boardwalks for your convenience. Over 200 bird species are known to live in the area, so keep your binoculars ready. Entry fee to the sanctuary is $12 with discounts for students. They're open seven days a week until 5:30 p.m.

Naples Botanical Garden

Beaches

The entire western edge of Naples is gorgeous coastline, with several white sandy beaches that are perfect for relaxing on. About a half hour drive north will bring you to a few good beach spots, including the **Delnor-Wiggins Pass State Park** *11100 Gulf Shore Drive N. Naples, FL 34108 (239) 597-6196.* Not only are there miles of beaches, the park has good facilities like picnic areas with BBQs, showers, restrooms and a boat-launch. Just south of the park is the smaller Vanderbilt Beach, which also has great facilities for a day at the beach.

Shopping

One of the top activities in Naples is shopping, and there are ample stores to browse.

The old fisherman's wharf, named Tin City, is home to a nice combination of artists, boutiques, gift shops and restaurants all under historical tin-roofed buildings. The Naples Winery is a must as they have free tastings and surprisingly good wine. There are boutiques, restaurants and galleries lining 5th Avenue

South and 3rd Avenue South.

Wine Tours

There are many world-famous vineyards and wineries in the Naples area, and spending an afternoon touring and tasting, appeals to many visitors. **The Naples Winery** *1200 5th Ave. S. Naples, FL 34102 (239) 732-WINE* is open daily for tastings, and you can sample their unique line of fruit wines.

Decanted *1410 Pine Ridge Road Suite 21, Naples, FL 34108 (239) 434-1814* hosts wine-tasting events frequently at their Naples shop, and they even run a cruise if you want to combine your wine tasting with coastal sightseeing.

Where to Eat

EJ's Bayfront Cafe *469 Bayfront Pl., Naples, FL 34102 (239) 353-4444* Across the Gordon River, you can get some of the best brunch dishes in all of Naples at EJ's. Omelets, waffles, scrambles and more can be the perfect start to your day. They do offer a nice selection of burgers, salads and sandwiches if you're not in the mood for breakfast. There is an outdoor patio, and being close to the water, you can enjoy the views while dining. $$

Captain Marcos Seafood *1716 Airport Rd N., Naples, FL 34104 (239) 262-1555* The menu at Captain Marco's is seafood with a Caribbean flair, with dishes like conch fritters, lobster creole and fish tacos. It can be a busy place at lunch because their tasty food is always very popular with the locals. They serve lunch and dinner, and the portions are always huge. $$

Bistro 821 *821 5th Ave S., Naples, FL 34102 (239) 261-5821* For a more upscale dining experience, have dinner at Bistro 821. The menu is mainly steak and seafood, and the style is elegant. Sea bass, snapper, prawns and the rib-eye steak are all constant customer favorites. The outdoor seating is as stylish as the indoor areas, and you'll receive attentive service no matter where you sit. $$$

Sandy's Cuban Cafe *1383 Airport Pulling Rd N., Naples, FL 34104 (239) 331-8204* Just a few short blocks north of the airport is this delicious little gem. The prices are really low, but the portions are generous. The menu is filled with classic Cuban dishes like empanadas, croquettes and Cuban sandwiches. It has a simple cafeteria-style interior, but for convenience to the airport, it's perfect. $

Where to Stay

LaPlaya Beach & Golf Resort Naples, *9891 Gulf Shore Drive, Naples, FL 34108 (239) 597-3123* If you're looking for some elegant peace and tranquility in Naples right on the beach, this is your place. If you want to be in the center of the

shopping and bars, then this isn't the place for you since the location is a few miles out of the center of Naples. The location on the gulf and river gives you wonderful sunrises and sunsets. Dolphins frequently come in along the shores. Multiple pools, tiki torches on the beach and open fire pits combined with outstanding service make this a Naples gem. For golfers, their 18-hole links golf course, just a few miles away is the perfect escape. Designed by Robert Cupp, this par 72, 6,907-yard championship layout is scenic and challenging. Since the David Leadbetter Golf Academy is located at the course, you might be able to book a school to coincide with your visit. $$$$

The Ritz-Carlton Golf Resort, Naples *2600 Tiburon Drive, Naples, FL 34109 (800) 542-8680* As you would expect, a very impressive hotel with impeccable Ritz-Carlton service and all the typical resort services. Not on the beach, but staying at the Golf Resort also allows access to the Beach Resort with a shuttle between the two every hour. While you don't have to play golf to enjoy the resort, golfers will enjoy the Greg Norman 36-hole championship course. This uniquely-designed course incorporates stacked sod-wall bunkers and coquina sand and does not contain rough. The Gold Course measures 7,288 yards from the Tournament tees and the Black Course measures 7,005 yards. The golf courses are also home to the PGA Tour Academy and the TaylorMade Performance Lab. $$$$$

Courtyard Naples *3250*

North US 41, Naples, FL 34103 (239) 434-8700 The Courtyard Naples is just half a mile from the airport if you're looking for easy-access accommodations. It's part of the Marriott chain, and the rooms are simple though attractively done. You'll get free Internet service, in-room coffee, and there is both a pool and fitness center on the premises. $$

Red Roof Plus Inn & Suites *1925 Davis Blvd., Naples, FL 34104 (239) 774-3117* Not far from the airport, but also close to the shopping along Fifth Avenue South, the Red Roof Inn offers some pet-friendly rooms with many amenities. There is free coffee, Wi-Fi and cable service available. Choose a standard room or let yourself stretch out in a larger suite. The suites offer lots of space as well as screened-in patio areas. $$

Naples Bay Resort *1500 5th Ave S., Naples, FL 34102 (239) 530-1199* If cost isn't an issue, stay in luxury at the Naples Bay Resort. This is a great location if you want to walk out to 5th and Tin City for the restaurants and shops. They have bicycles for rent if you want to pedal around town to see the sights (the beaches are within biking distance), or you can get on the water with a boat rental. On-site, there is a large waterfall pool, a full-service spa, and many rooms have views overlooking the bay and marina where you can rent a boat. The complimentary shuttle service will take you downtown when it's time to go shopping. $$$

Naples Municipal

KAPF

TOWER ©128.5
[0600-2200]

Ground Control **121.6**

Control Tower Phone
[239] 643-4929

Airport Manager Phone
[239] 643-0733

ASOS [239] 643-9886

ATIS 134.225 [239] 643-5230

®FORT MYERS App/Dep 119.75
[0600-2400]

®MIAMI CENTER App/Dep 134.75
[2400-0600]

CLNC DEL 118.0

UNICOM 128.825

Elevation	Traffic Pattern	Flight Service Station
8' MSL	1008' MSL [1000'AGL]	MIAMI RCO 123.6

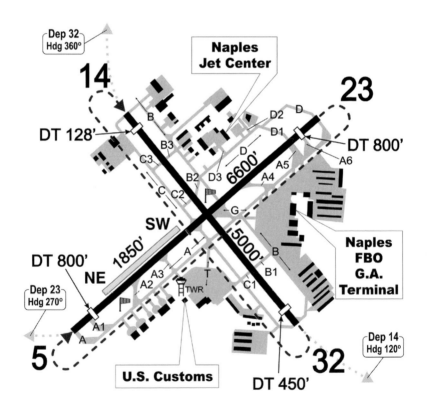

Dep 32
Hdg 360°

14

**Naples
Jet Center**

23

DT 128'

B

D2   D

B3

D1

DT 800'

C3

D

A5   A6

6600'

B2   D3   A4

C   C2

G

SW

**Naples
FBO
G.A.
Terminal**

1850'

5000'

A

B

DT 800'
NE

A3

T

B1

A2

⊟TWR

C1

Dep 23
Hdg 270°

A1

Dep 14
Hdg 120°

A

5

U.S. Customs

32

DT 450'

New Smyrna Beach

19 miles south of the more famous Daytona Beach, New Smyrna Beach has just as much to offer to visitors who enjoy spending time on the water without the congestion. It even has its own NASCAR track. And when you stay beachside, it makes a nice romantic getaway.

Blue skies meet over 13 miles of white sand in New Smyrna Beach. The extensive dune lined beach is made for long walks. Fishing, boating and surfing are also big activities along the beaches of New Smyrna. In fact, the town was named one of the world's top 20 surfing destinations by National Geographic. New Smyrna Beach was voted "Best Beach in Florida," by readers of Florida Monthly Magazine.

Natural areas like the Mosquito Lagoon Aquatic Preserve or the Smyrna Dunes Park can give you a chance to recharge after a busy day of sightseeing or water sports. Or just stick to the usual sandy beaches to relax on.

New Smyrna Beach is part of the "Fun Coast" for good reason. It's a total playground for all the coastal activities you can think of.

New Smyrna Beach

Flying There

Located right on the east coast of Florida, the airport is located under Daytona's outer Class C 1200 foot shelf. Approaching the airport from the south will bring you right past Cape Canaveral and its restricted areas, as well as Patrick Air Force Base (COF) and Melbourne (MLB). If you are not using flight following, then fly above 2,500 feet and stay just off the west bank of the intracoastal waterway, and you should be fine. Be cautious if you intend to overfly Massey (X-50) as it has skydiving, aerobatics, and glider operations. Contact Daytona approach on 125.35 when you are within 20 miles. From the north, you will be flying through Daytona Beach (DAB) airspace, so call Daytona Approach as you pass Flagler County Airport (XFL) on 125.8. From the west, call Daytona Approach before you pass Deland Airport (DED). Flying from the Southwest, your best bet is to have Orlando Approach 119.4 work you through the complicated airspace. If you are navigating on your own, beware of the permanent TFR within 3NM of Disney World up to 3,000 feet. Since it is not marked on the official charts you need to take care.

Airgate Aviation is the FBO and it has a café *(386) 478-0600*. Epic Aviation is a flight school next door that also offers FBO services. The city airport also offers self serve fuel (close to the tower) with public bathrooms a short walk away.

Walking Distance Activities

FBO Airgate has the Airgate Café (open from 6 a.m. until 2 p.m.) on the field. Also, Lost Lagoon Wings and Grill is a free-standing restaurant just at the entrance to the airport (a one minute walk) from either Airgate or Epic. Otherwise there is nothing interesting within a short walk.

Getting Around

Airgate has **Hertz** cars *(386) 478-0600*. Epic Aviation has **Enterprise** *(386) 423-1337*. **New Smyrna Taxi** *(386) 212-3333* is always happy to take you where you need to go when you don't need your own car.

There are some public transportation options in New Smyrna Beach. The bus does go right past the airport, and Route 40 will take you downtown. From there, you can get around town with Flex 43 or 42. Flex service runs like a combination taxi/bus that you have to call for, and they will pick you up at a point of your choosing and take you

anywhere within the service area. Fares are $1.50 per trip.

What to See and Do

Marine Discovery Center *520 Barracuda Blvd., New Smyrna Beach, FL 32169 (386) 428-4828* All sorts of marine activities can be found at the Marine Discovery Center, with the dolphin tours being the most popular. You can also take an eco-tour by kayak to see more of the local wildlife and scenery. They do a lot of volunteer projects if you want to join in and help out the local ecosystems. Dolphin tours start at $25, and you need to book ahead.

Arts on Douglas *123 Douglas St., New Smyrna Beach, FL 32168 (386) 428-1133* A unique commercial art gallery located in a converted warehouse. If you have any interest in art, it is well worth the trip. You will see many examples of local art both painting and sculpture. There is a reception on the first Saturday of the month, and it is the place to be for the art scene with great artists, and eclectic crowds.

Take a step back in time on the 53ft. schooner **Ondine**. *512 South Riverside Drive New Smyrna Beach, FL 32168 (386) 423-4940* This two masted sailing boat only takes one group on the river or inlet at a time so it is a private experience. (maximum six people). Pat and Jeannine and the crew are very friendly. They will adjust the cruise based on the weather and your desires.

New Smyrna Speedway, *3939 State Road 44, New Smyrna Beach, FL 32168 (386) 427-4129* If you are looking for action instead of romance,

the New Smyrna Speedway is a fun place for some up close NASCAR racing hometown style. There isn't a bad seat in the place to watch some exciting racing by local drivers beating and banging as they go around the high banks of this track for the win. Don't forget to bring your seat cushion.

Bob Ross Art Workshop *757 E 3rd Ave, New Smyrna Beach, FL 32169 (386) 423-4346* You have seen Bob Ross on TV, now you can make your own painting at this studio that he started many years ago. Four-hour classes for beginners take you step by step through the process of making a painting that you can fly home with. Lots of original Bob Ross paintings hang on the wall. They also have a 3-week certification course for artists that want to teach. Very fun.

Turtle Mound National Historic Site *(407) 267-1100* Take the main causeway over to the islands from town, and the Turtle Mound National Historic Site is just on the other side of the river. A large 2,000-year old burial mound is the historical element to the park, but you can also spend the afternoon just walking around the area on the paths and walkways. Turtles are everywhere.

New Smyrna Museum of History *120 Sams Avenue, New Smyrna Beach, FL 32168 (386) 478-0052* This is a local museum that highlights all aspects of New Smyrna Beach's past, including several interesting prehistoric collections of artifacts. Large items like the Native American canoe and vintage printing press are particularly fun to examine. The museum is free though they will take donations.

Beaches

The islands across the river are lined with beaches, so you shouldn't have any problems finding the perfect stretch of sand. The **New Smyrna Town Beach** on South Atlantic Avenue is a popular one, with a nice boardwalk for strolling, and there's plenty of free parking. Toward the southern end of the beach is the **Mary McLeod Bethune Park** *6656 S. Atlantic Ave.,* where you can find a more natural bit of shoreline that is populated with manatees.

If you want to head north instead, the **Smyrna Dunes Park** *(386) 424-2935* has lots of sand, views and 1.5 miles of boardwalk trails. It's more a nature park than a sunbathing beach but the surfing is pretty good in the area too.

Fishing

The fish are almost always biting around New Smyrna Beach, and there is a great se-

lection of boating charters you can choose from to help you get out onto the water. **The Fishing Guy** *1424 N. Peninsula Ave., New Smyrna Beach, FL 32169 (407) 948-5035* knows where to hook the amberjack, red snapper, mahi and kingfish.

Spot N Tail Charters *250 H.H. Burch Rd, New Smyrna Beach, FL 32759 (386) 566-1394* can help you cast your line out in the Mosquito Lagoon area of river inlets and wetlands for redfish, trout and tarpon.

Dinner and River Cruise

Combine a dolphin cruise with dinner and you have two activities in one! The **Dolphin View Seafood Dinner and River Cruise** *107 North Riverside Drive, New Smyrna Beach, FL 32169 (386) 402-8859* is a wonderful way to spend an evening. The evening begins with a buffet dinner while watching the dolphins that frequently swim right up. Once dinner is over, the cruise departs along the river. Watch the sunset, the intra-coastal scenery, wildlife and dolphins from the out-

side-seating areas, or head inside and enjoy the bar and DJ. The cost for this dinner and cruise is $19.95 per person.

Where to Eat

Lost Lagoon Wings & Grill, *2004 North Dixie Freeway, New Smyrna Beach, FL 32168 (386) 366-3360* A one minute walk from the FBO, this very popular place makes, what many people feel is, the best burger in town. Also known for their wings. Great place to fly in for Sunday Brunch.

The Garlic *556 3rd Ave., New Smyrna Beach, FL 32169 (386) 424-6660* You may have to cross the river to get there, but it's still only 10 minutes from the airport to one of the finest restaurants in New Smyrna Beach. Yes, they use a lot of garlic in their menu but it's not overwhelming. The roasted garlic appetizer is a big hit! They're only open for dinner, until 10 p.m. The place has a semi-outdoor feel that is fun, yet it is fully air conditioned. Take your pick from inside or outside seating. $$$

Crabby Chris Crab Shack *440 N Dixie Fwy., New Smyrna Beach, FL 32168 (386) 957-3878* It's a casual place with several umbrella-covered picnic tables outside. Portions are huge, and the seafood is always fresh. Crab cakes and fish tacos are crowd favorites whether you are grabbing a quick lunch or staying for dinner. Crabby Chris is in the center of downtown, but only a five minute drive from the airport. It's near the causeways that can take you over to the islands too. $$

J.B.'s Fish Camp and Restaurant *859 Pompano*

J.B.'s Fish Camp and Restaurant

Riverview Hotel

Ave., New Smyrna Beach, FL 32169 (386) 427-5747 This local landmark is off the beaten track and is a real slice of old Florida. More than a restaurant it has a boat launch, paddle board and kayak rental and a fishing dock. Go there for the throwback atmosphere, great views from their deck or dock area and spectacular sunsets over the Indian River. Bring your mosquito spray! $$

The Taco Shack *642 N Dixie Fwy., New Smyrna Beach, FL 32168 (386) 428-9882* The Taco Shack is the hidden gem that the locals are very proud of, and that most tourists never seem to find! There are no indoor seats, but the outside patio is covered and adorned with surfer decor. The cuisine is Mexican and they have a whole lot more than just tacos. They're closed Sunday and Monday, and open until 9 p.m. $

Where to Stay

Black Dolphin Inn *916 S Riverside Drive, New Smyrna Beach, FL 32168 (386) 410-4868* The hosts at the Black Dolphin really know how to treat their guests. Rooms and facilities are definitely four-star quality but without the high price tag. Spacious, beautifully decorated and very private, you'll certainly enjoy your stay. The grounds face the Indian River, and you can sit out on the dock and watch for dolphins or stay indoors to have

a drink with other residents at the common room bar. $$

Riverview Hotel *103 Flagler Ave., New Smyrna Beach, FL 32169 (386) 428-5858* Just across the river is the Riverview Hotel, a historic place with a lot of old Southern charm. It's a popular hotel for couples looking for a romantic place to celebrate an anniversary. There is a swimming pool, and every room has a private patio or balcony. Rooms and bathrooms are on the small side but cozy. Complimentary breakfasts are simple, but you can have yours delivered to your room if you want to sleep-in. You can walk to the nightlife, beaches or just stay at the hotel for some spa pampering. $$

Anchor Inn BnB *312 Washington St, New Smyrna Beach, FL 32168-7070 (386) 337-3319* Beautiful place. Two sisters, Marie and Ellen, own and run the inn. It is within easy walking distance to Canal Street which is the main street that houses many shops and restaurants and little museums. The breakfast is first-class. $$

Anchor Inn BnB

New Smyrna Beach Municipal — KEVB

SMYNA BEACH TOWER ©**119.67**
(0700-2200)

GROUND CONTROL **121.325**

Control Tower Phone
(386) 423-5024

Airport Manager
(386) 424-2199

AWOS–3 124.625 (386) 409–4705

ATIS 124.625

DAYTONA App ®125.35

UNICOM 122.95

Elevation 10' MSL	Traffic Pattern 800' MSL (790'AGL)	Flight Service Station 800-WX-BRIEF

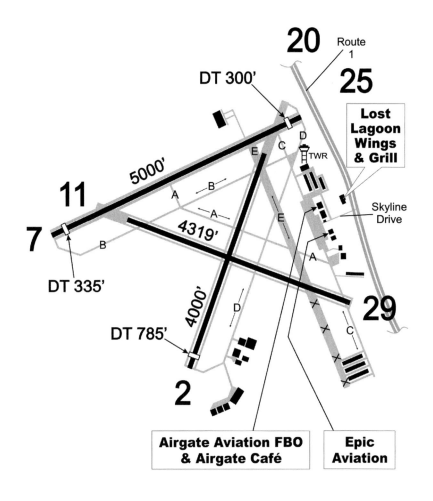

20

Route 1

25

DT 300'

Lost Lagoon Wings & Grill

5000'

11

7

DT 335'

B

A

A

B

E

C

D

TWR

E

Skyline Drive

A

4319'

29

C

4000'

DT 785'

D

2

X
X
X
X

Airgate Aviation FBO & Airgate Café

Epic Aviation

North Captiva Island

North Captiva Island is often confused with Captiva, but it is a very different island with its own character. Separated from Captiva by Red Fish Pass, it is accessible only by boat or airplane. The non-commercial remoteness of the island is its charm.

Well off the beaten track, North Captiva Island is accessible only by ferry, private boat or airplane. Due to this restricted access, the island is unlisted by almost every Florida travel guide, which suits the owners and residents of North Captiva just fine. It also makes visitors part of a very small insiders club.

This private island community reminds visitors of old Florida as it once was. On North Captiva, you will get around by golf cart or bicycle on sandy native trails. There are no cars or paved roads.

North Captiva Island

Flying There

If you are renting a home on North Captiva (also referred to as Upper Captiva) you can likely make arrangements to use the Salty Approach Airport (FL-90). The key is that you are renting from an airport owner. Be sure you confirm with your rental agent or owner that the property owner has rights to use the airport.

The strip is grass and approximately 2000 feet in length. The runway alignment is 10-28 and is clear of obstructions on both ends. The traffic pattern is a standard left-hand pattern to be flown at 800 feet. UNICOM is 122.75 and pilots are requested to start making calls at least five miles out. There are no night operations. For more information on the airport go to their website at saltyapproach.com.

The approach to the airport from the northeast, could take you over the Pine Island National Wildlife Refuge. Pilots are requested to avoid overflight below 2,000 feet MSL.

Other Ways of Getting There

For non-flying guests, there is hourly ferry service from Pine Island with **Island Girl Charters** *(239) 633-8142,* as well as water taxis and private charters from **Jensens Marina** *(239) 472-5800* and Pine Island.

Getting Around

North Captiva Island guests and owners get around by golf carts, bikes or by foot. One cart is usually provided with each rental. There are over 20 miles of trails and no paved roads.

What to See and Do

North Captiva Island's remote location means there is not a lot of activity, but that is the reason to come to this location.

Much of North Captiva Island is protected state preservation land. There are nature trails through the preserve (walking or biking only). North Captiva has about four miles of beache to walk. You will see many different species of migrating birds. From shore, you may also see dolphins manatees, sea turtles, and otters.

Kayaking is very popular on North Captiva Island as is biking on the 20 miles of trails winding over the island. The one-stop shop on North Captiva for renting Kayaks, bikes, and extra golf carts is **Boats and Fun** *(239) 214-8676*. They can also arrange boat tours around the island.

Fishing is very popular. Because of the island's location, fishing is very productive. You can fish from the land, or you can arrange a charter boat from Boats and Fun (see above).

Where to Eat

There are only four restaurants on the island. Some of them are available only to members and guests of clubs and resorts.

Barnicle Phil's *4401 Point House Trail, North Captiva Island, FL 33924 (239) 472-1200* Open to the public for lunch and sometimes dinner, it offers a casual dining experience. The location, right on Safety Harbor, is beautiful and the sandy beach, Adirondack chairs, and local fare add to a Caribbean feel. There is also an ice cream shop next door. $$

The Boathouse Restaurant *4421 Bartlett Parkway, North Captiva Island Club, North Captiva Island, FL 33945 (239) 283-3630* recently had a turnover in staff. Recent reviews are very good. Open to Island Club registered guests only. $$$

Mango's Cafe and Grill *Bartlett Parkway, North Captiva Island, North Captiva Island, FL (239) 395-1001* Combination pool bar/tropical restaurant, gets you in the vacation mood. Poolside dining is open only to members and guests of the North Captiva Island Club, but the public is invited to eat upstairs or enjoy takeout by the docks. $$

The Over the Waterfront is located at Safety Harbor townhouses. *4470 Escondido Lane, North Captiva Island, FL 33924 (239) 472-2387* The restaurant is truly over the water with a nice view of Safety Harbor and Pine Island Sound. There are viewing windows in the floor so you can look for sea creatures under the dock. Popular Chef David cooks and sometimes serves the food. The sign outside says that it is a private restaurant (for the benefit of Safety Harbor Club members), but some visitors say others can eat there also. If you are not staying at the Safety Harbor Club, call ahead to be sure you are welcome.

North Captiva Island and Salty Approach Airport

Salty Approach Airport

FL90

CTAF/UNICOM ©**122.75**

Airport Manager Phone
[239] 472-1079

ASOS 135.525 [305] 743–8373

®MIAMI App/Dep 133.5

Elevation	Traffic Pattern	Flight Service Station
6' MSL	800 MSL	800-WX-BRIEF

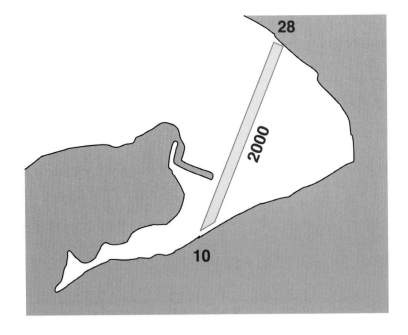

Ocala

Nicknamed Horse Capital of the World, Ocala is famous for its Thoroughbred horses, horse farms, attractive historical buildings, and for the nearby Silver Springs, Florida's first tourist attraction. There is a surprising art museum and an excellent car museum. Oh, and you can fly in for breakfast, lunch or dinner right at the airport!

The horse farm landscape that includes rolling hills and pastures is really quite different to the typical landscapes of Florida, making this an attractive and interesting place to visit. Add the large residential Historic District to your plans if you enjoy heritage buildings, plus a trip to the northeast of the city to visit Silver Springs to take a tour on one of their famous glass-bottom boats.

Ocala didn't become famous for its horses until the 1950s when the first Florida-bred thoroughbred, Needles, won the Kentucky Derby. Since then the city and surrounding county have become one of the major Thoroughbred centers of the world, home to around 1,200 horse farms of which around 900 are Thoroughbred farms. If you want to try horseback riding, Ocala would be a great place to do it.

Horses in Ocala

Flying There

Ocala is far enough from Orlando and Tampa to enjoy fairly simple airspace compared to many central Florida destinations, although pilots coming from the east will need to route around the Palatka 1 and 2 Military Operations Areas and several Restricted Areas to the south of them. OCF's Class D airspace is tower-controlled from 7 a.m. to 8 p.m.

Several non-towered airports are nearby, and pilots should, as always, be alert for traffic, including a celebrity-owned 707 based at the private **Jumbolair** airpark to the northeast of Ocala.

Sheltair runs the FBO on the northeast ramp. Full-service 100LL and Jet A are available, as well as self-serve

Ocala International-Jim Taylor

100LL. They offer courtesy cars and **Hertz** rentals. Business hours are 6 a.m. to 9 p.m. Radio 129.375. Telephone *(352) 237-3444* for customer service.

Getting Around

Rent a car at the airport with **Avis** *(352) 237-2714,* **Enterprise** *(352) 861-2528* or **Hertz** *(352) 861-1888),* or grab a taxi with one of the local firms including **A-1 Taxi** *(352) 299-1634,* and **Signature Taxi Shuttle** *(352) 207-2008.*

SunTran provides local public bus transportation services Monday through Saturday though none of their routes come out as far as the airport. If you get yourself into downtown Ocala, you can pick up the bus to travel out to Silver Springs. A one-way regular fare is $1.50.

Walking Distance Activities

Tail Winds Cafe is back. After becoming Thyme Fly's Bistro, it is Tail Winds again. Located at Sheltair, it offers fabulous views of airplanes taking off and landing. Open

for breakfast and lunch seven days a week. Read more below in the "Where To Eat" section.

What to See and Do

The Gypsy Gold Farm Tour is a wonderful experience for any horse lover. The Gypsy Vanner horses are a unique breed. Owner Dennis Thompson is a totally absorbing speaker with a wonderful sense of humor. The tour lets you see and even interact with some of the horses (some like to be pet and hand-fed carrots.) It's a most-enjoyable way to spend a morning. *12501 SW 8th Ave., Ocala, FL 34473 (352) 307-3777*

Appleton Museum of Art *4333 E. Silver Springs Blvd., Ocala, FL 34470 (352) 291-4455* For a relatively small city, the Appleton Museum of Art is an impressive museum if you're looking for a cultural fix while visiting Ocala. Featuring European, American and Contemporary art that includes sculptures and paintings as well as a collection of artifacts and antiquities from pre-Columbian times, there is also an attractive courtyard with

fountain and Asian statues. If you're interested in horses, the equestrian-themed room is for you. The museum is closed on Mondays, Thanksgiving, Christmas and New Year's Day. Admission is $8 for adults.

Don Garlits' Museum of Drag Racing *13700 SW 16th Ave., Ocala, FL 34473 (352) 245-8661* Don Garlits is the granddaddy of drag racing. While this is called a drag racing museum, it is much more than that. There are two buildings of roughly 300 classic, collector, antique cars and memorabilia that you're unlikely to see anywhere else. If Don is at the museum, which is often, you get to chat with him. Open every day from 9 a.m. to 5 p.m., except Thanksgiving and Christmas, a tour takes around two to three hours. Admission is $20 for adults.

Silver Springs

While technically just outside Ocala, Silver Springs is one of the area's best known attractions. In fact, Silver Springs was the first tourist attraction in Florida, operating its glass bottom boat since 1878 so vis-

Appleton Museum of Art

Don Garlits' Museum of Drag Racing

itors could see the world's largest artesian springs. Today the famous glass bottom boats still operate 30 minute tours allowing you to see the crystal clear waters for yourself. There's also two State Parks, Silver Springs and Silver River, where you can hike the trails or paddle a kayak on the river. Prices vary depending on which activities you choose to do.

Downtown Ocala

Ocala has managed to retain its small-city charm and this, coupled with its historic architecture, make the downtown area a very attractive place to visit. Ocala Historic District features a number of buildings listed on the National Register of Historic Places and if you enjoy seeing Victorian homes, head to East Fort King Street. In the heart of the city, Ocala Downtown Square has a quaint and friendly atmosphere and hosts farmer's markets, live concerts and other events through the year. At Christmas the square is especially nice.

Horse Riding and Tours

As the Horse Capital of the World, you cannot visit Ocala without having some interaction with at least one horse! If you'd like to try horseback riding, **Cactus Jack's Trail Rides** *The Florida Horse Park, 11008 S Highway 475, Ocala, FL 34480 (352) 266-9326* can take you out on a guided trail ride on the Ocala Greenway Trail System. Riders over six years old can enjoy a trail ride but phone ahead for reservations.

If you're celebrating a special occasion, then a scenic tour on a horse-drawn carriage will fit the bill! **Horse Country Carriage Co & Tours** *5400 NW 110th Ave., Ocala, FL 34482 (352) 727-0900* offer one-hour, fully-narrated tours in which you'll travel through the heart of horse country, passing famous horse farms. Tours must be reserved in advance.

The Ocala Drive-In *4850 S Pine Avenue, Ocala, FL 34480 (352) 629-1325* If you are staying overnight in Ocala, this will give you a throwback night of entertainment under

the stars. Every showing is a first-run double-feature. The concession stand has pizza, hot dogs, popcorn, candy, etc. and is open throughout the shows. The drive-in features a brand new Digital HD Projector with outstanding picture quality and the sound is broadcast on the FM band through your car radio. A great place to make memories in your rental car!

Where to Eat

Tail Winds Cafe *1200 SW 60th Avenue, Ocala, FL 34481* It doesn't get much more convenient than this! Located within the **Sheltair** FBO at Ocala Airport, Tail Winds is a great little place to eat if you love watching airplanes taking off and landing. The former Tailwinds Cafe morphed into Thyme Fly's Bistro and has now transformed back to Tail Winds Cafe again! Open seven days a week for breakfast and lunch. $$

La Hacienda *4185 W Hwy 40, Ocala, FL 34482 (352) 512-0746* On the way into Ocala are numerous fast food chains if you want a quick fill up of the usual burger fare or stop by La Hacienda for something a little different. Part supermarket, part bakery, and part restaurant (with dine-in area), La Hacienda serves tasty and authentic Mexican cuisine, home cooked from scratch and at very reasonable prices. $

Harry's Seafood Bar and Grille *24 SE 1st Avenue, Ocala, FL 34471 (352) 840-0900* You'll find many great restaurants in downtown Ocala though Harry's stands out as one of the best-rated in the city. Set right on Ocala Downtown Square, this restaurant and bar has a friendly and lively atmosphere. They serve American, Cajun and Creole inspired dishes with a focus on seafood so you'll get a taste of New Orleans in Ocala with dishes like Mardi Gras Shrimp and Shrimp etouffee. $$

Where to Stay

Red Roof Inn & Suites *120 NW 40th Avenue, Ocala, FL 34482 (352) 732-4590* The Red Roof Inn and Suites is the closest accommodation to Ocala Airport, accessible by a five minute drive or a 50 minute walk. The hotel offers comfortable and affordable rooms with free Wi-Fi, complimentary continental breakfast, a year-round outdoor swimming pool, and pets stay free too. Convenient to the airport, and less than a 10 minute drive to downtown Ocala. $

Seven Sisters Inn *828 SE Fort King Street, Ocala, FL 34471 (352) 433-0700* There are surprisingly few hotels or B&Bs within walking distance of downtown Ocala, and the

Ocala Drive-In

Seven Sisters Inn is one of them. Set on a residential, tree-lined street, this historic Inn was built in 1890 in the Gothic Victorian architectural style. All the suites have antique charm and grandeur mixed in with modern-day bathroom comforts. A great breakfast is included and the hosts are very friendly. With its expensive room-rates and historic charm, this would be the perfect place to spend a special occasion. $$$

Holiday Inn Express Ho- **tel & Suites** *5360 E Silver Springs Blvd., Silver Springs, FL 34488 (877) 859-5095* If you're hoping to spend some time exploring Silver Springs, to the northeast of Ocala, then the Holiday Inn is a good base. Offering comfort and service typical of the Holiday Inn brand, this larger hotel has a swimming pool, free hot breakfast and Wi-Fi, a microwave and fridge in the rooms, and a fitness center and business center all within minutes of the attractions of Silver Springs. $$

John Travolta's Boeing 707 at his House in Jumbolair

Ocala International-Jim Taylor — KOCF

OCALA TOWER ©119.25
[0600-2100]

Ground Control **121.4**

Airport Manager Phone
[352] 629-8377

AWOS-3 128.125 [352] 237-8525

ATIS 128.125

®JACKSONVILLE App/Dep 118.6

UNICOM 123.00

Elevation 89' MSL	Traffic Pattern 1089' MSL [1000'AGL]	Flight Service Station GAINESVILLE RCO 122.1R 113.7T

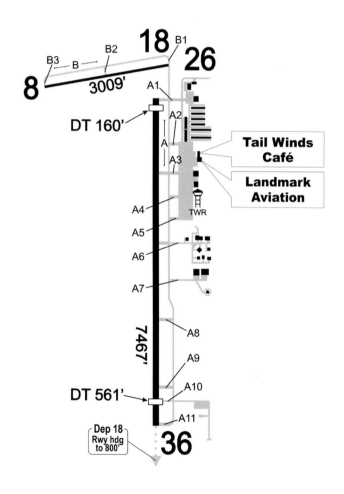

Okeechobee

Okeechobee is best known to pilots as the home of the Landing Strip Café. It is an easy flight from either the west or the east coast of Florida. But if you want to fish, camp, or gamble, you can do it here.

The Landing Strip Café

Pilots will notice the big lake south of the airport also called Okeechobee, which means "big water" in the Seminole language. It is the second largest fresh water lake in the U.S., and it provides many recreational opportunities. There are actually three airports around the lake: Okeechobee (KOBE) to the north, Pahokee (KPHK) officially known as Palm Beach County Glades on the southeast shore of the lake, and Airglades (21S), 9 miles west of the lake's southwest shore. KOBE is the located where the city is, and where the restaurant is located.

Flying There

The approaches into Okeechobee are generally free of obstacles and conflicting airspace. Pilots should be aware of the R-2901 Restricted Areas, which lie as close as 10 nm to the northwest and require avoidance if coming from that direction.

Okeechobee's quiet location also makes it a popular destination for instructors and students looking to escape the busy airspace around the large training centers on the coast.

Okeechobee Jet Center is the field's FBO. Self-serve 100LL and Jet A are available 24/7. Full-service Jet A is offered during their regular business hours of 8 a.m. to 5 p.m. Enterprise rental cars are available. Radio on UNICOM 123.0 or call *(863) 467-5888.* The adjacent Landing Strip Cafe is open 6 a.m. to 3 p.m.

Walking Distance Activities

The **Landing Strip Café** at the airport is really the only thing you will want to walk to here.

Enterprise doesn't have a local office, but they do keep a car on-site, available for rent. Call Alex Mendoza, the FBO manager to arrange for a car *(863) 467-5888.*

What to See and Do
Fishing

Besides having breakfast or lunch, fishing is a good reason to fly in. Okeechobee is well-known for largemouth bass, but it is also a good place to fish for crappie and bluegill. There are many fishing guides and bait stores around. One place that is close to KOBE (a 14 minute ride) is **Fast Break Bait and Tackle** *1505 State Road 78 West Okeechobee, FL 34974 (863) 763-2474.* They not only have the supplies you need but also have seven captains available for charters. You have to love their confident "No Fish, No Pay!" pledge.

Airboat Tours
GatorHunt Airboat Rides *(863) 763-7433* has a boat that can carry up to six guests through the shallow parts of the lake. You might see alligators, birds, turtles and more. They launch it from a ramp on the north part of the lake, so it is not far from the airport.

Biking (or Hiking) Around the Lake
The lake is ringed by a 110 mile path on top of the Okeechobee dike, roughly 35 feet high. It goes by the unfortunate acronym of LOST (Lake Okeechobee Scenic Trail). 66 miles of the trail are paved and 44 miles are gravel. You can enjoy walking, hiking, rollerblading, bicycling or even horseback riding (if you can fit a horse in your airplane) around Lake Okeechobee. Being on top of the trail gives you a wonderful vantage point to view everything from the scenic lake to agricultural landscapes. To get on the trail you need to find an access point, of which two are near the town of Okeechobee. The closest access point to an airport is by KPHK. If you want to take your time on your journey, there are 14 camping areas available on or adjacent to the trail of which nine are primi-

tive campsites you can use. No fees or permits are required for trail use. Beware that construction on the dikes is currently causing sections of the path to be closed. Check online or call the Army Corps of Engineers at (863) 983-8101.

Gambling
If you don't have a casino near you, a 30 minute drive from the airport will bring you to the **Seminole Casino Brighton** *17735 Reservation Rd, Okeechobee, FL 34974 (863) 467-9998.* If you have been to Vegas, Coconut Creek or the Hard Rock in Tampa, you will be surprised at this casino. It is small (if you can call a 27,000-square-foot casino small) and not very grand on the outside. Inside it is comfortable. The personnel are friendly and there is a nice ambiance about the casino. The casino features slot machines and a big bingo hall. They no longer have card tables. There is one restaurant which gets mixed reviews. Occasionally they have shows which in the past have included variety

shows as well as comedian Bill Engvall.

Where to Eat
Landing Strip Café *2800 NW 20th Trail, Okeechobee, FL 34972 (863) 467-6828* This is the highest rated restaurant in Okeechobee and a very good place to eat. No, it's not fancy, but the staff are very friendly, and the prices are reasonable. You can sit in air conditioning inside or if the weather is nice, go to the patio outside and look at the airplanes. If you flew in alone, you can sit at the bar to eat. They are open for breakfast and lunch, seven days a week.

Where to Stay
There are not a lot of fancy places to stay in this rural area.

Hampton Inn Okeechobee *1200 State Road 70 East, Okeechobee, FL 34972 (855) 271-3622* Hampton Inn is Hilton's budget brand, but this is a modern, clean hotel whose staff gets consistently high marks from guests. Very popular breakfast room.

Biking in Okeechobee

Okeechobee County

CTAF/UNICOM ©123.0

Airport Manager Phone
[863] 763-3955

AWOS–3 118.675 [863] 467–1148

®MIAMI App/Dep 132.25

Elevation	Traffic Pattern	Flight Service Station
33' MSL	833' MSL [800'AGL]	800-WX-BRIEF

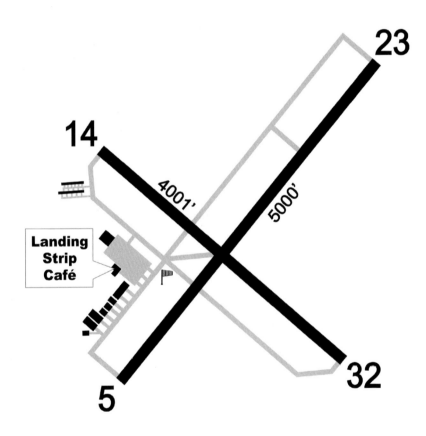

14

23

Landing Strip Café

4001'

5000'

5

32

Palm Beach County Park

The motto of Palm Beach sums up this coastal town very accurately: "The Best of Everything." Palm Beach does indeed appear to offer a little of everything from its beaches, to golfing, boating, shopping and dining, but why choose Palm Beach for a flying visit over any other attractive coastal town?

P alm Beach is the ultimate resort town, established by oil baron Henry Morrison Flagler when he connected the barrier island to the mainland via his Florida East Coast Railway. Flagler then had two luxury hotels built, the Royal Poinciana and The Breakers, the latter of which still stands today. The town developed into a hugely-popular tourist destination, especially with the wealthier of society, who would come for parties and to enjoy the boating, golfing, tennis and fishing that are still popular today.

Flying in to the small airplane-friendly Lantana Airport puts you a little way inland, away from the beaches and the larger crowds, and provides the opportunity to do something a little different from the norm. You can still head to Palm Beach, for a day on the sand, to visit the impressive historic Breakers Hotel; the attractive

Palm Beach looking at the Breakers on the Right

Four Arts Gardens; the upscale stores of Worth Avenue; and the striking Flagler Museum, if you want to, though there are different and unique things to see and do here too.

Designed to feel like an old farmhouse, the breezeway of Lantana airport's FBO has Old-Florida charm. **Galaxy Aviation** inherited the building from the last FBO operator **Florida Airmotive,** and plans to replace it with a modern building soon, so if you haven't visited Lantana before, you might want to land for a look at some disappearing history.

Flying There

Lantana provides pilots of small general aviation aircraft visiting the Palm Beach area with an excellent alternative to jet-oriented PBI. All jets are prohibited from using LNA.

Approaching from the north or south along the beach makes for easy navigation and great scenery. Just be sure to contact Palm Beach Approach on the appropriate frequency for flight following and airspace transitions.

Coming from the west is also easy, with good visual landmarks along the way. Highway 441 is very visible from the south end of Lake Okeechobee and runs due east before a series of bends. The second bend is marked on the sectional chart as the "20 Mile Bend Pumping Station." From there, fly southeast about 10 nm to clear three tall towers, the highest of which is 1,548 feet MSL, before turning east to fly up to Lantana. The Class C airspace comes down to 1,200 feet MSL, which is below the tops of the towers, so it's really best to contact Palm Beach Approach for clearance through the airspace instead of trying to get under it.

Lantana is an uncontrolled airport, so if you depart to the north, you'll need to turn quickly to avoid PBI's Class C surface area.

The preferred runway for noise abatement is 3/21, but there are two other runways. All three are a little over 3,000 feet long. All three have left-hand traffic patterns, which need to be kept tight to avoid PBI's airspace immediately to the north.

Galaxy Aviation of Lantana is the centrally-located FBO, offering full-service fuel from 8 a.m. to 6:30 p.m. **Courtesy** cars are available. No ramp fee. Call *(561) 656-9815.*

Getting Around

PalmTran *(561) 841-4200* runs the public bus system for the entire Palm Beach County and Route 63 has a stop right

Galaxy Aviation

outside the airport. A standard one-way fare is $2 though the 24-hour pass represents far better value for money at only $5. If you know where you're headed, then a taxi may be a better bet – there are numerous cab companies serving the Palm Beach area so take your pick from **Center Yellow Cab** *(561) 357-9779,* **All Transportation Services** *(561) 450-5858* or **PBFC Local Yellow Cab** *(561) 474-2222* to name a few. There are no car rental companies at this airport, though all the major national companies are present in Palm Beach. Galaxy can help you arrange a rental.

Walking Distance Activities

Right at the airport is **Skywalker Pilot Shop** *(561) 963-3737* where you can pick up everything for your flying needs as well as souvenirs and aviation memorabilia. They are open seven days a week. A ten-minute walk brings you to **Airport Square** where **Jo Jo's Café** *3246 Lantana Rd, Lantana, FL (561) 966-2111* serves breakfast and lunch seven days a week. It's a small and friendly place, good for a quick

bite. Another few minutes walk will bring you to a variety of chain options including Burger King and Pizza Hut, or you can walk a few minutes north for the more independent offerings at Shoppes of Atlantis, including **Atlantis Grill & Bar** *(561) 641-3330,* **Rosalita's Tex Mex Grill** *(561) 964-5747* and Payathai Asian Restaurant – see the "Where to Eat" section for more info.

None of the major Palm Beach attractions are within walking distance, and the neighborhood surrounding the airport is mainly residential with some shops, restaurants and services.

What to See and Do

We've already touched on and the fact that you can do pretty much anything around here (from fishing to shopping and everything in-between) so just to be different, here are three more unique activities.

Palm Beach Par 3 Golf Course *2345 South Ocean Blvd, Palm Beach, FL 33480 (561) 547-0598* Golfing may not sound especially unique in Palm Beach, considering the number of golf courses and country clubs that are within the city, but Palm Beach Par 3 Golf Course is really quite special. The course covers the width of the narrow barrier island, so you have water on two sides, making for some wonderful views, while you're wandering the fairways. The course itself is well-maintained, and players always report this to be a fun course; in fact it's been rated among the Top 50 Most Fun Golf Courses in the

Theatre Building could be it. Listed on the National Register of Historic Places, this impressive building was opened in January 1927. For over 50 years this was the place to come for first-run movies, but in 1980 it was closed. Surviving various attempts to have it demolished, the building's historical architecture and features have been retained, and it's now a multi-use building that houses a church as well

Kiteboarding Palm Beach offers two, three, or six hour private or semi-private lessons as well as three or five day camps, from a qualified IKO instructor. Make the most of the winds coming off the Atlantic Ocean and enjoy surfing like you never have before!

Where to Eat

Payathai Asian Restaurant *5879 S Congress Ave., Atlantis, FL 33462 (561) 967-0333* The first great thing about this restaurant is the location, about a 15 minute walk from the FBO. The second great thing is the food – authentic Thai and Japanese cuisine that is raved over by anyone who visits. In fact, some people say this is the best Thai food in Palm Beach so if you're looking for a meal that's different than the typical seafood and grill restaurants that are so abundant in the area, Payathai is the place to go. They serve sushi, sashimi, pad thai, curries, and their own special signature dishes. The lunch specials are very affordable and they do take-out too. They are open Monday to Friday for lunch and dinner, and just for dinner on the weekends. $$

Shopping in Palm Beach

USA by *Golf Digest!* If you don't want to lug your clubs on your airplane, you can rent a set along with a riding cart from the club. After a round you can enjoy a drink or a meal in the clubhouse restaurant, Al Fresco. It offers some of the best dining views in Palm Beach and a varied menu to go with the views. Call *(561) 273-4130* for reservations.

Paramount Theatre Building *139 N County Rd, Palm Beach, FL 33480 (561) 835-0913* Palm Beach features numerous historic buildings that you could visit, though if you're looking for something unique, then the Paramount

as art galleries, jewelry stores and clothing stores. The best thing about it is the extensive historical photograph exhibit which is a must-see for anyone interested in the movies. The exhibit is free and it's open every day.

Kiteboarding Palm Beach *6990 N Ocean Blvd, Palm Beach, FL 33434 (561) 502-8623* You can try all the usual water sports activities while you're visiting Palm Beach, though among the most thrilling is Kiteboarding. Apparently this is the fastest growing water sport in the world, and you can head to Ocean Inlet Park to try it out for yourself.

Victoria's Peruvian Cuisine *111 South 3rd Street, Lantana, FL 33462 (561) 588-9606* One of the top-rated restaurants in the Lantana neighborhood of Palm Beach, Victoria's specializes in tasty Peruvian cuisine which is recommended if you've never tried it before. The restaurant is run by a Peruvian family so you can be sure you're eating authentic dishes, of which the ccviche is usually excellent. The only drawback to this restaurant is its size because, being so popular, it is usually packed, and you'll have to wait to get a table. Make a reservation in advance if you're keen to sample the Peruvian food and friendly atmosphere. $$

Old Key Lime House *302 E Ocean Ave., Lantana, FL 33462 (561) 582-1889* Old Key Lime House is more the kind of restaurant you'd expect to find in Palm Beach, serving locally-caught seafood. This one stands out for its fabulous waterfront location on the Intracoastal, and because it is said to be the oldest waterfront restaurant in Florida at over one hundred years old! The restaurant has a great atmosphere and is suitable for a lively lunch or evening out – they have live music Wednesdays to Sundays – and the Tiki bar is said to be the largest in south Florida if you'd like to dine outside enjoying the gator viewing site. This is also the place for a romantic meal thanks to the fabulous sunset views. The menu is heavily seafood, though there are other options such as chicken wings,

quesadillas and burgers, and you must finish your meal with a slice of their famous home-made key lime pie. $$

Where to Stay

The Breakers *1 South County Road, Palm Beach, FL 33480 (888) 459-7063* From one extreme to the other, The Breakers is among the most expensive places to stay in Palm Beach but most who stay here appreciate that it's well worth the cost. If you're looking for a special experience, you'll find it at The Breakers. The original hotel that put Palm Beach on the map, this historic gem is stunning in every way – the location, the service, the atmosphere, the rooms, the swimming pools, the dining, and the recreational activities, and to top it all, this is an all-inclusive hotel so you don't have to go out to restaurants if you're staying here. $$$

Palm Beach Historic Inn *365 South County Road, Palm Beach, FL 33480 (561) 832-4009* When you feel like staying in the heart of downtown Palm Beach, among the

historic buildings and close to the exclusive boutiques of Worth Avenue, this is the place to stay. Palm Beach Historic Inn dates from 1923 and has an attractive Mediterranean Revival style of architecture that's listed as a Historic Landmark. Despite the historic status, this small hotel has all the mod-cons including newly renovated rooms, HDTVs and internet, and the hotel is fully pet-friendly. The complimentary breakfast is self-serve and includes bagels, pastries and cereals. $$

Fairfield Inn & Suites Palm Beach *2870 S Ocean Blvd, Palm Beach, FL 33480-5507 (561) 582-2585* Fairfield Inn is a small, clean, service-oriented hotel located in the historic and beautiful town of Palm Beach. The staff is friendly and attentive. Located on the intracoastal waterway, you get great sunset views. Conveniently located 4 minutes from public beach access, shops and restaurants. Good value for the money. $$

Sun Fest

Palm Beach County Park/Lantana

KLNA

CTAF ©122.7

Airport Manager Phone
(561) 471-7412

AWOS–3 119.925 (561) 964-0308

®PALM BEACH App/Dep 125.2

Elevation 14' MSL	Traffic Pattern 1014' MSL (1000'AGL)	Flight Service Station MIAMI 122.4 122.1R 115.7T

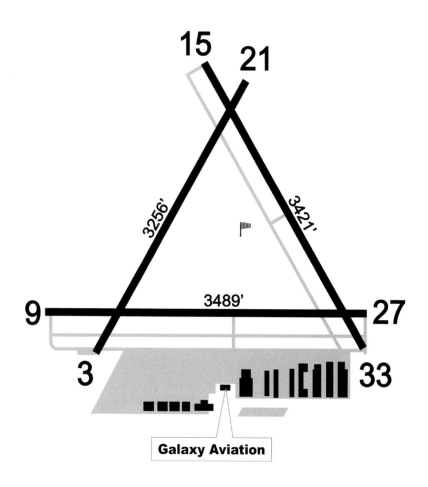

Galaxy Aviation

Pensacola

Located at the western tip of the Florida panhandle, the city of Pensacola is home to white sand beaches as well as a large Naval Station. There is lots to see and do for an aviation enthusiast, including a visit to the National Naval Aviation Museum.

Various tribes of Native people lived in the Pensacola area, but the first European settlement was a Spanish fort built in 1698. It's a very old city, and you can find all kinds of historic places, including the old forts and many other buildings that are hundreds of years old.

For pilots, the **National Naval Aviation Museum** is the biggest attraction in Pensacola. Just don't get so caught up in the museum and the Naval Station that you forget to see the rest of the city!

National Naval Aviation Museum

The historic downtown hosts several large-scale festivals each year. In May it's the **Pensacola Crawfish Festival** where the specialty is one of the largest crawfish boils in Florida. There are also arts and crafts tents and live entertainment. The Pensacola Seafood Festival happens each September and has been running annually for nearly 40 years. Live music and one of the largest arts and crafts fairs in northwest Florida complement the exquisite seafood that's on offer. This festival has free admission, but the Crawfish Festival is $5 for adults.

The city is connected to the popular Gulf Islands National Seashore, where you can find beaches that go on for miles and miles. The boating and fishing around the island as well as the mainland coast is also impressive, and there are countless water-based activities to keep you busy.

Flying There

Heavy military flight training activity around Pensacola is generally confined to the numerous Special Use Airspaces in the area. Instrument training flights are sequenced into the normal flow of military and civilian IFR traffic. Many of the military aircraft use UHF radios, while approach controllers transmit simultaneously on both VHF and UHF, so you may hear only half of their conversations.

The best way to avoid the military traffic is to follow published Victor Airways and expect vectors to the airport once you get closer in. VFR flights along the coast from the east and west are complicated by several Restricted Areas and the FAR Part 93 Special Traffic Rule airspace in the Eglin terminal area to the east. IFR arrivals may be vectored directly through the Eglin airspace, depending on traffic.

It may sound complicated, but Pensacola is actually not a difficult place to reach by air. From the north or east, follow the airways to the Crestview (CEW) VORTAC, then contact Pensacola Approach for arrival instructions.

Coming in from the west, be alert for towers over 2,000 feet tall along Interstate 10.

Innisfree Jet Center is the newer of PNS's two FBOs, located on the eastern ramp facing runway 8/26. They're open from 6 a.m. to 10 p.m. and offer a full range of FBO services including crew cars, **Enterprise,** and **Hertz** rentals. Radio 122.85 or call *(850) 436-4500.*

Pensacola Aviation Center is on the south ramp, facing runway 17/35. They're open 24 hours and boast five crew cars, dog treats, and a pilot shop. **Avis, Hertz,** and **Enterprise** rental cars available. Radio 129.575 or call *(850) 434-0636.*

Getting Around

More than a dozen cab companies operate out of the airport, so you'll have no trouble getting a ride when you arrive. **A&A Airport Taxi** *(850) 478-4477* and **Royal Taxi Service** *(850) 934-0123* are two options if you prefer to call ahead to make sure there's a car waiting.

Public bus service is very good in Pensacola, and you can get all around the city for just $1.75 per trip. Route 42

serves the airport.

Walking Distance Activities

Not much to walk to here because the general aviation parking is on the opposite side of the airport to the main terminal. It's more residential on this, the east side, of the airfield, though if you can get to the terminal building, there are restaurants and a couple of stores there and easy access to countless fast-food and other restaurants located around the Cordova Mall.

What to See and Do

National Naval Aviation Museum *1750 Radford Blvd., NAS Pensacola, Pensacola, FL 32508 (800) 327-5002* Pilots don't come to Pensacola without at least one stop at the National Naval Aviation Museum. Actually, you could probably visit every time you're in town and still see something new. Over 150 complete aircraft are on display, featuring planes from all aspects of Navy and Coast Guard duty. Inside, there are thousands of aeronautical items in a number of themed exhibits. You might also see the **Blue Angels** fly. This is their home base, and they practice from March to November every Tuesday and Wednesday usually at 11:30. You can go to the flight line and watch the show for free. Please note that backpacks, daypacks, luggage, or similar items are NOT allowed on the flight line during Blue Angel practice air shows.

There are also two state-of-the-art **MaxFlight Simulators** available that can perform fully aerobatic (360-degree pitch

and roll) movements. They are under your control, and these high definition 3D simulators are capable of air-to-air combat and stunt flying. Cost is $20. There is also an **IMAX** theatre to add a little extra excitement to your visit ($8.75), and you can shop for great aviation souvenirs at the **Flight Deck Store.** There is even an atomic bomb replica on display. Admission to this popular museum is completely free. If you plan on being there a while, you can have a snack or lunch at the **Cubi Bar Cafe** which is a neat former airmen's club relocated here from the Philippines. The National Naval Aviation Museum is open daily from 9 a.m. to 5 p.m., year-round, with the exception of Thanksgiving, Christmas and New Year's days.

Fort Barrancas *Pensacola Naval Air Station, Pensacola, FL (850) 455-5167* Part of the larger Pensacola Naval Air Station, the fort is the remaining structure from the first naval yard built in 1821. Some sections are even older, with some Spanish fort construction still in place. It's very close to the National Naval Aviation Museum so you can easily get from one to the other while you're at the southern end of the city.

Historic Pensacola Village A twenty minute ride east from the Naval Aviation Museum, Historic Pensacola Village is well worth the visit. This is the site of Pensacola's first permanent settlement in 1559, beating St. Augustine by six years. But the original settlement was wiped out after two years by a hurricane. Much of the current downtown district was built in the late-1800s and

T.T. Wentworth Jr. Florida State Museum

it is a great place to wander around with many museums and historic houses. You can roam the area for free, but you will need a ticket to get into some of the houses which costs $8. Get it at the Village Gift Shop in the **Tivoli House,** *205 E Zarragossa St., Pensacola, FL 32502 (850) 595-5985* Included with your access ticket is a guided tour of the homes and buildings. The tours go three times daily at 11:00 a.m., 1:00 p.m., and 2:30 p.m. and last approximately 1 to 1.5 hours.

Go Retro Ghosts and Graveyard Tour *610 N. Spring St. Pensacola, FL 32501 (850) 466-5220* Go Retro has a number of historic tours through Pensacola, but the Ghosts and Graveyard one is something a little different. It's an hour and a half tour through the older parts of town, and the guide will entertain you with tales of the many scary sightings as well as details on the history of

Pensacola. You can even get a closer look at the local cemetery at the end of the tour. The tour runs on Thursdays and Saturdays, and tickets are $20.

Minor League Baseball

The Pensacola Blue Wahoos are the Class Double A affiliate of the Cincinnati Reds major league team. They play their home games at a new stadium right on the water. Pensacola Bayfront Stadium *351 W. Cedar St., Pensacola, FL 32502 (850) 934-8444*

Water Adventures

Your standard boating tours can get dull after a while, but Pensacola is home to a number of charters that specialize in sailing ships for a whole new boating experience. **Condor Sailing Adventures** *997 S. Palafox St. (850) 637-7245* is a popular one, and you will get the chance to sail on a racing trimaran. You'll be skimming

over the water at high speeds, and you can learn a bit about running a sailboat as you go.

Aquatic Charters Chase-N-Fins *655 Pensacola Beach Blvd, Pensacola Beach, FL 32561 850-492-6337* "Chase-n-Fins" is Pensacola Beach's original Dolphin Cruise boat and still the most popular. They also do a sunset dolphin cruise. Sometimes you can see the Blue Angels practice during your 2-hour cruise. $25 per person.

And if you area headed over to the Gulf Islands and Pensacola Beach, **Jolly Sailing** *655 Pensacola Beach Blvd. (850) 723-6142* is your sailboat connection. They run tours with a 34' yacht, and they have a host of activities available besides just taking a tour. They've got equipment for paddle boarding and snorkeling too.

Beaches

Down through the city, you can take a causeway over to the Gulf Islands, and that is where you'll find the best beaches in Pensacola.

The **Gulf Islands National Seashore** is the best stretch of beach around, running for more than 150 miles along the long, narrow island. Raised boardwalks make great routes for walking along the soft white sand beaches to enjoy the water or look for shore birds. There are public boat docks too, in case you're coming over from the mainland in a kayak or other rented boat. It costs $8 in park fees per vehicle if you're entering by car.

If you're looking for a bit more activity, **Pensacola Beach** has restaurants, bars and a few shops. Still part of the Gulf Islands Park, this specific beach is right at the point where the causeway comes from the mainland. Head to the west if you want a more remote beach visit.

Where to Eat

O'Brien's Bistro *4350 Bayou Blvd., Ste 8, Pensacola, FL 32503 (850) 477-9120* If you don't mind the strip mall location, O'Brien's Bistro is the closest restaurant to the airport – about a 50 minute walk or a seven minute drive, and it's one of the top-rated restaurants to eat. This comfortable place has a fine selection of seafood such as shrimp Tuscany, seared scallops and pan-fried grouper. They're open for lunch and dinner, and they even have a special menu of brunch delicacies for early diners. $$

The Tuscan Oven *4801 N 9th Ave., Pensacola, FL 32503 (850) 484-6836* Their wood-fired oven helps create some of the finest pizza in the city, making this one of the best-rated restaurants in

Pensacola. The pizzas are the specialty, though their menu covers a bigger range of Italian dishes too. Just a little past the Cordova Mall, you can drive here in 10 minutes or walk in a little over an hour. They're closed Sunday and Monday but otherwise open for lunch and dinner (until 9 p.m.). $$

Jackson's Steakhouse *400 S Palafox Street, Pensacola, FL 32502 (850) 469-9898* Set within an attractive historic building in the heart of the historic downtown of Pensacola, Jackson's Steakhouse makes a nice change from the many seafood restaurants in the city. Rave reviews slate this as one of the best restaurants in Florida, so if you're looking for somewhere to celebrate a special occasion, this could be it. $$$

Where to Stay

Hyatt Place Pensacola Airport *161 Airport Lane, Pensacola, FL 32504 1-888-882-1234* The closest hotel to the airport, the Hyatt Place offers comfort,

quality and convenience if you don't want to travel all the way into downtown. Their facilities include everything you'd want in a hotel, like a gym, business center, bar, pool and a very good restaurant on the premises. If you worry about the noise, being so close to the airport, don't; previous guests often comment on how quiet their stay was. $$$

Homewood Suites by Hilton *5049 Corporate Woods Drive, Pensacola, FL 32504 (855) 277-4942* Also right near the airport grounds is the Homewood Suites and they will have a free breakfast waiting for you in the mornings. The great thing about staying here is you don't have to worry about transportation as they run a complimentary shuttle service to get you around the city. Their guest rooms are large, or choose extended suites if you want to stretch out during your stay. There's also a pool, tennis courts and gym. $$

Noble Manor B&B *110 W. Strong St., Pensacola, FL 32501 1-877-598-4634* The highest ranked B&B in the city is a gorgeous old brick Tudor home that has just five guest suites, and you'll be within walking distance of much of downtown Pensacola. All the rooms are very large and decorated with a lot of style, or ask for the Carriage House in a separate cottage from the main house if you're seeking additional space or privacy. Your hosts can help you with your sightseeing and they're sure to serve a sumptuous breakfast every morning. $$

Tivoli House in the Historic Pensacola Village

Pensacola International | KPNS

TOWER ©**119.9**
(0630-2400)

Ground Control **121.9**

Control Tower Phone
(850) 444-5615

Airport Manager Phone
(850) 436-5000

ASOS (850) 436-4799

ATIS 121.25

®PENSACOLAApp/Dep 118.6 (251°–339°) 119.0 (340°–159°) 120.65 (160°–250°)

CLNC DEL 123.725

UNICOM 122.95

Elevation 121' MSL	Traffic Pattern 1121' MSL (1000'AGL)	Flight Service Station GAINESVILLe RCO 122.2 122.6

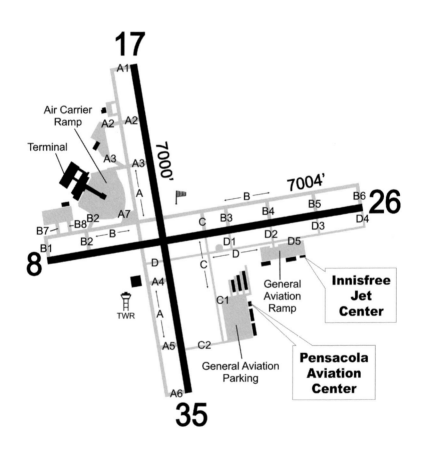

Punta Gorda

It may seem like a small town, but there are loads of things to see and do in Punta Gorda. For pilots, flying in to eat at the Skyview Café is a no-brainer. But Punta Gorda is full of opportunities to go boating and to see the local mangroves too. The town also has some interesting and unusual museums that are worth a visit. The Tampa Bay Rays have spring training here.

The name "Punta Gorda" comes from references on early maps from 1851 that simply marked a point of land in Charlotte Harbor. When it was starting to be settled, about a decade after the end of the Civil War, the town was officially named Trabue. After another 12 years, the growing town was incorporated and the name went back to Punta Gorda.

Sitting on the sheltered coast of Charlotte Harbor, it's a great city for anyone who enjoys boating. The calm waters are ideal for paddling a kayak, though motor boats can take you out farther to the islands of Gasparilla Sound and the Charlotte Harbor Preserve State Park. There may not be the usual beaches you associate with Florida here, but there is plenty of coastline to explore.

Punta Gorda

Flying There

The airspace surrounding Punta Gorda is uncomplicated Class D. Arrivals from the west and northwest need to be aware of some wildlife refuges between Punta Gorda and Sarasota and in the Charlotte Harbor area.

Coming in from the northeast, there's plenty of room to maneuver around the Lake Placid Military Operations Areas and R-2901 Restricted Areas near Okeechobee and Sebring.

Several towers reach over 1,500 feet MSL approximately 13 nm southeast of PGD in the Tucker's Corner area.

The nearest major airspace is Fort Myers to the south. If you're coming up from the Florida Keys, Naples, or Marco Island, call Fort Myers Approach for flight following and airspace transitions. If they're closed for the night, call Miami Center on 134.75. Fort Myers Approach also monitors 127.05 to provide clearance delivery services when Punta Gorda's tower is closed.

Charlotte County Airport Authority provides 24-hour 100LL and Jet A fueling from the FBO on the southwestern ramp. Self-serve 100LL is also available. Contact on UNICOM 122.75 or call *(941) 639-4119*.

Muscle Car City Museum

Getting Around

A taxi can get you into Punta Gorda in no time. Just call **Airport Limo** *(239) 850-5466* or **Salem Taxi** *(941) 249-1385* to get picked up. If you prefer to take control of your travels, there are several rental car outlets at the airport where you can rent a vehicle for your stay. Take your pick from **Avis** *(941) 575-7597*, **Hertz** *(941) 575-7983* or **National** *(941) 205-5015*. There is no public bus system in Punta Gorda.

Walking Distance Activities

The SkyView Cafe is right in the airport, about a minute's walk from the GA terminal. There are large model airplanes hanging from the ceiling. Since Charlotte County Airport also serves commercial flights, there is a mix of travelers, locals and private pilots eating here. It tends to be busy especially on Sunday. The consensus is that the food is good as are the prices. There is also a pilot shop in the GA Terminal at **Harborside Aviation** *(941) 639-0057*.

The town of Punta Gorda is about an hour from the air-

port on foot, and there aren't too many sights or stops along the way.

What to See and Do

Muscle Car City Museum *3811 Tamiami Trail, Punta Gorda, FL 33950 (941) 575-5959* Who doesn't love the beauty and power of restored vintage sports cars? Displayed among antique gas pumps and a mix of other memorabilia, the collection of 200+ cars are in splendid condition and span all makes and models. There is a gift shop and 50s diner on site too. Tickets are $12.50 for entrance, and it's closed on Mondays. The museum is a little outside of town, but easy to access if you're driving.

Military Heritage Museum *1200 West Retta Esplanade, Unit 48, Punta Gorda, FL 33950 (941) 575-9002* At the north end of Punta Gorda, this little museum is right in the Fishermen's Village area and is an interesting stop if you're seeing the waterfront sights. The exhibits cover many different wars dating as far back as the Civil War. It's run by veterans so you know you can

get great information and lots of stories if you start asking questions. Admission is free, but donations are welcome.

Octagon Wildlife Sanctuary *41660 Horseshoe Road, Punta Gorda, FL 33982 (239) 543-1130* It's not a typical zoo but rather a refuge where abandoned or injured exotic animals come for care. Their collection typically has many big cats (including lions and tigers), primates, reptiles, bears, and many birds too. The park is just a half-hour drive from the airport. Tickets are $10, with discounts for kids and seniors. Open weekends only, unless you make an appointment.

Sandman Book Company *16480 Burnt Store Rd, Punta Gorda, FL 33955 941-505-1624* Sandman Books is located well-outside of Punta Gorda but is worth the trip if you like bookstores. From the new books and the huge inventory of used books to the friendly knowledgeable staff and wonderful "book archway," this place is a real treat.

Boating and Fishing
The King Fisher Fleet

(941) 639-0969 has a whole list of potential boat cruises and fishing charters that should suit any interest or schedule. Go out looking for dolphins or just enjoy the water at sunset. You can stay close to home or book a longer trip out into the Gulf for deep-sea sport-fishing. You'll get similar options with **Calusa Queen Excursions** (941) 301-8687 though they operate a bit farther south down the coast at the Burnt Store Marina. They do several excellent tours out to the Gasparilla Islands, Charlotte Harbor Preserve, and the Cape Haze Aquatic Preserve.

If you don't want to take an organized tour and just need a boat, then see what's available at **Holidaze Boat Rental** (941) 505-8888. They have a selection of modern motorboats so you can get out on the water on your own for the afternoon. **Tampa Bay Rays** *Charlotte Sports Park 2300 El Jobean Road, Port Charlotte, FL 33948.* While the Rays play their regular season in an air-conditioned stadium in St. Petersburg, in March they move to Port Charlotte for Spring Training. The stadium is about 28 minutes from Punta Gorda airport (KPGD).

The City

Spending time right in Punta Gorda itself is also recommended. Being a historic city, there is an assortment of historic buildings, ten of which are listed on the National Register of Historic Places including the beautiful Queen Anne style **A.C. Freeman House** (941) 639-2222. It is now home to a local history museum and the Chamber of Commerce.

Be sure to wander along the waterfront as well, then head to the Fishermen's Village area of the city for some shopping, in their range of boutique stores, and stay for lunch or dinner in one of the restaurants.

Where to Eat

Perfect Caper *121 E Marion Ave., Punta Gorda, FL 33950* (941) 505-9009 The cuisine at Perfect Caper is an international mix of flavors with a focus on seafood with a French flair. It's downtown and close to the harbor, so you won't have to stray too far if you're already sightseeing by the water. Just keep an eye out for the (very small) sign. $$$

Jack's on Marion *201 W Marion Ave, Punta Gorda, FL 33950* 941-637-8800 A favorite place for locals but always attracts visitors with its central location near hotels. Great to sit outside and watch people or listen to the live music they offer several nights a week.

Hurricane Charley's Raw Bar and Grill *300 W Retta Esplanade, Punta Gorda, FL 33950* (941) 639-9695 For the ultimate seafood experience down by the harbor, try a few delicacies at Hurricane Charley's. Lots of seafood but with a mix of Italian, Asian and Creole flavors. Don't let the name scare you off. There is a lot more to the menu than their raw oyster bar. Sit out by the water on the outdoor deck and watch the boats on the river. $$

Sandra's Restaurant *111 W Olympia Ave., Punta Gorda, FL 33950* (941) 575-0177 Tired of the usual Southern seafood fare? Get a platter of Schnitzel and a dark German beer at San-

dra's. Not a lot of small towns in Florida are going to have this kind of authentic German food, so take advantage of your chance while in Punta Gorda. It's just a couple of blocks from the harbor. $$

Where to Stay

Fisherman's Village *1200 West Retta Esplanade, Punta Gorda, FL 33950* 1-800-639-0020 Part resort, part shopping plaza and part marina, the Fisherman's Village is filled with things to do if you're staying there (and even if you're not). If you don't mind the higher price tag, this is the place to stay if you want to be close to the waterfront. They've got a pool, free Wi-Fi, tennis court, BBQ grills and you can even borrow a bike if you want to pedal around town. $$$

Knights Inn Punta Gorda *9300 Knights Drive, Punta Gorda, FL 33950* (888) 424-0138 For a quick check-in after landing, you should book with Knights Inn. It's just five minutes from the airport, and it won't cost an arm or a leg. You'll get a simple room with a free continental breakfast in the morning. They do have Wi-Fi and a small swimming pool too. $

Four Points by Sheraton Harborside *33 Tamiami Trail, Punta Gorda, FL 33950* (941) 637-6770 Spending time by the water and want a few more amenities than the usual motel? The Four Points is a solid choice. There are rooms overlooking Charlotte Harbor and there is a thatched outdoor Tiki bar for some drinks in the evening while watching the sunset. $$

Punta Gorda — KPGD

CTAF ©**121.0**
[10700-2200]

Ground Control **119.55**

Airport Manager Phone
[941] 639-1101

ASOS 135.675 [941] 639-0076

®FORT MYERS App/Dep 125.15
[0600-2400]

®MIAMI CENTER App/Dep 134.75
[2400-0600]

UNICOM 122.975

Elevation 25' MSL	Traffic Pattern 1025' MSL [1000'AGL]	Flight Service Station ST PETERSBURG 122.025

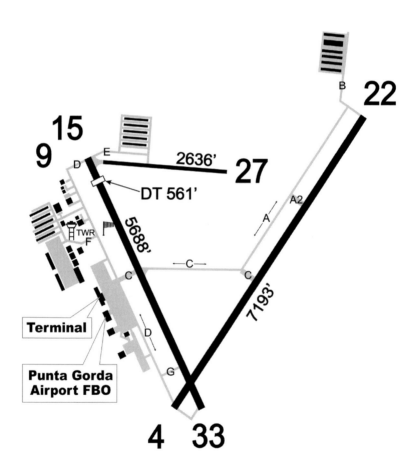

River Ranch

Looking for a dude ranch getaway adventure? Or to see a professional rodeo? It doesn't get much more convenient than River Ranch with the airstrip located right in the resort. Fly in, enjoy your adventure, and fly out again! Fly in for lunch on weekends.

River Ranch is an authentic dude ranch where you really can live like a cowboy or cowgirl for the duration of your stay. You may not think of Florida as being a place for cowboys but the state has more than 1 million head of cattle, which means there are lots of cowboys here. This authentic dude ranch offers everything you would expect, from horseback riding to rodeos, dinner at the saloon, and accommodations to suit all tastes and budgets. They even have Glamping (if you don't know what that is, see below).

Horseback Riding

River Ranch dates back to the 1960s when it was planned that it would become the heart of a huge resort-style property called River Ranch Acres. In the following years, a large motel was constructed, as well as a Western-style saloon and café; the airstrip; and a few other facilities and services. The huge resort never happened, but this means that River Ranch has retained its rural feel and allows guests to experience how Flor-

ida would have been hundreds of years ago when cowboys drove cattle through here.

Today River Ranch is a Westgate Resort property and it's the largest dude ranch east of the Mississippi. It has recently had a multi-million dollar renovation, with new activities added, so expect to get real value for your money when you stay here.

They are even planning a new **River Ranch Aviators Club,** a community of luxury homes with adjacent hangars.

Flying There

There are no airports with controlled airspace in the vicinity of River Ranch, but pilots must avoid the R-2901 Restricted Areas immediately to the west and south of the airport. Runway 34 uses a nonstandard right-hand traffic pattern. Stay north and east of the field as much as possible.

The surprisingly long, paved runway is surrounded by tall trees, making it difficult to see from the east. Landing on runway 16, stay north of Highway

---

60 as it crosses the Kissimmee River and you'll be set up on a left base by the time you're able to see the runway. The trees also mean there's usually very little wind directly over the runway surface.

Landing runway 34, fly toward the water tower until you see the runway, then keep your pattern tight to avoid the restricted area.

There are no taxiways, and the parking area is at the south end of the runway. In light winds, it's not unusual for aircraft to land from the north and depart back to the north. Be sure to listen to the CTAF 122.8. The field is sometimes used by ultralights, powered parachutes, and other aircraft without radios.

The Air Strip

Self-serve 100LL fuel is available. The building adjacent to the parking area is a combination airport terminal and golf pro shop with a weather computer but otherwise somewhat limited FBO services. If it's not attended, use the phone in a call box at the west entrance to contact the resort's front desk for courtesy golf cart transportation or to rent a golf cart.

Westgate River Ranch Resort & Rodeo *3200 River Ranch Blvd, Lake Wales, FL 33867 (863) 692-1321*

What to See and Do

The Saturday Night Rodeo is one of the most talked about activities at River Ranch, so make sure you're here on a Saturday night at 7:30 p.m. The rodeo is not just for show, it's an actual competition, making this the longest running Saturday night championship rodeo in the country. Join roughly 1,200 other guests and non-guests in watching the thrilling evening of events that include bull riding, trick riding and barrel racing. When it's over, you can try your hand at riding the mechanical bull (available seven days a week) at the Saloon. The rodeo ends with a fun Dance Party outside the River Ranch Saloon, so grab a partner, dance to the DJ's music, and play some games. Tickets for the rodeo cost $17 for adults, and the mechanical bull ride is an additional $8.

The River Ranch Saloon is just what you'd expect from the Wild West, so don your cowboy hat, your checkered shirt and your jeans and take a seat at the full bar. Watch the line-dancing and listen to the live music, and on Friday nights you'll even get line-dancing lessons for no charge. The Saloon is only open Friday and Saturday from 6 p.m. to midnight.

Horseback Riding

With miles of untouched scenery surrounding River Ranch, this is the perfect place to hone your horseback riding skills or take lessons if you're a beginner. One-hour guided trail rides are available and are led by experienced wranglers, or if you're craving more time in the saddle (and you're experienced), you can take the extended two-hour trail ride. Lessons are available for beginners though you must book your lessons and trail rides in advance to be guaranteed a spot when you visit. Trail rides begin at $45 per person for riders eight years and over *(863) 692-1321, ext 40015.*

Boat Rides

The full-service marina at the ranch is the place to go to have fun on the water. Several of the ranch's popular activities start here, including the airboat ride and guided fish-

There is a Professional Rodeo every Saturday Night

ing trips, plus you can rent a pontoon boat by the hour and take yourself and up to seven other people out on the water.

The airboat rides are one of the most popular activities at the ranch. You take a thrilling high-speed, one-hour tour in which you could see alligators, turtles, eagles and plenty more wildlife and birds while listening to the guide giving interesting information on the Kissimmee River. Get your tickets and start your tour from the marina. The cost is $27.50 for adults.

Swamp Buggy Rides

Swamp Buggy Rides also start at the marina and provide a fun way to see more of the 1,700 acres that the ranch

The Airport at River Ranch

is set in. These high vehicles take you on a one-hour tour along a wooded trail and because you're high up, they're great for spotting wildlife and checking out the scenery. Tickets are $27.50 for adults.

Archery and Shooting Ranges

River Ranch has both an archery range and a trap and skeet range. If you've ever wanted to shoot with a bow and arrow, here's your chance. The price is $8.

The trap and skeet range is a little more sophisticated and expensive. For $38.50 you get 25 rounds as well as shotgun rental, earplugs and eye protection. Beginners are welcome, and there are experts who can

teach you what to do as well as the differences between trap shooting and skeet shooting.

Other Activities

Among the other activities you can try out while staying at the ranch are mini-golf, 9-hole golf, horseshoes, rock climbing, zip lining, tennis and basketball, or simply wander around the resort on your own time, taking everything in.

Where to Eat

There aren't any towns close by to River Ranch, but that's not a problem seeing as there are several great places to eat right on-site.

Westgate Smokehouse Grill This restaurant serves breakfast and dinner. On weekends they serve lunch, so if you are flying in for lunch, weekends are the time to go. They have a breakfast buffet that includes an omelet bar and pancakes. Lunches and dinners include barbecue favorites like chicken wings, steaks, ribs and brisket. The atmosphere is friendly and relaxing, and the restaurant overlooks the Kissimmee River. Sit out on the screened-in porch when the weather's nice. Days and hours of operation vary by season, so call ahead if you are flying in just for a meal. $$

Deli at the General Store sells an assortment of groceries as well as beverages and ice cream, and if you'd like a quick lunch, this is the place to go. The deli serves made-to-order sandwiches, pizza and salads.

Dinner Hayride If you'd like a completely different dinner experience, book your place on the Dinner Hayride. All in the price you get a 45 minute tractor-pulled hayride into the adjoining Kissimmee Island Cattle Company Wildlife Management Area, and a family-style cookout buffet that includes hamburgers, hot dogs, grilled chicken, corn on the cob, baked beans, coleslaw and apple cobbler, plus drinks. The price is $25 for adults and $15 for children.

Where to Stay

The River Ranch has many different options when it comes to accommodations from camping to suites to cottages and cabins, and even a railcar.

Glamping

In case you don't know, glamping is "glamorous camping!" A large tent is all set up and ready to stay in and it comes fully-furnished with real beds, dressers, table and chairs, picnic table, and of course there's a campfire. Each tent has its own private bathroom though these are set away from the tents in a building that only you have access to. The tents even have air conditioning, a mini fridge, and

Glamping

a microwave, and they sleep up to four people! If you'd like to save money and go for real camping, you can bring along your own tent and camp in the resort campsite.

The Lodge has a variety of different options. Standard guest rooms are very nice; they have only recently been refurbished and include a TV, microwave, mini fridge, coffee maker and wet bar and of course a bathroom.

If you'd like more space and the option to cook in your room, choose a Lodge Suite or Deluxe Lodge Suite as these have kitchenettes.

The Lodge also has one and two bedroom cottages that have a lovely living room, full kitchen, screened-in patio and more.

The **Saddle Club** also has several different types of accommodations. One of the most unique places to stay at River Ranch is in a Saddle Club Rail Car. Each cabin is stand-alone so they're very private, has a queen bed and bunk bed, full bathroom, living area and a compact kitchen as well as two TVs and a gas grill and picnic table outside.

There are also Studio Cabins with kitchenette, two-bedroom cabins, and one-bedroom grand cabins, both with full kitchens.

Cottage at The Lodge

River Ranch Resort

CTAF/UNICOM ©122.8

Airport Manager Phone
(863) 692-1321

Elevation 55' MSL	Traffic Pattern 1100' MSL (1045'AGL)	Flight Service Station 800-WX-BRIEF

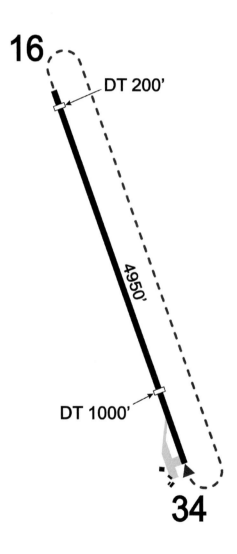

16

DT 200'

4950'

DT 1000'

34

Sanibel & Captiva Islands

Sanibel Island is famous for its seashells, glorious beaches and laid-back atmosphere. There is a cute little town at one end of these islands, and the rest is made up of beaches and nature reserves.

Captiva, with its white sugar sand beaches is just north of Sanibel. If you're looking for a quiet place to relax, this could be it! The island still has a "small town" feel to it, as regulations were put in place to keep buildings under three stories tall and to not allow any new chain restaurants on the island. Everything is unique and there are lots of family-owned businesses to explore. The town portion of the island is at the eastern end, where the causeway bridge connects Sanibel to the mainland and Fort Myers.

Sanibel is probably most famous for being the "world's best shelling location." Named **Costa de Caracoles,** or Coast of Seashells by explorer Ponce de Leon, every day beachcombers count on the tides to bring in another crop of shells.

Since you can drive to the island, it's easy enough to have a car during your stay, but you might find it just as convenient to walk. The town is quite small, and you can probably walk across the main business

Sanibel Island, the World's Best Shelling Location

area in under an hour.

Whether you prefer the small-town appeal or just want to relax on the beach, you should enjoy your visit to Sanibel Island.

Flying There

The closest airport is Fort Myers Page Field. (KFMY). Located 6.5 miles north of Southwest Florida International Airport (KRSW), Page Field is tucked under the 1,200 foot outer-shelf of KRSW's class C airspace. It is suggested you contact Ft. Myers approach on 125.15 within 20 miles to

transition you to Page Field. If you choose to duck under the shelf, beware that 12 miles to the north there are four 1549 foot antennas you need to avoid. Coming from the south, there is another 1054 foot antenna to avoid.

Walking Distance Activities

It will take about half an hour by car to get to the island from the mainland airport (Causeway Blvd links it to the mainland), but once you are there, you may find it easier to do more walking. Most of the main town is easy to see on foot, though a car would be handier for the farther out beaches and nature areas.

Getting Around

To get to Sanibel Island from the airport, you'll need a taxi or a rental car. **Hertz** *(239) 454-9750* is right at the airport making this the easiest choice for a rental car, and **Sanibel Taxi** *(888) 527-7806* offers good service from the airport as well as for getting around town.

What to See and Do

J.N. Ding Darling National Wildlife Refuge *One Wildlife Drive, Sanibel Island, FL 33957 (239) 472-1100* A large part of the island is taken up by this wildlife park, including sections of the Sanibel Bayou. You can take your car on a drive through the reserve or go walking on the trails. Alligators are a sure sight, and there can be hundreds of migratory birds around. Keep an eye on the water too. It's very clear and you can see fish and the occasional manatee. The park is open six days a week (closed on Fridays), and the education center is closed on most major holidays. Access is free.

Bailey Matthews National Shell Museum *3075 Sanibel-Captiva Road, Sanibel Island, FL 33957 (239) 395-2233* This is a fun little museum for anyone who loves shells and the seashore. There are more than 30 separate exhibits of shells and mollusks from around the world, including facts on history, fossils and details on local specimens. Check out the shell jewelry in the gift store for a lovely and unique souvenir.

Sanibel Historical Museum and Village *950 Dunlop Road, Sanibel Island, FL 33957 (239) 472-4648* Get a feel for the history of the island at the local history museum. Seven original buildings from around the island have been moved here to create this authentic village that represents the life of the original pioneer settlers. A school house, post office, general store and several private homes make up this little village. Admission is $10 and they're open Wednesday through Saturday.

Beaches

There are several excellent beaches all along the southern coast of the island, where you can go walking, swimming or just relax with some sunbathing. Gulfside Beach is just on the outskirts of town, and there is a whole park there with picnic areas and beach chairs. If you enjoy shell collecting, this is probably the best place on the island for finding shells.

Right at the tip of the island near the causeway from the mainland, is the Lighthouse Beach Park. Not only can you visit the old lighthouse, but the sandy beach is excellent too.

You can do a little fishing off the pier if you want to.

At the other end of the island, Bowman's Beach is a very popular spot. Since it faces the west, it's the place to go for romantic sunsets. The beach has parking, washrooms and picnic tables too.

Boat and Fishing Tours

You certainly can't visit an island and not spend some time out on the water. Boating charters are easy to find, whether you want a tour or plan on doing a little fishing. **Mangrove Masters** *(239) 410-0890* and **Tarpon Bay Explorers** *(239) 472-8900* both have great wildlife tours that will take you out around the island to see the mangroves or to spot wild dolphins.

For a good all-around boating tour of the island, check out **Sanibel Island Cruise Lines** *(239) 472-5799*. They have a mix of tour options so you can just enjoy the scenery, go snorkeling, visit some of the more remote beaches, or watch the waves for dolphins.

For some fishing, charter a boat with **Hey Mon Sanibel** *(612) 804-0947* to hook some redfish, snapper, grouper or tarpon. Their 25' boat is great

Sanibel Island

Sanibel Island

for you or a small group, and the captain knows the waters like the back of his hand.

Where to Eat

Sweet Melissa's Cafe *1625 Periwinkle Way, Sanibel, FL 33957 (239) 472-1956* For a gourmet treat, have a meal at Sweet Melissa's Café. Don't let the name fool you; this is a high class restaurant serving dinner with a French twist. Beef tenderloin, seared tuna, grilled asparagus and pork confit are some of their specials. It's a busy place so you should try to get a reservation unless you don't mind a wait. The outside patio is a refreshing spot to enjoy your meal if it's crowded in the dining room. $$$

Lazy Flamingo *1036 Periwinkle Way, Sanibel, FL 33957 (239) 472-8484* You'll get a casual dinner of southern seafood at the Lazy Flamingo. The clam chowder and fried grouper sandwiches are popular, but you can just settle down with a basket of wings and a beer if you want to relax in the evening. It's right in town and easy to get to. $$

Bennett's Fresh Roast *1020 Periwinkle Way, Sanibel, FL 33957 (239) 312-4651* Bennett's is a very popular coffee shop in Sanibel, and though they are quite famous for their coffee and fresh-made doughnuts, they do offer a wider menu with sandwiches and soups too. It's a bright and busy place, with both indoor and outdoor seating. For a bite to eat when you're on the go, you can't beat it. $

Doc Ford's Rum Bar and Grille *975 Rabbit Rd., Sanibel, FL 33957 (239) 472-8311* Located more in the interior of the island, Doc Ford's Rum Bar and Grille would be a perfect place to eat if you're heading to the Ding Darling Wildlife Park. It's a casual place with a full bar, and they're open until 10 p.m. Most of the menu is seafood, but apparently their rib-eye steak is amazing too. $$

Where to Stay

South Seas Island Resort *5400 Plantation Road, Captiva Island, FL 33924 (866) 565-5089* The South Seas Island Resort is on the far end of the island, technically on the smaller Captiva Island that is connected by another causeway. To stay in luxury, away from the crowds, or to celebrate a special occasion, this is the place. Choose from lovely rooms or larger stand-

alone villas. In true resort style, there are many activities to keep you busy. There are several swimming pools, and easy access to the local beaches, along with boat rentals and a marina. Restaurants and shops are all right at-hand, and you can unwind at the spa. If you do want to sight-see around the island, they have a complimentary shuttle. $$$

Anchor Inn *1245 Periwinkle Way, Sanibel, FL 33957 (239) 395-9688* These adorable little cottages are very private and offer lots of space during your stay. The Inn does have more standard motel rooms as well if you prefer, though the cottages are popular with their homey feel. You won't be right on the beach, but it's just a short stroll away. $$

Waterside Inn on the Beach *3033 W Gulf Dr., Sanibel, FL 33957 (239) 472-1345* If you do want to stay right on the beach, then try the Waterside Inn. You'll have room to stretch out in their huge, brightly-colored cottages. Even if you're just staying for one night, the kitchenettes can be handy. It's really the location that makes the Waterside Inn great. A few steps out your front door, and you're on the beach. $$

Sanibel Inn *937 E Gulf Dr., Sanibel, FL 33957 (239) 472-3181* To stay a little closer to town, the Sanibel Inn puts you right on the beach but yet you're still within walking distance of the shops and other businesses on the island. The Wi-Fi is free, and there is an outdoor bar by the pool. They have regular rooms and larger suites, and most have views of the beach. $$

Page Field; *Fort Myers* — KFMY

PAGE TOWER ©119.0
(0700-2300)

Ground Control **121.7**

Control Tower Phone
(239) 936-7867

Airport Manager Phone
(239) 590-6601

ASOS (239) 936-2318

ATIS 123.725

FT MYERS App/Dep ®126.8 (0700-2300)

MIAMI App/Dep ®134.75 (2300-0700)

CLNC DEL 121.7

Elevation 17' MSL	Traffic Pattern 800' MSL (783')AGL	Flight Service Station 122.65 122.2 122.1 MIAMI

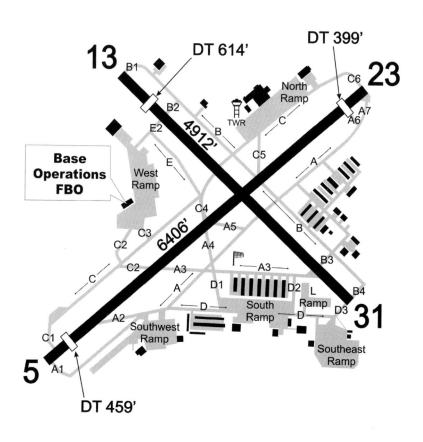

13   DT 614'   DT 399'   23

B1   North Ramp   C6
B2   C   A7
4912'   B   A6
E2   TWR
E   C5   A
Base Operations FBO   West Ramp   A
C4   A
C3   A5   B
6406'   A4   B3
C2   A3   A3   B4
C2   A3   D1   D2   L Ramp
C   A   South Ramp   D   D3   31
A2   D   Southwest Ramp   D   Southeast Ramp
C1   A1

5   DT 459'

KSRQ

Sarasota

Sarasota gives you access to great water and smaller island keys and offers the attractions of a large urban center. You can have a romantic weekend or a party weekend here. A good nearby restaurant, a classic car museum, and a great art museum, all within a 15 minute walk from the FBO, make for a great day trip. In the spring the Baltimore Orioles and Pittsburgh Pirates are in town.

The **Ringling Brothers Circus** made Sarasota its winter home, and the wealthy family had quite an impact on the city during its early growth. Their large family museum is still a major attraction in Sarasota today, and you can see the name Ringling in various places around town. And of course, you can see circus performances if you are there during the winter months when they are in town.

Compared to other beach towns, Sarasota is pretty big and you have a large metropolitan area to explore. You can get some of the Florida Keys experiences without going all the way south. Boating, fishing, wildlife parks, and great city museums will fill your time in Sarasota. Lido Key is particularly busy with boats and nature tours.

Downtown and Marina of Sarasota

Flying There

Sarasota's Class C airspace is carved out of the southern extreme of the Tampa Class B. Arriving from directions other than north is free of other airspace considerations. A single tower 16 nm east of the airport reaches up to 1,749 feet MSL.

Dolphin Aviation operates a 24-hour FBO on the west ramp featuring a coffee shop, sandwiches, and pilot supplies. Crew cars and rental cars are available on site. Radio on UNICOM 122.95 or telephone *(941) 355-7715*.

Rectrix Aerodrome Centers services turbine aircraft on the east ramp and piston aircraft on the north ramp. Self-serve 100LL is available on the north ramp. Courtesy cars and rentals from Hertz and Enterprise are available, but consider calling ahead to clarify which location you should taxi to if you're renting a car. They're open Sunday through

Friday 6 a.m. to 10 p.m., and 6 a.m. to 9 p.m. on Saturday. The jet center monitors 130.225, or call *(941) 358-9600* (jet center) or *(941) 355-8100* (light general aviation).

Getting Around

There are **Alamo** *(888) 826-6893* and **Hertz** *(941) 355-8848* outlets right in the airport for immediate access to rental cars. If you just need a lift downtown, grab a taxi with **Sarasota Yellow Cab** *(941) 955-3341* or **Downtown Taxi Service** *(941) 536-7855*.

Public buses can take you all around Sarasota, courtesy of the Sarasota County Area Transit (SCAT). Several routes serve the airport and will get you downtown for $1.25. If you want to use the bus to get around the city, a pass is $4.00.

Walking Distance Activities

Dolphin Aviation has a coffee shop with sandwiches as well as a Pilot Shop. A five minute walk to the south from Dolphin Aviation will bring you to the excellent **Captain Brian's Seafood,** open Monday through Saturday from 9 a.m. to 8 p.m. The **Ringling Museum of Art** is a 15 minute walk to the south. The **Sarasota Classic Car Museum** is also about a 15 minute walk, so you can easily spend a full afternoon without having to really leave the airport area.

What to See and Do

Sarasota Classic Car Museum *5500 N. Tamiami Trail, Sarasota, FL 34243 (941) 355-6228* Literally at the entrance to the airport, this couldn't be more convenient to visit after

Ringling Museum of Art

you land. A fifteen-minute walk from Dolphin Aviation will take you to more than 100 vintage automobiles on display. The staff know all the vehicle's histories and can share many great stories about the cars. Some cars are particularly notable, like the Mercedes once owned by John Lennon. The Museum has self-guided tours daily from 9 a.m. to 6 p.m., seven days a week. The museum is closed on Christmas Day, and tickets are $12.85.

St. Armands Circle *300 Madison Dr, Sarasota, FL 34236 (941) 388-1554* An eclectic mix of tourist friendly shops, bars and restaurants in a very neat and tidy district separated from the mainland by Sarasota Bay. With the palm-lined medians, a park-like setting, and tropical plantings, this shopper's Paradise has a mixture of very high-end stores and moderate priced places. The Circle, from

which all the streets radiate, features Italian statuary from the circus magnate John Ringling's personal collection. Close to beaches, Mote Aquarium and lots of other neat places. St. Armands Circle is a fun place to people watch.

Ringling Museum of Art *5401 Bay Shore Road, Sarasota, FL 34243 (941) 359-5700* Located directly across from the Classic Car Museum, a 14 minute walk from Dolphin Aviation will take you here. The Ringling name may make you think of the circus, but this huge museum complex shows a whole other side to their family. There is a large artistic collection, as well as exhibits that specifically showcase the history of the circus. The Ca' d'Zan Mansion is a unique part of the museum that should not be missed. It's a fully-furnished 1920s Venetian mansion that was once home to the Ringling family. Admission to the entire complex is $25 for adults, with discounts for seniors, military and students. If you need more time, get a three-day pass instead. Open daily, 10 a.m. to 5 p.m., Thursdays until 8 p.m. Closed on Thanksgiving, Christmas and New Year's Day.

Baltimore Orioles Baseball takes place in March at Ed Smith Stadium. *2700 12th Street, Sarasota, FL 34237 (941) 893-6300* The recently renovated stadium is a mini-Camden Yards. If Camden Yards is a cathedral (45,000 seats), then this Ed Smith Stadium is a chapel (8,500 seats). The sun is brutal on the third-base side. Best chance for some shade is the upper seats on the first-base side. Free admission to watch Rookie baseball in the summer.

Pittsburgh Pirates *1611 9th Street W. Bradenton FL 34208* They play at McKechnie Field, which was built in 1923 and last renovated in 2012, for a good mix of old-school charm with modern amenities. It is a 14 minute drive from Sarasota-Bradenton (SKRQ) airport.

Boating

Take advantage of the great coastline and do some boating in Sarasota. There are rentals and charters in all shapes and sizes to fit your needs. **Sea Life Kayaking Adventures** *190 Taft Drive, Sarasota, FL 34236 941-400-2740* can take you on a group tour or you can just rent your own kayak. Similar options are available with **Liquid Blue Outfitters** *(941) 306-1220* to paddle around the Lido Key mangroves.

Sarasota Paddleboard Company *690 Ben Franklin, Sarasota, FL 34234 (941) 650-2241* Based on Lido Key, Sarasota Paddleboard Company provides rentals lessons and excursions seven days a week. All necessary instruction and safety equipment is provided. They also do a Lido Mangrove Tunnel tour and an Illuminated Night Tour with boards outfitted with underwater L.E.D. lights.

Surfit *6225 Ravenwood Dr., Sarasota, FL 34243 (941) 952-8245* They offer guided, stand-up paddleboard tours through the famed mangrove tunnels and at the beach. With any luck you may see manatees and dolphins.

Key Sailing *2 Marina Plaza, E-18, Marina Jack, Sarasota, FL 34236 (941) 346-SAIL* Key Sailing lets you take a bit more of a sophisticated trip that you don't have to work so hard at enjoying. Their motto is: "Fresh Air, Fine Chocolates, and a few hours of peace on Earth." Husband and wife Jan and Tim take you out on their 41-foot Morgan sailboat. You can charter the whole boat for up to six or join other couples. Captain Tim is also a minister, (he was a chaplain for the Cincinnati Reds) and can perform your wedding ceremony onboard or renew your marriage vows!

Sarasota Jungle Gardens *3701 Bay Shore Road, Sarasota, FL 34234 (941) 355-5305* Jungle Gardens is a smaller wildlife park that doesn't have the same busy hype as major zoos, making it a bit more peaceful for an afternoon stroll. The free-roaming flamingos are very fun, and you can see more than 150 different animals at the park. Admission is $16 for adults, and the park is open until 5 p.m. every day.

Siesta Key Rum *2212 Industrial Blvd., Sarasota, FL 34234 (941) 702-8143* Hidden on an industrial estate, this destination is a real gem. A friendly husband and wife distilling team, who are passionate about rum, give free tours. It takes about 40 minutes and includes an explanation of the equipment and the rum-making process. You must pre-register on their website or by phone to attend tours. Summer hours are Thursday through Saturday from 12 to 5. In-season the tasting room is open Tuesday through Saturday from 12 to 5.

Marie Selby Botanical Gardens *811 South Palm Ave., Sarasota, FL 34236 (941) 366-5731* The Marie Selby gardens have about 14 acres of lush groomed gardens to visit, including a hot-house full of orchids. Round out your visit with a cup of tea at the cafe, and a browse through the garden gift shop. Admission is $19 and that covers both indoor and outdoor gardens.

Mote Marine Aquarium *1600 Ken Thompson Parkway, Sarasota, FL 34236 (941) 388-4441* Tanks and outdoor marine enclosures hold manatees, sharks, stingrays and jellyfish to give you an opportunity to see these creatures up close. Located on the tip of Lido Key Island, you can drive to the aquarium via a causeway in about 20 minutes from the airport. Admission is $20 and they're open 365 days a year. You can also book eco-boat tours if you want to see more ocean sights out in the wild.

Marietta Museum *2121 North Tamiami Trail, Saraso-*

Ringling Museum of Art

ta, FL 34234 (941) 364-3399 If you're a fan of fun and quirky, the Marietta Museum is a must-visit. They have an odd-ball collection of sculptures and paintings that are fun, colorful and well-worth exploring. Admission is free, and you can't miss the bright pink building.

Where to Eat

Captain Brian's Seafood Market, *8441 N Tamiami Trl, Sarasota, FL 34243-2015. (941) 351-4492* A local favorite for many years and just a short walk from the airport. Captain Brian's is a family-style restaurant serving the freshest seafood. Select the fish or lobster you would like straight from the tank and have them cook it just the way you like it, or stick to the menu and choose a filling Seafood Combo Platter, Norwegian Salmon, or a wonderful Swordfish Steak. The lunch menu is a little more casual with burgers, baskets and Po'boys on offer though whatever you choose, you won't leave hungry! $$
Coffee Loft *5025 N Tamiami Trail, Sarasota, FL 34234 (941) 706-4047* The Coffee Loft is a trendy coffee shop that

has a menu with every fancy coffee drink around along with sweet desserts and sandwiches. The prices are great, and you can relax upstairs in the loft with your drinks. Hang out and take advantage of their free Wi-Fi as you enjoy your coffee. $
Euphemia Haye Restaurant *5540 Gulf Of Mexico Dr., Longboat Key, FL 34228 (941) 383-3633* Located on Longboat Key, this is a romantic restaurant with excellent food. The atmosphere is adorable as the restaurant is adorned with show posters and wine corks and cases of wine. The wait staff is friendly without being overbearing. The signature Prime Peppered Steak gets raves. The fish is excellent, and the service is attentive. After dinner, you go upstairs to the dessert bar. $$$$
Selva Grill *1345 Main St., Sarasota, FL 34236 (941) 362-4427* For a fancier meal, you'll have to head right down into the city center, but that's still just 10 minutes by car from the airport. They serve a mix of Peruvian and Spanish food, and the ceviche always gets rave reviews. Selva is only open for dinner, though they stay open

fairly late (11 p.m.) if you want to stop in for drinks. Their patio is very nice for fresh air dining and people watching. $$$
Toasted Mango *430 N. Tamiami Trail, Sarasota FL (941) 388-7728* They serve fresh and delicious breakfast and lunch every day (they close at 3 p.m.), and you can choose the dining room or the private outside patio for your meal. Many consider it the best breakfast in Sarasota and the Ritz Carleton staff have been known to recommend it. $$

Where to Stay

Longboat Key Club and Resort *220 Sands Point Road, Longboat Key, FL 34228* Beautifully landscaped, it is one of the best places to play golf in Florida. You can only play the 27 hole harbor-side course if you are a guest of the resort. They also have a great 20-court tennis installation. The resort is ideally located on a beautiful, soft white sand beach. For those who like pools, they have a great hot tub and a large pool. Most rooms have a balcony. $$$$
Hyatt Regency Sarasota *1000 Boulevard of the Arts, Sarasota, FL 34236 (941) 953-1234* The outdoor bar and waterfall lagoon pool are a few of the lovely touches that make the Hyatt Regency a special place to stay. A $15/day resort fee gives you Wi-Fi, kayak and paddleboard rentals and a few other handy amenities. The hotel is right in downtown Sarasota by the coast and the causeway over to the islands. You can be checking into your room within about 10 minutes of leaving the airport. $$$

Sarasota/Bradenton International — KSRQ

SARASOTA TOWER ©**120.1**
(0600-2400)

Ground Control **121.9**

Control Tower Phone
(941) 355-3105

Airport Manager Phone
(941) 359-5200

ASOS 124.375 (941) 359-0117

ATIS 124.375

®TAMPA App/Dep 119.65 124.95
(4000 and below)

CLNC DEL 118.25

UNICOM 122.95

Elevation 30' MSL	Traffic Pattern 1030' MSL (1000 'AGL)	Flight Service Station ST PETERSBURG 122.1R 117.0T

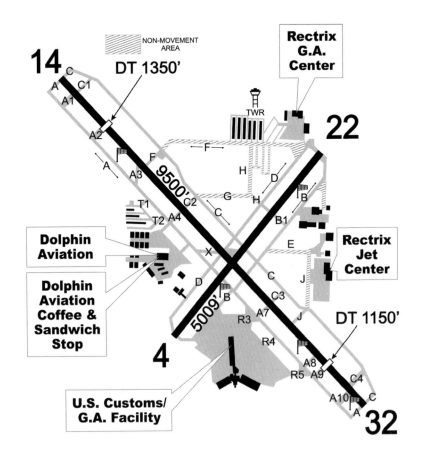

Not for navigation or inflight use | © 2017 Adventus Media LLC

Sebastian

Sebastian Inlet is the premier fishing spot in Central Florida. There is also a good restaurant on the field that few pilots know about.

The town was founded in 1882, with a small fishing industry to keep it going. The very first National wildlife refuge in the USA was established nearby at **Pelican Island** in 1903, and it is still a major attraction for Sebastian. Between that and Sebastian's Inlet park, you'll be able to do many hours of fishing, bird-watching and nature walking while you are in town.

Treasure hunters often tour the waters near Sebastian looking for wrecks or signs of sunken booty under the waves. Seven Spanish ships sunk in 1715 and most of their precious cargo was lost. Professional salvagers like **Mel Fisher** have recovered some, but much is still out there under the waves. Local museums have many of these unique items on display.

It's not as well-known as many larger beach towns, but that means you won't be fighting the crowds in Sebastian.

Flying There

There is no controlled airspace in the immediate vicinity of the Sebastian Airport. The closest controlled airspace to Sebastian is Vero Beach to the south. Be alert for heavy flight

Sebastian Inlet Looking East

training traffic to the west and to the east along the beach.

Sebastian hosts a very active skydiving facility. Jump planes broadcast on CTAF 123.05. Landings and departures during jump operations are usually not a problem but avoid flying directly over the airport.

Runways 23 and 28 use right-hand traffic patterns to keep traffic away from populated areas. All traffic patterns are oriented north of the field.

On the CTAF frequency, key your microphone three times for an automated weather broadcast.

Pilots Paradise operates an FBO on the west ramp offering full-service 100LL from 8:30 a.m. to 5 p.m. Monday through Saturday and 9 a.m. to 1:30 p.m. on Sunday. They monitor CTAF/UNICOM and can be reached at *(772) 589-0800.*

Sebastian Municpal Airport runs the main terminal building on the east ramp and has self-serve 100LL fuel available 24/7. Call *(772) 228-7001* or visit www.sebastianairport.org for information regarding services and noise abatement.

Getting Around

There is public bus service in Sebastian, and you can pick up Route 5 out on Main Street to take you to the coast or towards downtown. Fares are by donation.

Jetty is one of the Best Fishing Spots in Central Florida

There aren't any car rental booths in the airport, but there is an **Enterprise** outlet *(772) 646-4965* just out on Route 1 that can bring a car to you. If you want taxi service, **Caravan Transportation** *(772) 985-4830* can be waiting for you if you call ahead. They will take you anywhere you need to go in Sebastian.

Walking Distance Activities

One of the best activities in town is right at the airport. You can just taxi your airplane to **Skydive Sebastian,** and you're ready for your high-altitude thrills. **The Zoo Bar and Cafe** is located at Skydive Sebastian and serves breakfast and lunch (see below). All around the airport is the **Sebastian Municipal Golf Course.** They like to cater to pilots, so you'll not only get a discount if you play, they can have a golf cart waiting for you at the airport.

What to See and Do

Fishing at Sebastian Inlet The inlet and surrounding areas are part of the Sebastian Inlet State Park. (see below). If you love to fish, load up your airplane with fishing gear and visit the premier fishing spot in central Florida. You can fish from the shoreline south of the jetty, under the bridge from the southern entrance to the park, or the ocean-side jetty walkway accessed by the north park entrance. At the north jetty a catwalk goes out over the ocean. Snook and redfish are what Sebastian Inlet is best known for, but bluefish, Spanish mackerel, pompano, and tarpon are frequently caught there too. In season you can find flounder, mangrove snapper and sheepshead too.

If you want some professional help **Captain Mike Peppe** *326 Fleming Street Sebastian, FL 32958 (772) 581-0062* knows all about light tackle and flyfishing and can help you land the big game fish of the area. **Going Coastal** *(321) 863-8085* takes fishermen (and women) out all through the Sebastian Inlet area for sea trout, snook, flounder and redfish. You can also do a little inland fishing by kayak or head out in deeper waters for a longer trip seeking amberjack and snapper. You

can also book with **Big Easy** *(772) 538-1072* and bring in a catch almost every time, even the hard-to-land cobia.

Pelican Island National Wildlife Refuge *4055 Wildlife Way, Vero Beach, FL 32963 (772) 581-5557* Take a walk through the Pelican Island park to see dozens of waterbird species, including pelicans, egrets, herons and more. Various trails and boardwalks will take you through the wetlands to enjoy the scenery and do some birdwatching. The park is pretty much directly across the river from the airport, but you'll have to head down through town to get the causeway to take you over. Unless you have rented a boat and plan on seeing the area from the water.

Sebastian Inlet State Park *9700 S Hwy A1A, Melbourne, Fl. 32951 (407) 589-2147* Miles of walking trails will take you all through the park to see the wildlife and island landscapes. There is a great beach for swimming, fishing and surfing too. If you rent a boat at one of the marinas, this should be on your list of places to see from the water. It's farther to the north on the same island as the Pelican Island park, and there are always fewer crowds here. Even so, it's only half an hour by car from the airport.

Also at the park is the small **McLarty Treasure Museum,** that shows off some of the finds from the salvage of a 1715 Spanish galleon off the coast. Admission is $2 and they are open seven days a week.

Mel Fisher's Treasure Museum *1322 U.S. Highway 1, Sebastian, FL 32958 (772) 589-0432* Small local museums are always a fun visit, and the Mel Fisher Treasure Museum is no exception. They have an impressive collection of artifacts and treasure from local sunken-ship discoveries. Learn more about local ship wrecks, and see recovered cannons and displays of gold coins. There is a little gift shop too if you want some nautical souvenirs. Plan ahead if you want to visit though. They're only open on weekends.

Sebastian Skydiving *400 West Airport Drive, Sebastian, FL 32958 (772) 388-5672* The Skydive Sebastian headquarters are right at the airport, making it the easiest attraction in town to get to. It's a popular drop zone in the area, with great staff and amazing views from 13,500 feet. Novices can take a tandem dive with an instructor and more-experienced jumpers can go solo.

If you are coming to Sebastian to do a little skydiving, you can spend the entire day at the airport. There is even a restaurant at the Skydive Center where you can get some lunch between jumps. The casual little Zoo Bar does breakfast and lunch, and you can eat there whether you are diving or not.

About Kayaks River Rentals *25 Airport Dr W, Off Roseland Road, across from Wimbrow Park, Sebastian, FL 32958 772-589-3469* Enjoy a eco-friendly way to immerse yourself in the beauty and wonder of nature. They'll set you up with guided tours or a 2-3 hour self-guided tour. Take your choice of sit-inside, sit-on-top single or tandem kayaks.

Capt. Christy's Casual Cruisin *806 Indian River Dr, Sebastian, FL 32958-4162 772-633-0987* Sailing out of the marina at Mulligan's Beachhouse Bar & Grill, six different tours are offered on her pontoon boat. Captain Christy has a great sense of humor and a vast knowledge of the Sebastian Inlet. Christy's love for the area and her clear expertise on all things histor-ical, marine and aviary, make this a fun experience for young and old alike. She also does Kayak and Stand Up Board Tours.

Where to Eat

The ZooBar and Café *400 Airport Dr W, Sebastian, FL 32958 (772) 388-5672* Best described as a small beer and wine bar with excellent food. They serve breakfast and an extended lunch. You'll find normal lunch items: hamburgers, hotdogs, and french fries as well as daily specials that can be far more gourmet. The ZooBar is open from 7

Fishing in Sebastian

a.m. to 5 p.m. daily.

Mo-Bay Grill *480 US Highway 1, River Park Plaza, Sebastian FL 772-589-4223* First rate Jamaican restaurant. Owner and Chef Wesley Campbell has won multiple awards in his carcer including Chef of the Year in Jamaica and it shows in his food. Great jerk chicken and curry chicken. The conch fritters are excellent. The atmosphere and service is also great. Right across from the river.

Las Palmas Cuban Restaurant *1929 US Hwy 1, Sebastian, FL 32958 (772) 388-5188* Minutes away from the airport is your chance to try some excellent local Cuban food. Platters of seafood paella are huge, and the flan is a popular choice for dessert. The restaurant is very casual and can be a noisy spot when it's busy. They've got Wi-Fi if you need it, but there is no outside patio. $$

Tiki Bar & Grill *1130 Indian River Dr., Sebastian, FL 32958 (772) 388-1080* The name says it all. This spot is all-outdoor seating with thatched umbrellas over most of the patio. Relax with some new friends, with a few drinks and a bite to eat. They're open for both lunch and dinner. The Tiki Bar is right on the shore so you can enjoy the view of the Indian River while you're there. $

Squid Lips *1660 N Indian River Dr., Sebastian, FL 32958 (772) 589-3828* Who can resist a restaurant called Squid Lips? It has a classic surfer style, and a line-up of seafood dishes like Mahi-Mahi, coconut shrimp and bacon wrapped scallops. They also have a raw bar for the more daring with a selection of oysters, clams and sashimi scallops. $$

Where to Stay

Camping

If you bring a tent, there is a campground at the **Sebastian Inlet State Park** *(772)589-9659.*

Surfing in Sebastian

The Inn at Captain Hiram's *1580 US Highway 1 Sebastian, FL 32958 (772) 388-8588* This is the resort where you stay when you want a lot of activities at your fingertips. Very tropical feel with Bahamian-style SandBar (yes, it is outside and the "floor" is beach sand), regular live entertainment, waterfront rooms and much more. There is a marina, restaurant, bar and a comfortable hotel all rolled into one. Boat rentals at the marina give you the freedom to explore the river and the islands on your own, but the hotel also has a swimming pool and live entertainment if you prefer to stay closer to home. $$

Disney's Vero Beach Resort *9250 Island Grove Ter., Vero Beach, FL 32963 (772) 234-2000* Across the river on the island, and about 20 minutes from the airport, the Disney's Vero Beach Resort is waiting for you. This oceanfront resort was Disney's first resort built outside of their parks. There are rooms and suites in the main hotel or more private villas right on the beach. While it is Disney-themed, its not an amusement park by any means. There are lots of kids activities including character breakfasts. It's more than suitable for families as well as couples. There is more than one place to eat on the premises, and the staff is super attentive to your every need. $$$

Sportman's Lodge *412 Indian River Drive, Sebastian, FL 32958 (772) 589-2020* It's hard to believe you can get really good accommodations for these low prices. Though the hotel doesn't have many features, the rooms are clean and there is a swimming pool for guests. It's minutes from the airport and located right on the shore for easy access to the water. $

Sebastian Municipal

CTAF/UNICOM ©123.05

Airport Manager Phone
(772) 388-8228

Weather: Automated Unicom: 3 clicks for short airport advisory. Three more clicks for extended advisory.

PALM BEACH App/Dep 123.625

Elevation	Traffic Pattern	Flight Service Station
21' MSL	1000' MSL (979'AGL)	800-WX-BRIEF

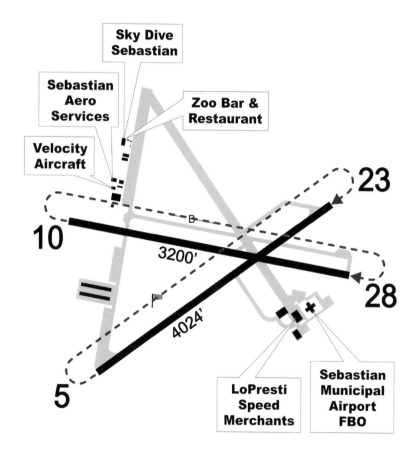

Sky Dive Sebastian

Sebastian Aero Services

Zoo Bar & Restaurant

Velocity Aircraft

23

10

3200'

28

4024'

5

LoPresti Speed Merchants

Sebastian Municipal Airport FBO

KSEF

Sebring

Pilots love to fly here for a restaurant on the field. But they also know Sebring for the U.S. Sport Aviation Expo held in January. The rest of America knows Sebring as the home to Sebring International Raceway.

Sebring International Raceway is America's oldest road racing track. Built on a few closed runways at KSEF, this has to be the easiest racetrack in the country for a pilot to fly to.

You can also pilot a car on the track if you sign up with the racing school.

Flying in for the the U.S. Sport Aviation Expo is also fun. The Expo has expanded from just a sport pilot show to more of an "affordable aviation" show and is worth a visit.

Sebring

Flying There

The main challenge to arrival into Sebring is the group of Restricted Areas to the north and east. Sebring also lies below the Lake Placid East Military Operations Area, which includes the airspace above 7,000 feet MSL. Contact Miami Center on 127.2 to determine the status of the MOA.

Every January, Sebring hosts the **U.S. Sport Aviation Expo.** A temporary control tower is established and controls the airspace during the event, including several days prior. Pilots flying into and out of the airport must read and heed a special NOTAM available at http://www.sportaviationexpo. com/notam/.

Mandatory special arrival and departure procedures are in effect during the Expo.

Sebring Flight Center (operated by Volo Aviation) is the FBO. They offer full-service 100LL and Jet A, and self-serve 100LL, Jet A, and Mogas. The terminal has the usual general aviation amenities, plus a restaurant. Weekday hours are 7:30 a.m. to 6 p.m., and they're open from 7:30 a.m. to 5 p.m. on weekends. Courtesy cars and Hertz and Enterprise rentals are available. Radio UNICOM 122.7 or call *(863) 655-6455.*

Getting Around

While most pilots will end up just staying at the airport, Volo Aviation has a courtesy car and they will help you arrange for a taxi or car rental.

Walking Distance Activities

All the action is at the airport. In addition to the Aviation Expo, race track and racing school, there are many

Not for navigation or inflight use | © 2017 Adventus Media LLC

U.S. Sport Aviation Expo

aviation business located on the field.

Lockwood Aviation, the Rotax engine specialist is based there with over 8,000 parts on hand. They fix Rotax engines as well as train light sport repairmen. They also have an LSA pilot school. Additionally they sell LSAs as well as manufacture the AirCam Twin.

Tecnam USA *(863) 655-2400* Tecnam is also based at Sebring, selling everything from their well-known LSAs and their new Part 23 Certified four passenger plane and twin to their airborne surveillance twin.

FPNA *(863) 655-3770* The initials stand for Floatplanes and Amphibians and they're into water flying, as the name implies. They import and manufacture FAA certified Special Light Sport Aircraft (S- LSA) and Experimental Light Sport Aircraft, (E-LSA). They also offer flight instruction.

Paradise Aircraft USA *(850) 758-2967* They build the P1-NG here. This roomy high wing LSA is unique in the light sport world in that it has dual control yokes, and a central power quadrant, more like a Cessna than a light sport. It also has a rare feature in an LSA — a rear cargo door.

What to See and Do
U.S. Sport Aviation Expo

Held every year in Sebring, the Expo began as a light-sport aircraft event, but now includes homebuilts, ultralights and other aircraft. The Expo also offers onsite overnight camping for those who fly in. The event is typically held the last week in January. In 2015, more than 18,000 people attended the Expo.

Sebring International Raceway *Sebring Air Terminal, Sebring, FL 33870 (800) 626-RACE* Originally the track used parts of a retired runway and old ramps along with parts of the active runways to run the famous **12 Hours of Sebring** race. Through revisions over the years, the current course can now be used without interfering with airport operations. **The Annual 12 hours of Sebring** is held in March.

Another race at the track is the **Lamborghini Super Trofeo,** a one-make series taking place in November. www.supertrofeo.com/

Skip Barber Racing School *108 Golden Eagle Dr., Sebring, FL 33870 (863) 655-6566* Want to learn to drive a race car? Using the Sebring International Raceway as your classroom, Skip Barber will put you in the seat of a race car, and give you anything from a one Day Driving School ($995) to more advanced programs. They also have a Teen Safety and Survival School, great for new drivers. When you have honed your skills, they also have racing weekends.

Airboat Wildlife Adventures *4971 US Hwy 98, Sebring, FL 33876 (863) 655-4737* If you feel you have to leave the airport, consider an airboat ride. Captain John

12 Hours of Sebring Race

narrates the tour up and down the Arbuckle Creek and Lake Istokpoga. You'll see beautiful scenery, all kinds of birds, gators, remains of a plane crash, a llama, and possibly a monkey.

Lost Mines of Atlantis *10404 US Hwy 27S, Sebring, FL 33876 (863) 655-4044* There is no actual mine on the property, but it is a place where you can "mine gems." You can purchase buckets filled with fine gravel that are generously salted with crystals, amethyst, quartz, gem stones (rubies, sapphires, emeralds, fire opals), minerals and fossils. A sluice technique is used as you scoop the contents of your bucket into a wire mesh box. As the fine gravel is washed away, it is pretty amazing what the water reveals. Kids, of course love it, and most adults do too. You actually keep everything you find. Buckets range from $20 to $150, and there is a $60 minimum for your group. There is a very interesting gift shop, with many unique items from around the world, next to the mine. Cash only. Call ahead to verify the hours.

Where to Eat

The Runway Cafe *128 Authority Lane, Sebring Airport, Sebring, FL 33870 (863) 655-0732* Very popular place for pilots to fly in. Open for breakfast and lunch. Some people keep flying back for breakfast just to have more of their homemade jam! You can eat inside in the air conditioning or underneath the ceiling fans out on the patio which overlooks the runway. Open seven days a week, the café features a full menu for breakfast and lunch.

Terminal, Home of the Runway Café

Esperante Restaurant *(863) 655-7200* Located in the Chateau Elan Hotel on the airport property, it is one of the nicest restaurants in Sebring. The evening menu tends toward Italian, but they also have salmon and steaks.

Where to Stay

Chateau Elan Hotel & Conference Center *150 Midway Dr., Sebring, FL 33870 (888) 844-6835* Located right on the airport grounds next to the race track, the property is beautifully manicured; the staff professional and helpful. Very nice pool. If you are not staying here during race week, it is a great resort for a romantic, reasonably priced weekend.

Inn On The Lakes *3101 Golfview Road, Sebring, FL 33870 (877) 897-6023* This is a grand old hotel with lots of history. Rooms are very comfortable, well-maintained, nicely-appointed. The property is lovely, well-manicured with lots of flowers, and a great view of the lake. The pool area has flowers and trees throughout with tables and chairs, loungers, and wicker booths. At night propane mantel lanterns light the area creating a romantic mood. **Chicanes Restaurant** is on-site, and you can dine with a lakeside view.

Inn on the Lakes

Sebring Regional

KSEF

CTAF/UNICOM ©**122.7**

Airport Manager Phone
(863) 655-6444

AWOS-3 119.475 (863) 655-6424
®MIAMI CENTER App/Dep 127.2

Elevation 61' MSL	Traffic Pattern 900' MSL (839'AGL)	Flight Service Station ST PETERSBURG 122.25

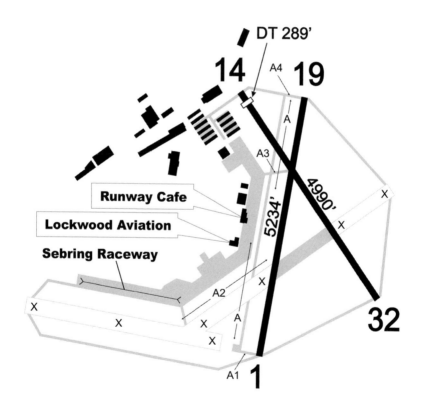

Spruce Creek

A gated village set around a private airfield, where almost all the residents own an airplane and have hangars with direct access to the runway… welcome to Spruce Creek! Oh, and there is a restaurant on the field, so you can fly in for breakfast, lunch or dinner.

You may be wondering why **Spruce Creek** is being featured in this guide since it is a private airfield. Generally it remains private and inaccessible to the public though a little-known secret will get you access into this exclusive community, at least into part of it anyway. **The Downwind Café** is located right in the heart of Spruce Creek on two taxi ways, and it is open to the public whether you fly in or drive in. Sit and enjoy breakfast, lunch or dinner while watching the planes going by and get a taste of what life in this private community is all about.

Spruce Creek Airport

The Community

Spruce Creek is the largest and most famous fly-in community in the country. Located in Port Orange, seven miles south of Daytona Beach, the airport started life as an outlying field to Naval Air Station DeLand and NAS Daytona Beach during World War II. At that time it had four paved, 4,000 foot runways, but when the war was over, it was no longer needed and the U.S. Navy abandoned it much like they did many other military strips across the country.

Recognizing that there were so many strips and such a high number of trained pilots following the war, the Civil Aeronautics Administration (predecessor to the FAA) suggested that they be put to good use – it seemed silly to let the strips deteriorate and become unusable, so the CAA proposed that 6,000 residential airparks be constructed all across the country. Of course, such a high number of fly-in communities never happened, but today there's about a tenth of that number and they are all popular and highly-desirable places to live.

Spruce Creek became famous for a couple of reasons – first it is the largest fly-in community in the country:

home to around 5,000 residents spread across the village's 1,300 homes. Second, it has been home to some prominent names, the most famous being John Travolta who moved out following a number of disagreements with other residents.

While it's the appeal of having your own hangar; a driveway leading directly to the runway; and many neighbors who love everything about aviation as much as you do, Spruce Creek does also feature some other highly-desirable traits. The Spruce Creek Country Club encourages active living with its 18-hole golf course, tennis, swimming pool and fitness center, though you do have to be a member to be able to enjoy these activities.

Flying Here

Spruce Creek features a 4,000-foot paved, lighted runway located below the Daytona Beach Class C airspace and immediately adjacent to the surface area. Contact Daytona Beach Approach for airspace transition clearance and flight following.

Visit www.scpoa.com/airport for detailed information about local procedures. The "Creek Arrival/Departure" to and from the airport passes through the narrow space between the Daytona Beach Class C and New Smyrna Beach Class D surface areas and below Daytona Beach's 1,200-foot Class C shelf. This follows roughly a 070 track out of Spruce Creek at 800 feet AGL. Pilots flying the procedure should announce their position on CTAF 122.975 when arriving over the shoreline or departing over the interstate. The "Tank Departure" consists of flying northwest out of Spruce Creek to a large water tank, then maintaining a 290 heading until clear of Interstate 4 and Highway 92 before turning on course.

Airport weather information is broadcast on 121.725. Left traffic patterns are used for runway 5/23 in both directions, and the traffic pattern altitude is 800 feet AGL. Larger, faster aircraft may use a 1,000-foot AGL traffic pattern.

Parking areas for visiting aircraft are on the east side of Beech Blvd; the large taxiway exiting the runway to the south at midfield; and additionally on the west end of Cessna Blvd., which runs east-to-west from the approach end of runway 5. Visitor parking areas are designated by blue lines.

Prior permission is not required to visit the restaurant. All visitors should post a note inside the left-hand cockpit windshield of their aircraft showing the pilot's name and either a local or cell phone number to contact the pilot.

Yelvington Jet Aviation *(386) 257-7791* runs a small FBO on the field with self-serve 100LL, Jet A, and Mogas available 24/7 with major credit card.

Visiting Spruce Creek

While strictly-speaking Spruce Creek is an entirely private airstrip, this doesn't mean you cannot visit at all. If you're lucky enough to know a resident of Spruce Creek, you can get invited to fly in and park your plane for free for up to three nights.

If you don't know a resident, all is not lost! You can fly-in to this exclusive community to enjoy a meal at The Downwind Café.

The Downwind Café *100 Cessna Blvd, Port Orange, FL 32128 (386) 756-8811* It seems like a contradiction to have a public restaurant in the heart of a private, gated community, but The Downwind is open to the public whether you've flown in or driven in to Spruce Creek.

This family-owned and operated restaurant has a lot going for it – an extensive and varied menu, a full bar, live music on Friday and Saturday nights, and interesting décor. Perhaps the most appealing thing (for pilots) about visiting The Downwind is the chance to sit and watch the airplanes come and go. With two taxiways right outside the window, there's always something to see, not to mention some of the unique airplanes you're likely to see when taxiing yourself from the runway.

The restaurant is open every day except Monday and opens for breakfast at 8 a.m. Closing time isn't fixed as such – about 9:00ish on weekdays and 10:00ish on Fridays and Saturdays. Favorite dishes from the menu include New York Style pizza, said to be the best around, plus there are quality steaks, burgers, seafood, pasta, chicken and salads, so something for all tastes. $$

When flying in, you have automatic approval to land if you're coming to dine at The Downwind. You'll just need to be sure to park in one of the guest parking spots and familiarize yourself with the Spruce Creek Airport Procedures before visiting so that you know what to expect.

Spruce Creek Airport 7FL6

CTAF/UNICOM ©122.975

Airport Manager Phone
(386) 872-1430

AWOS 121.725 (617) 262-3825 and
when prompted for an airport, enter
7356 for 7FL6

®DAYTONA App/Dep 125.35

Elevation	Traffic Pattern	Flight Service Station
23' MSL	823' MSL (800'AGL)	800-WX-BRIEF

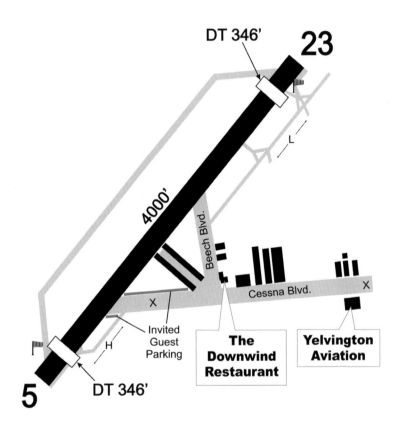

St. Augustine

As the oldest, continuously-inhabited European-established settlement and port in the continental United States, St. Augustine is a beautiful city that's big on history. Visit for the historic architecture, the riverside setting, the scenery and wildlife, and the wide variety of tours. Fly in for a meal at the Fly-by Café.

Nicknamed "Ancient City," St. Augustine is ancient in U.S. terms! Established in 1565 by the Spanish, the city served as the capital of Spanish Florida for more than 200 years before coming under British rule for a brief period. When the Florida Territory was established St. Augustine remained the capital until 1824 when it moved to Tallahassee.

Many of the major buildings from the Spanish and British rule are still standing in St. Augustine today and they have been attracting visitors to the city since the late 19th century when the city had its heyday. Plenty of investment went into the city at that time to build lavish hotels and homes that would house the tourists coming here, and now these themselves are also tourist attractions for the modern-day visitor. Places like the impressive Ponce de Leon Hotel and the Casa Monica Hotel, to name a few.

Carriages on King Street

Flying There

St. Augustine enjoys a location in relatively quiet airspace between the Jacksonville Terminal Area to the north and the Daytona Beach Terminal Area to the south. Contact Gainesville Radio on 122.2 to determine the status of military flight activities in the area. The control tower operates from 7 a.m. to 9 p.m.

Atlantic Aviation runs the FBO on the main ramp west of the airline terminal. Full-service 100LL and Jet A fuel are available during business hours of 6 a.m. to midnight on weekdays and 6 a.m. to 10 p.m. on weekends. Courtesy cars and rental cars are available. Radio 130.05 or call *(904) 824-1995*.

The **Northeast Florida Regional Airport** also operates a self-serve 100LL pump near the control tower that's available 24/7 with credit card.

Getting Around

You can easily rent a car.

The FBO has rentals and the big four rental companies have offices in the terminal building so you won't have to walk far to get to them. Take your pick from **Budget** *(904) 824-6372,* **Avis** *(904) 825-1505,* **Hertz** *(904) 826-1374* or **Enterprise** *(904) 823-1767.*

The **Sunshine Bus Company** *(904) 209-3716* has six different routes serving the city, one of which passes the airport, though service times are limited so catching a taxi or renting a car will be more useful. There are several taxi cab companies serving the city. Choose from **Abraxi Taxi** *(904) 599-6666,* **First Coast Taxi** *(904) 825-9999* or **Castillo Cab Company** *(904) 392-1422.*

Walking Distance Activities

The airport is four miles north of the city center so a little too far to comfortably walk the distance. The **Fly-By Café** *(904) 824-3494* is right on the airport grounds next to FBO Atlantic Aviation. If the weather is nice, you'll enjoy the outdoor balcony right on the field. Large model airplanes decorate the ceiling. Many locals come to the airport to eat here, so that is a good sign. They are open from 6:30 a.m. to 3:30 p.m. weekdays, closing an hour later on the weekends.

What to See and Do
Historic Walking Tours

The major thing to experience in St. Augustine is the history. You can happily wander around the streets of the city on your own, seeing the historic buildings, but you'll get far more out of your visit if you join one of the many walking tours. These guided tours ensure that you see the best of the city's history and learn a lot about what you're seeing as you go. Some walking tours are themed – ghost themed ones are popular, or

Castillo de San Marcos

you can go for a more standard history tour. **Secrets of St. Augustine Ghost Tours** *9 Saint George St., St. Augustine, FL 32086 (904) 814-1174* is highly rated for the tour guide's great stories and enthusiasm on this 90 minute walking tour. Another option is **St. Augustine Historic Walking Tours** *69 St George St., St. Augustine, FL 32084 (904) 392-7137* This tour company offers a variety of different tours depending on your tastes, including a Historic Pub Crawl, Family Tours, and Food Tours.

Old Town Trolley Tours of St. Augustine *167 San Marco Ave., St. Augustine, FL 32084 (in the Old Jail) (904) 829-3800* If you want to see more of the city in a shorter time the Old Town Trolley Tours are a great choice. Operating as a hop-on/hop-off tour you can stay on the trolley and enjoy

the guided commentary or step off when you come to an attraction that interests you. Look around, and then catch the next trolley when you're done. The trolleys stop at all the major points in the city including the Lightner Museum, Castillo de San Marcos, and the Colonial Quarter. Tickets cost $25.74 for adults and are valid for three consecutive days.

Horse Dawn Carriage Tours

Perhaps a more unique way to see the city's history is by horse-drawn carriage. There's nothing quite like being taken around town in a carriage, making this the perfect way to celebrate special occasions or for a romantic getaway. The best company offering horse-drawn carriage tours is **Country Carriages** *(904) 826-1982.*

St. Augustine Lighthouse and Museum *100 Red Cox Rd, St. Augustine, FL 32084 (904) 829-0745* Set on Anastasia Island, across the water and to the southeast of downtown, is this historic lighthouse that

St. Augustine

was lit in 1874. It is the city's oldest surviving brick structure and has been restored to its historic colors and materials. The striking combination of black and white stripes means you cannot miss this structure. Self-guided tours allow you to see the lighthouse, the keeper's house and the exhibits, or take a special guided behind the scenes tour. General adult tickets are $9.95.

San Sebastian Winery *157, King Street, St. Augustine, FL 32084 (904) 826-1594* A visit to the San Sebastian Winery is more than just an opportunity to buy some great wines; it is several attractions in one. For starters, the winery is located within one of the city's historic buildings: one of Henry Flagler's East Coast Railway buildings that's close to the historic downtown. Secondly the winery offers free tours and wine tasting seven days a week between 10 a.m. and 5 p.m. Monday to Saturday and 11 a.m. to 5 p.m. on Sundays. Guided tours run about every 20-25 minutes and last around 45 minutes, followed by the wine tasting. A visit is a great opportunity to learn more about wines and pairings with the chance to buy a bottle or two direct from the makers.

Where to Eat

Fly By Café See details above in the "walking distance activities" section.

Collage Restaurant *60 Hypolita Street, St. Augustine, FL 32084 (904) 829-0055* St. Augustine is not lacking in quality restaurants, but if you're looking for the best, try Collage. It is the number-one-rated restaurant out of hundreds in the city and is located right in the heart of the characterful Colonial Quarter. Their menu makes a refreshing change from the many similar seafood restaurants of the Floridian coast. They serve an eclectic mix of seafood, steaks, lamb and veal with an international twist on their dishes. Come here to celebrate a special occasion or for a date night to remember. $$$

Old City House Inn & Restaurant *115 Cordova Street, St. Augustine, FL 32084 (904) 826-0113* As the name suggests, this is both an inn and a restaurant so you could stay the night after enjoying a tasty dinner in pleasant surroundings. The restaurant is smaller and more intimate than some of the bustling city restaurants, making it a nice place to eat for a quiet dinner and good conversation, and there's a very nice patio within the lush gardens. Located just across the street from the Lightner Museum, this building once housed the stables that served Henry Flagler's hotels. The food is tasty and includes nice features such as homemade salad dressing. $$

The Bunnery Bakery & Café *121 St. George Street, St. Augustine, FL 32084 (904) 829-6166* When you don't need a big lunch, the Bunnery is a good option. Their central downtown location makes this great for a quick bite while on the move. Their breakfasts are very good and all the bakery goods are made and cooked right on-site. For lunch try a pastry, cinnamon bun, sandwich, panini or salad. $

Crave Food Truck *134 Ribera Street, St. Augustine, FL 32084* Despite being a food truck and despite being located in a sometimes hard-to-find location, Crave is one of the top rated places to eat in St. Augustine. Open Monday to Saturday from 11 a.m. to 4 p.m., this is basically a place to grab a healthy lunch. There are wraps, salads and sandwiches on the menu and they're created using locally-grown fresh produce. The truck is parked off Ribera Street and among units used by marine companies, but this means you benefit from seats (picnic tables) overlooking the water. $

Where to Stay

Bayfront Marin House Bed and Breakfast *142 Avenida Menendez, St. Augustine, FL 32084 (904) 824-4301* The Bayfront Marin House probably isn't what you would expect from a typical B&B; this is a luxurious place with a beautiful setting right by the water and is ideal for honeymoons and anniversaries. Set right on the bay and still within the city's historic centre puts you steps away to everything. The rooms are elegantly decorated and furnished, some with four-poster beds. Many of the rooms have fireplaces and Jacuzzis and the majority are pet-friendly too. In addition to the rooms and suites, the B&B has a couple of cottages, one with private pool. $$$

St. Augustine Reenactors

Casa Monica Hotel *95 Cordova Street, St. Augustine, FL 32084 (888) 213-8903* The wonderful thing about staying at the Casa Monica Hotel is that you'll be experiencing a true part of the city's, and the country's, history. This is one of the oldest hotels in the United States, opened originally in 1888 by Franklin W. Smith who later sold it to Henry Flagler. Along with Flagler's other St. Augustine hotels, this hotel is luxurious and majestic, and while it still retains that historic charm, it has been completely renovated to today's modern standards. Stay here for a night to remember. $$$

Jaybird's Inn *2700 N Ponce de Leon Blvd, Saint Augustine, FL 32084 (904) 844-0558* For a reasonably priced room, this motel is a good choice. It has renovated rooms and is close to the beaches as well as close to downtown. It may not look like much on the outside, but inside the renovated rooms are clean with a contemporary feel. There are bikes you can check out for the 10-minute bike ride to downtown.

The Cozy Inn *202 San Marco Ave., St. Augustine, FL 32084 (888) 288-2204* Another more affordable option, the Cozy Inn is about a 15 minute walk into the heart of the city. Comprising of two different locations (on either side of the street), this Inn has motel-style accommodation as well as rooms within an old southern-style house, completely modernized for today's travelers. Service, price, cleanliness and comfort are just some of the reasons why this is among the top places to stay in St. Augustine. $$

Sidewalk Dining on Aviles Street

ST AUGUSTINE TOWER ©**127.625**
[0700-2100]

Ground Control **121.175**

Control Tower Phone
[904] 824-2644

Airport Manager Phone
[904] 209-0090

AWOS-3 [904] 824-7084

ATIS 119.625

®JACKSONVILLE App/Dep 120.75
UNICOM 122.95

Elevation 10' MSL	Traffic Pattern 1010' MSL [1000'AGL]	Flight Service Station GAINESVILLE 122.3

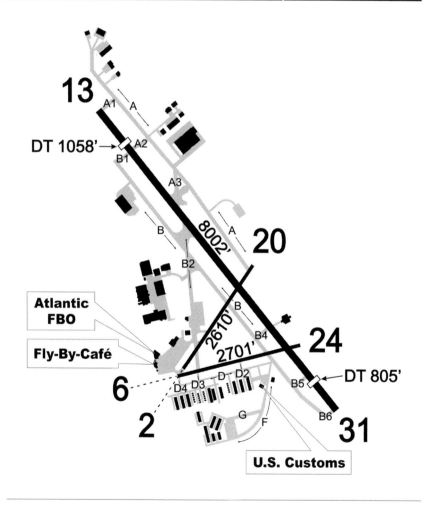

Atlantic FBO

Fly-By-Café

U.S. Customs

St. Petersburg

Albert Whitted field is right in downtown St. Petersburg on the bay with a restaurant on the field. It may be the most perfect pilot's destination in Florida with its combination of walking-distance culture, dining and sports events.

St. Petersburg

St. Petersburg, called by locals St. Pete, also has the nickname, "Sunshine City." Located just south of Tampa, it has built its Tampa Bay waterfront neighborhood next to the airport as an arts and cultural center. Pilots will find an amazing number of cultural and culinary destinations within easy walking distance.

For the $100 hamburger, the on-field **Hangar Restaurant and Flight Lounge** serves breakfast, lunch and dinner.

Located one block from the FBO is the new Salvador Dalí museum. Next door is the Mahaffey Theater, featuring Broadway roadshows, touring pop headliners and classical performances by the Florida Orchestra.

Walk 10 blocks to the west and you can catch the Tampa Bay Rays playing the Red Sox, Yankees, Orioles and other teams in their domed, air-conditioned stadium.

You can even play golf if you choose to stay overnight at the luxury 1920's era Vinoy Renaissance Resort located in St. Pete's charming Old Northeast.

For motor racing fans, the annual Grand Prix of St. Petersburg takes place March 11-13, 2016, and actually uses runway 7/25 as part of the race course.

If you have kids or grandkids along, don't miss the airport-themed playground next to the airport. There is also a 20-screen theater with an IMAX screen two blocks from the Pier Muvico Baywalk 20, *(727) 502-0965.*

Flying There

Flying to **Albert Whitted** (KSPG) takes you into Tampa's Class B airspace. Contact Tampa Approach on 119.65 from the east and 125.3 from the west.

There are multiple TV towers starting 14 NM to the east of the airport with heights from 1549 to 1670 feet, so maintaining an altitude above that is advisable.

Eleven miles to the south is Sarasota's Class C air space. Tampa Approach 125.3 can be contacted at or below 4,000 feet.

Also note the heavy, fast military traffic to the northeast

Salvador Dalí Museum

and south of MacDill Air Force Base (KMCF) from 1,000 to 2,500 feet over Tampa Bay.

Sheltair *(797) 824-2880* has tie downs, fuel, Wi-Fi, and crew cars available. It is located in the terminal on the northwest part of the field at the beginning of runway 7.

Getting Around

You don't need to rent a car. If you want to stay in the waterfront area near the airport, there is enough to do. For some of the destinations further out, like the Sunken Gardens (2.2 miles and 44 minute walk), you can call a cab or take the trolly. If you do want a car rental, **Hertz** *(727) 823-8612* has a desk at the terminal.

The **St. Petersburg Trolley Downtown Looper** *(727) 540-1900* route connects to many of the city's major museums and attractions. The fare is either free or 50 cents depending on where you get on. It can also connect you to the **Central Avenue Trolley** *(727) 540-1900* which takes you down to the the Grand Central District where you can walk to galleries, antique stores, restaurants, and unique shops. Fare range from 50 cents to $2 depending on how far you go.

Walking Distance Activities

Almost everything is within walking distance. The Dalí museum and Mahaffey Theater are right next door to the the airport terminal.

On the field you can check out **Biplane Rides** *(727) 895-6266* who give air tours in a 1933 Waco once owned by William Randolph Hearst.

What to See and Do

The new **Salvador Dalí Museum** (2011) *(727) 823-3767* has a spectacular bay-front location adjacent to the airport. It is worth a visit just to see the museum's architecture. Walk the maze outside before entering or when you leave. The museum has the largest collection of Dalí's works outside of Spain. Definitely take the tour with a docent or the audio tour with headphones if you want to go at your own pace. Even people that aren't sure they like Dalí's art seem to like the experience. Admission is $24 but Thursday night is half price.

Mahaffey Theater Located next to the Salvador Dalí Museum, this 2000+ seat theater is worth a visit if there is a performance going on when you are in town. In fact, if you are looking for an excuse to visit St. Pete, check the theater's schedule and plan your visit around a performance you want to see. The Florida Orchestra performs weekly from October through May. Pop stars, ballet, comedians, and touring theater shows are also booked. *(727) 892-5767*

Chihuly Collection *400 Beach Drive NE, St. Petersburg, FL 33701 (727) 896-4527* A sixteen minute walk (.8 miles) north of the airport. Those strolling by might think this looks like just another gallery. Inside has a stunning, permanent collection of world-renowned glass artist Dale Chihuly's unique artwork. (Visitors to the Atlantis Hotel in the Bahamas or the Bellagio Hotel in Las Vegas have probably seen examples of his work). Admission is $14.95. For $5 more you can purchase a combination ticket that includes free glass blowing demonstrations at the Morean Hot Shop, a working glass studio nearby.

St. Petersburg Museum of History *335 2nd Ave NE, St. Petersburg, FL 33701 (727) 894-1052* Located a 20 minute walk north of the airport, pilots should visit at least once. The first airline and commercial flight was started in St. Pete. The museum's World's First Airline gallery proudly features a full-size working replica of the Benoist Airboat, the airplane that started it all. The museum also tells the history of St. Petersburg, dating from the prehistoric era. New is Schrader's Little Cooperstown, a baseball museum whose collection of over 4,600 baseballs is is recognized by the Guinness Book of World Records as the largest private collection of autographed baseballs in the world.

Museum of Fine Arts *255 Beach Dr NE, St. Petersburg, FL 33701 (727) 896-2667* Located across from the St. Petersburg Museum of History, the museum is housed in a lovely Palladian-style building near the Pier. The wide ranging collections include pre-Columbian, ancient, Asian, American and European works of art. It is noted for its collection of French Impressionist paintings by Gauguin, Monet, Renoir

Tropicana Field is just 10 Blocks from the Airport

and Cézanne. Other artists represented include Georgia O'Keeffe and Auguste Rodin. There is also a 14,000 photograph collection the photography exhibit draws from.

Sunken Gardens *1825 4th St N, St. Petersburg, FL 33704 (727) 551-3100* Built over 100 years ago, it is home to some of the oldest tropical plants in the region. The five-acre setting is a drained ancient lake, giving the garden its name. This peaceful setting has waterfalls

and more than 50,000 tropical plants and flowers. The gardens feature a butterfly garden, a walk-through aviary with exotic species of birds and an orchid arbor. You may also see turtles, and flamingos within the gardens. Remember to bring bug repellant for this outdoor attraction. $8 for adults. The location is 2.2 miles north of the airport and will take 44 minutes to walk. From the airport you can take the bus (PSTA) Route 4 to the Gardens. The bus leaves every 15 minutes and the ride takes 23 minutes.

Great Explorations *1925 4th St N, St. Petersburg, FL 33704 (727) 821-8992* Located next to Sunken Gardens, this is a children's museum with a hands-on approach to the arts, health and science. Designed for children 10 and under, although many older children and adults find it interesting. There is a nice indoor playground, hula hoops, a play grocery store, pneumatic tubes as well as the Touch Tunnel, a dark maze for kids to explore. $10

Doo's Amazing Tours *475 2nd Ave NE, St. Petersburg, FL 33701 727-278-9799* Located by the Central Yacht Basin,

about a fifteen minute walk from the FBO, Doo's offers three different Segway tours around St. Pete. The owner (Doo) leads the tours. Headsets are provided as well as a bottle of water for those hot days.

Where to Eat

The Canopy Rooftop Lounge *Beach drive, Birchwood Inn, St. Petersburg, FL (727) 896-1080* Located six blocks west of The Pier, in a renovated historic building, it commands a fabulous view of downtown St. Petersburg and the Bay. Has a South Beach feel with the couches and fire pits. Cabanas are available for more private seating (with a minimum bar tab). The air-conditioned and covered open-air bar is nice during some of the warmer summer afternoons. A limited but trendy light menu. $$

BellaBrava, *204 Beach Dr NE, St. Petersburg, FL 33701 (727) 895-5515* Popular Italian trattoria centrally located on Beach Drive near museums, parks and galleries. Dine on the sidewalk or inside. Tuscany influenced menu as well as wood fire cooked pizza and flatbreads. $$

Crowley's Downtown, *269 Central Ave., St. Petersburg, FL 33701-3325 (727) 821-1111* Inviting place with inviting Irish Pub atmosphere and excellent food. Some creative menu items including macaroni and corned beef, and reuben egg rolls. Outside seating available. $$

Z Grille, *104 2nd St S, St. Petersburg, FL 33701 (727) 822-9600* Z-Grille is a fun, lively place to go. The menu is unique, a bit eclectic, and has great variety. Signature

The Canopy Rooftop Lounge

dishes include unique deviled eggs and the locally famous Dr. Pepper fried ribs.

Ceviche Tapas Bar and Restaurant *10 Beach Dr NE, St. Petersburg, FL 33701 (727) 209-2302* The restaurant is adjacent to the hotel Ponce de Leon. Great atmosphere with seating inside as well as on the balcony. $$

La V, *441 Central Ave., St. Petersburg, FL 33701 (727) 820-3500* Vietnamese. A classy, clean, and stylish restaurant. Some customers who know Vietnamese food say this is the best Vietnamese restaurant in the state. $$

Red Mesa Cantina, *128 3rd St. S, St. Petersburg, FL 33701-4224 (727) 896-8226* Self-described as a modern Mexican taqueria, it features a more upscale decor than the typical Mexican restaurant. Menu features some creative items like Ahi Tuna tacos and duck tacos in addition to a more standard fare. $$

Where to Stay

Vinoy Renaissance Resort & Golf Club *501 Fifth Ave NE, St. Petersburg, FL 33701 (727) 894-1000* The place to

stay if you want the full resort experience. Built in 1925 with wonderful Mediterranean Revival architecture and totally restored in 1992. Many Major League Baseball teams stay here when they are playing the Tampa Bay Rays. Features include a spa, and 12-court tennis complex. They also have an 18-hole course located 1.7 miles from The Vinoy on Snell Isle. Choose the original building if you like historic touches or choose the tower for larger, newer rooms. Ask for a room overlooking the water for stunning bay views. Rooms overlooking the old courtyard also have a charming view. $$$

Hilton St Petersburg Bayfront, *333 First St. S, St. Petersburg, FL 33701 (855) 271-3621* Closest hotel to the airport, four blocks from the FBO. Right in the center of the downtown action with a free shuttle service and a Starbucks. Bay view rooms showcase the bay, beautiful bay side parks and also let you see the airport. $$$

The Birchwood *340 Beach Dr NE, St. Petersburg, FL 33701 (727) 896-1080* The Birchwood was originally constructed in 1924 as the Lantern

Lane Apartments. The Spanish Mission-style building, listed in the National Registry of Historic Places, was beautifully renovated into 18 rooms featuring oversized bathrooms with claw foot tubs. Set in the center of the action, this boutique hotel doesn't have a pool, gym or room service, but it has an inviting charm. Its Canopy Rooftop Lounge (see left) is very popular. $$$

Larelle House Bed & Breakfast *237 6th Avenue, NE, St. Petersburg, FL 33701 (727) 490-3575* Larelle House is a Queen Anne Victorian three-story residence constructed in 1908. Guests approach via a charming cobblestone street. All of the rooms are decorated in true vintage fashion. The first floor of the house is open to all guests and is very inviting. The four available guest rooms are upstairs. Lovely front porch with wicker chairs, a garden Jacuzzi and available bicycles for the guests round out the experience. Unlike other B&B's where the food is placed out and you serve yourself, here you will be served like a guest in hosts Larry and Ellen's home. $$$

Watergarden Inn at the Bay *126 Fourth Ave. N.E., St. Petersburg, FL 33701 (727) 822-1700* A bed & breakfast in two restored buildings, the Inn combines charming antiques and modern amenities in its 14 rooms. All rooms are available to pre-view online. Guests comment on the comfortable beds. A true oasis in the city, its quiet location is just three blocks from the Pier. Unusual for a B&B is the pool with tropical landscaping. Bikes are available for guests. $$$

Albert Whitted; *St Petersburg* | KSPG

TOWER ©**127.4**
(0700-2100)

Ground Control **121.8**

Control Tower Phone
(727) 823-8897

Airport Manager Phone
(727) 893-7657

ASOS 118.875 (727) 821–4334

®TAMPA App/Dep119.65 (East) 125.3 (West)

UNICOM 122.95

NOTE: St Petersburg FSS monitors 121.8 when tower closed.

Elevation	Traffic Pattern	Flight Service Station
7' MSL	807' MSL (800'AGL)	800-WX-BRIEF

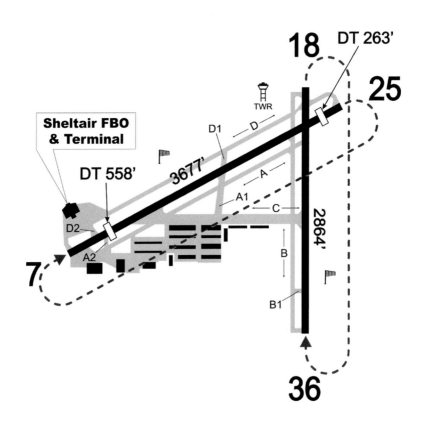

Steinhatchee/ Cross City

The small town of Steinhatchee offers a taste of Old Florida from its scenic location on the banks of the Steinhatchee River, just before the river flows into the Gulf of Mexico. This is a place for a quiet, natural getaway. Come for the peaceful river boating and fishing, the quaint and friendly town, and the resort facilities of Steinhatchee Landing.

Visiting Steinhatchee is like stepping back in time, to a time before big towns and cities existed and almost everyone worked the land or the waters for a living. Since the early 19th century the community has played an important part in the forestry industry, and of course in fishing, crabbing and scalloping. Despite its beautiful coastal location Steinhatchee really hasn't grown much in the last hundred or so years. Today it's home to just over 1,000 people though thousands more come to visit over the course of each year, drawn by the peaceful and laid-back atmosphere and the chance to fish and boat away from the masses in Southern Florida.

This region of Florida is known as the Big Bend because of the way the coast curves around to the Panhandle,

Steinhatchee Sunset

though it's also known as the Nature Coast for its unspoiled and undeveloped beauty. This is somewhere you come specifically to get away from the hustle and bustle of everyday life.

Fishing and boating are the top activities in the village, and

there are several restaurants, motels and inns right in the village of Steinhatchee if you're planning to stay. The popular Steinhatchee Landing Resort (see the What to See and Do section) offers more options and activities.

Steinhatchee River and the Steinhatchee Landing Resort

Flying There

Cross City is far away from any controlled airspace, terrain, or obstacles impeding the approach from any direction. Pilots can contact Gainesville Radio on 122.2 to determine the status of activity in the Live Oak Military Operations Area to the north.

Dixie Aviation Services offers self-serve 100LL and Jet A fuel 24/7 and assists with service during their business hours of 8 a.m. to 5 p.m. Restrooms, internet access, courtesy cars, and rental cars are available. Radio on UNICOM 122.8 or telephone *(352) 498-6656.*

Walking Distance Activities

Cross City Airport isn't within walking distance of Steinhatchee, in fact the village is a good 20 miles from the airport so you will need transportation to get there. If you're hoping to grab something to eat at the airport there is a pilot's lounge where you can buy snacks though these are pre-made, microwave snacks rather than freshly prepared.

Getting Around

As Cross City Airport is on the outskirts of a small city there's not much in the way of transportation services. There are no taxi cab companies based right in Cross City so the best option is to rent a car through **Hertz** *(352) 373-8444.* They have an office in Cross City.

What to See and Do

Steinhatchee Landing Resort *203 Ryland Circle, Steinhatchee, FL 32359 (352) 498-3513* Steinhatchee Landing Resort sits on the edge of the village where it offers easy access to the surrounding untouched Floridian countryside, and to the **Steinhatchee River.** You will relax here, because Steinhatchee Landing Resort's two-bedroom, two-bath Victorian or Florida Cracker-style cottages have spotty cell phone service. The internet, however, has finally appeared here, and you may be able to get a wifi connection. This is not one of those crowded luxurious resorts with countless activities, it's more a nature-based resort where you come to get away from it all and to enjoy the pic-

turesque surroundings. Boating on the river is the top thing to do. Though it's strikingly beautiful the river remains surprisingly quiet making this a great stretch of water to explore by kayak or canoe, both of which are available for rental from the resort. Bicycles can also be rented if you want to take a leisurely ride around the resort and the village, or head a little farther and go across the river for wilderness trails. Of course all these places can be hiked as well, if you prefer.

Also at the resort you can rent equipment for a game of croquet or shuffleboard, or try out some archery or tennis. There is a new 55 foot swimming pool and pavilion that has a sauna and fitness center. If you'd rather see the river while letting someone else do the hard work you can take a trip on the resort's river and Gulf view pontoon boat cruises, or contact a local boat rental or charter company for more options (see below).

The resort does not have its own restaurant though the cottages you can rent here do have kitchens. You can make your own meals or wander into the village where there are several places to eat. Every morning the resort puts on complimentary tea and coffee in the welcome center and you can buy muffins, Danish, juice and donuts in the Gift Shoppe.

All in all Steinhatchee Landing Resort is a great place to bring the family or the grandkids, or to come with your partner and enjoy the peace and quiet.

Boat Rentals and Charters

In Steinhatchee village there are a number of options for boat rentals or charters. The **Sea Hag Marina** *322 Riverside Drive, Steinhatchee, FL 32359 (352) 498-3008* has a fleet of seventeen rental boats available. Their 24' Skiffs can be rented by the day or half day and you can take a boat out on the river or head into Deadman Bay and the Gulf of Mexico. If you're planning to fish they can sell you live bait and tackle, plus they have all the equipment you'll need for scuba diving too, including rentals.

River Haven Marina *1110 River Side Drive, Steinhatchee, FL 32359 (352) 498-0709* is a little closer to Steinhatchee Resort and further inland from the Gulf. There's a selection of charters and guides operating out of this marina making this a good place to come to find a captain for a charter. Give the marina a call to see who's available when you're planning to visit. Of course, if you're an experienced captain yourself, you can also rent boats from here, anything from a 19' Skiff to a 24' deck boat, as well as single or tandem kayaks.

Scalloping

Scallops used to be prevalent all along the coast from Palm Beach to Pensacola, but today one of the few remaining places you can go scalloping is here in Steinhatchee. The season roughly runs from July to September and you are free to wade and find scallops yourself but if you're planning on diving or snorkeling you will need a fishing license. Captains operating out of the marina will be able to take you to some great spots for the best scalloping opportunities, and if you're doing it from a chartered boat you won't need a license because the boat operator will already have one.

Where to Eat

Taste of Dixie Diner *16840 SE 12 Ave., Cross City, FL 32628 (352) 498-8008* For real local flavor, their menu of real Dixie food makes this a popular place for the locals and anyone passing through. Try swamp cabbage plucked right from the local swamps and a number of other Southern foods in their filling buffet. If you're here in the evening there's also regular live music performances.

Roy's Restaurant *100 1st Avenue, Steinhatchee, FL 32359 (352) 498-5000* There aren't too many restaurants in Steinhatchee but Roy's has been here on the waterfront since 1969 and is the best rated place in town. Enjoy dinner or cocktails while watching the water and the sunset. Seafood features highly on the menu though they also serve steaks and chicken and have a children's menu. Open seven days a week from 11 a.m. to 9 p.m. $$

Fiddler's Restaurant *1306 Riverside Dr., Steinhatchee, FL 32359 (352) 498-7427* You can dine inside or outside at Fiddler's Restaurant, and it has a lovely riverside setting. The menu is similar to other places with seafood prominently featured, though their steaks and ribs are highly rated. Before or after dinner you can relax in their full-service lounge. Open seven days a week from 6 a.m. to 10 p.m. and they serve a very popular buffet on Sunday, from 11 a.m. to 2 p.m. $$

Who Dat Bar and Grill *7022 Hwy 358 SW, Steinhatchee, FL 32359 (352) 498-8088* Part of the Good Times Motel and Marina this laid back restaurant and bar is the place to go for a fun and relaxing evening among friends. Have a drink in the full bar or relax over your meal in the

One of the Steinhatchee Landing Houses set on the Water

outside dining area where you can watch the boats coming in. The menu includes locally caught fresh fish and a variety of other dishes. $$

Where to Stay

Steinhatchee Landing Resort *203 Ryland Circle, Steinhatchee, FL 32359 (352) 498-3513* At Steinhatchee Landing accommodations consists of private cottages, nestled in the trees, close to the river. From the outside they look quaint and cute in Victorian or Florida Cracker style, though inside they have everything you'd need. Cottages range from one to four bedrooms and can sleep up to 14 guests. They have fully equipped kitchens, washer and dryer, screened porches with views, linens and towels, and TVs with DVD players. Fifteen of the cottages are pet friendly (up to 28 pounds). Some of the cottages are specially set aside as Honeymoon Cottages, perfect for celebrating your honeymoon or anniversary. $$

Bay Street Mobile is a step-up from the motel, perfect for a family it sleeps up to eight and features a full kitchen and everything you'd need for self-catering. Prices start at $120 per night. The River Haven Cottage is a little different; set right on the river you can watch the boats come and go from your private verandah. It sleeps up to six and starts at $125 per night.

Finally, the **River View House** is a 3,500 sq ft home with four bedrooms, three baths, game room and a private swimming pool. Prices start at $300 per night.

River Haven Marina and Motel *1110 River Side Drive,*

Steinhatchee Landing

Steinhatchee, FL 32359 (352) 498-0709 The River Haven Marina has a couple different options for accommodations also, including their simple but comfortable motel rooms, decorated in tropical Florida and nautical themes. Rooms start at $60 per night.

Sea Hag Marina *322 Riverside Drive, Steinhatchee, FL 32359 (352) 498-3008* The Sea Hag Marina also has a wide variety of lodging including renovated motel rooms that they fondly call "Shacks," plus five units that are directly across the street from the marina. Capacities vary from 4 to 15 people.

Good Times Motel and Marina *7022 Hwy 358 SW, Steinhatchee, FL 32359 (352) 498-8088* This quaint hotel looks like it's stuck in the past but the rooms are spacious, clean and comfortable and the service is always top class. Some rooms have kitchenettes. $

Canoeing on the Steinhatchee River

Cross City

KCTY

CTAF/UNICOM ©122.8

®JAX CENTER App/Dep 127.8

Airport Manager Phone
(352) 498-6656

Elevation 42' MSL	Traffic Pattern 1000' MSL (958'AGL)	Flight Service Station GAINESVILLE 122.1R 112.0T

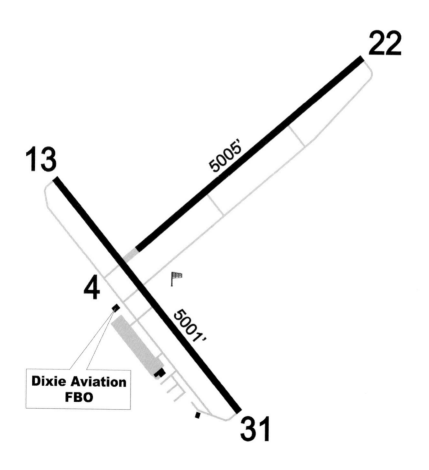

22

13

5005'

4

5001'

31

Dixie Aviation
FBO

Stuart

"The Sailfish Capitol of the World" caters to fishermen and beach-lovers alike. They also have a must-see auto/boat/baseball+art museum right next to the beach. If you really want to get in the spirit of the Treasure Coast, you can always try a little wreck diving.

One of the first recorded mentions of the Stuart area was in 1832 when an infamous pirate, Pedro Gilbert, used the coastal sandbar as a base for raids on passing ships. Even today, the island along the coast is known as Gilbert's Bar.

As a town, it was first settled in 1870, and within a few years, there was a rescue station set up just outside of town. You can still visit that site as the House of Refuge Museum.

The town has declared itself to be the **Sailfish Capitol of the World** due to the amazing population of these huge fish offshore. People come from around the country for the sport fishing around Stuart. But there are also some impressive boat cruises, including one aboard an old wooden sailing schooner that will make you feel like you've gone back in time.

Fishing

Flying There

There are no other controlled airports in the vicinity of Stuart.

Pilots should avoid a pair of antennas up to 1,548 feet MSL located 10 nm west of the airport, and another antenna 9 nm south up to 1,038 feet MSL. Avoid loitering around the nuclear power plant on the barrier island 10 north of Stuart.

The tower operates from 7 a.m. to 8 p.m. Stuart doesn't have any large flight schools based on the field, and caters mainly to business and private flights. Both of the FBOs on the field offer typical jet-center amenities and full-service 100LL and Jet A fuel.

Atlantic Aviation occupies the central/western portion of the ramp. Courtesy cars and shuttle, with Hertz rentals on site. Fueling hours 6 a.m. to 10 p.m. Radio 130.85 or call *(772) 781-4720*.

Stuart Jet Center is on the east end of the ramp and offers courtesy cars, a shuttle, and Hertz rentals from 6 a.m. to 10 p.m. Call *(772) 288-6700*.

Getting Around

Hertz *(772) 283-9627*

and **Avis** *(772) 283-9627* have rental cars available at the airport. If you don't really need a whole car all to yourself, you can grab a taxi with **Paradise Cab** *(772) 781-8088* for a few trips around Stuart.

Martin County Transit Service has public bus service around Stuart though it's really just one route that goes around town (coming about a block away from the airport). Bus service isn't really practical since the nearest bus stop is a 40 minute walk from Stuart Jet Center. Fares are $1.50

Walking Distance Activities

Witham Field is adjacent to the commercial part of Stuart. There are no restaurants on the field. The closest walking distance restaurant is **Taqueria Los Mexicanos**, *2425 SE Bonita Street, Stuart, FL 34997* which is a 20 minute walk south of the Stuart Jet Center. They serve authentic Mexican food with in-house made taco shells.

What to See and Do

Elliott Museum *825 Northeast Ocean Boulevard, Stuart, FL 34996 (772) 225-1961* It is worth flying in for the day just to visit this museum, which is a 20 minute drive to the barrier island from the FBO. Their new building opened in 2013 and they have an eclectic mix of vintage cars, baseball collectibles, and local nautical history. The real star of their collection is actually the three-story high mechanized car delivery system. The cars are held in an enormous glass "vending machine." Choose which car you want to see,

Elliott Museum; "Auto Vending Machine" can be seen in the Background

perhaps their 1914 Packard, or the 1926 Bugatti T-35 racer, and an elevator system picks out that car and brings it down to the viewing area for you to examine. The Elliott Museum has one of the largest collections of historic Ford Model A and Model AA commercial vehicles in the world. They also have an early seaplane on display. To keep things fresh, the museum has rotating fine art shows. The museum is open seven days a week until 5 p.m., and tickets are $14 with discounts for members of the military. There is a little cafe in the museum for a snack or a light lunch.

The House of Refuge Museum *301 SE MacArthur Blvd., Stuart, FL 34996 772-225-1875* Out on the barrier island is the House of Refuge Museum, commemorating local history when there were stations placed along the coast to help shipwrecked sailors. The tower is still standing, and the museum has exhibits and artifacts from more than 100 years ago when

the station was still running. It provides an interesting look at some local nautical history, and the views are breathtaking from the point. There is a good wreck site not far from the museum, where an Italian barkentine Georges Valentine went down. If you're into scuba diving, check it out. The museum is open 7 days a week, and the admission is $8 with discounts for seniors and military.

The Riverwalk *SW St. Lucie Ave., Stuart, FL 34994* The Riverwalk is part of the busy, trendy part of Stuart, where you can follow the boardwalk to see the river as well as browse around through many little shops and boutiques. Several old historic buildings are along the way, and there are always boats going to and from the marina. The stage hosts musical events on most Sundays, like the popular Rockin' Riverwalk concerts. Also on Sundays is the Green Market near the City Hall building.

Collect Shells Along Bathtub Reef *1585 SE MacArthur*

Blvd, Stuart, FL As the name suggests, the water is really shallow out around the reef, so you can easily go wading even without a swimsuit. It's a bit of a round-about drive from the airport across Sewell's Point but it's still just 15 minutes by car. If you've gone to visit the House of Refuge, you're pretty much there already. The sand is just loaded with shells, and the clear water makes for amazing snorkeling if you want to explore even further.

Fishing Charters

Well, you can't come to the Sailfish Capital of the World and not get out on the waves to do a little fishing.

To get at those really big sport fish, go out with **Off the Chain Charters** *3585 SE Saint Lucie Blvd., Stuart, FL 34997 (772) 285-1055* Even a fishing novice will have the chance to bring in a wahoo, tuna, or a huge trophy sailfish. It's not a pleasure cruise, it's a real sportsman's trip. **The Lady Stuart I Deep Sea Fishing Charter** *555 NE Ocean Blvd., Stuart, FL 34996 (772) 286-1860* can take you out on their comfortable 65-foot cruiser in small groups, to cast for snapper, trigger fish and sea bass. You might see a few dolphins while you're out.

Boating Tours

You don't necessarily have to go fishing to enjoy the coast and all the great sights on the water. **Treasure Coast Sailing Adventures** *121 SW Flagler Ave., Stuart, FL 34994 (772) 267-7076* is one great example. Get aboard a historic wooden sailing schooner to see the coast in style. The classic

three-masted ship is a sight all on its own, and it's an exciting way to see the river. Or take a popular eco-tour with **Sunshine Wildlife** *(772) 219-0148* to see the birds and wildlife in Indian River Lagoon. It's a little farther south than the rest of Stuart, but still only 10 minutes from Witham Field.

Where to Eat

District Table and Bar *900 SE Indian St., Stuart, FL 34994 (772) 324-8357* Only a few minutes drive from the airport, you can sit down to an elegant meal at the District Table and Bar. They use lots of locally grown farm-fresh ingredients and they keep the menu creative and tuned to the seasons. The cuisine is heavy on the seafood with a classic Southern twist. They're closed Mondays, and only open in the evenings for dinner. $$$

Anthony's Coal Fired Pizza *2343 SE Federal Hwy., Stuart, FL 34994 (772) 287-7741* In the shopping plaza near the airport is one of the finest pizza places in Stuart. Everything is fresh and home-made, putting it well above the usual chain pizza joints. Come here for classic pizzas baked fresh in the coal-fired oven. Try their ribs, wings or salads too on the side. They're open for lunch as well as dinner. $$

Chef's Table *2313 SE Ocean Blvd., Stuart, FL 34996 (772) 287-5599* Head around the airport to the north for about five minutes by car, and you're there. The menu is classic American fare but it's served with a gourmet French style twist. There is a nice outdoor patio for dining, and you probably should make a

reservation. Their hours are a little irregular but they're open for dinner on most nights but closed Sundays. $$

Where to Stay

Inn Shepard's Park B&B *601 Southwest Ocean Boulevard, Stuart, FL 34994 (772) 781-4244* Less than 10 minutes by car from the airport, this quaint B&B is situated right on the shores for some lovely river views and is in the heart of the historic downtown. Enjoy your breakfast out in the cheerful enclosed veranda and get a good start to your day in Stuart. Maybe stroll a few blocks to check out the Riverwalk. The entire inn only has four rooms, so know it will be quiet and private, and there is Wi-Fi in the rooms too. Three of the rooms have ensuite bathrooms while the fourth has a private bathroom just down the hall. The inn offers kayaks, bicycles, beach gear and coolers for your use, at no charge. $

Marriott Beach Resort and Marina *555 NE Ocean Boulevard, Stuart, FL 34996 (772) 225-3700* If you are planning a visit that involves beaches and the sights out on the islands, you should book your room at the Marriott Beach Resort. Also ten minutes from the airport, you can be relaxing in your room in no time. It's a quiet beach location, far from the busy noise of downtown. As the name says, it's a complete resort so you'll get a fitness center, swimming pool, on site restaurants and bar, Wi-Fi and access to the private stretch of beach. Several fishing charters operate out of the marina here as well. $$

Witham Field; *Stuart*

TOWER ©**126.6**
(0700-2000)

Ground Control **121.7**

Control Tower Phone
(772) 221-0109

Airport Manager Phone
(772) 221-2374

AWOS–3 134.475 (772) 692–7399
ATIS 134.475 [AWOS is broadcast over ATIS when tower is closed]

®PALM BEACH App/Dep 128.3

Elevation 16' MSL	Traffic Pattern 1000' MSL (984'AGL)	Flight Service Station 800-WX-BRIEF

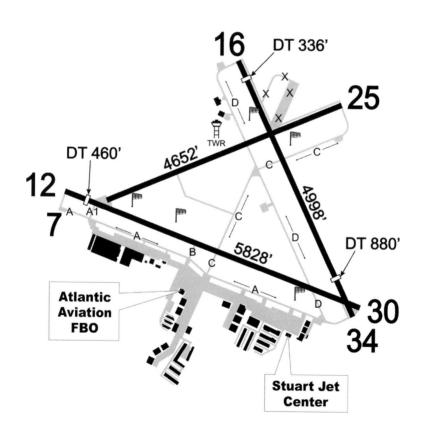

Atlantic Aviation FBO

Stuart Jet Center

Sugarloaf Shores

Sugarloaf Key is one of the lower Florida Keys, 14 miles east of the far more famous Key West. The Sugarloaf Shores Airport is a private airstrip specifically for the Sugarloaf Lodge on Sugarloaf Key.

S ome people come to stay at Sugarloaf Key for better prices and smaller crowds, while still having very easy access to the sights of Key West. The fact is there is plenty to do right on Sugarloaf Key, and the Sugarloaf Lodge is a central hub for the island's activities. Boating, fishing, skydiving, biking and scuba diving are just a few things that can fill your time at the Sugarloaf Lodge.

The style of the lodge will remind you of the old-fashioned hotels of the 60s with retro decor and a vintage look. There is pleasant nostalgia that comes from staying at the Sugarloaf Lodge, but don't worry it's fully modernized with flat-screen TVs and free Wi-Fi. You'll be comfortable no matter how long you stay.

Sugarloaf Key has also been the location of a few movies. In the James Bond movie, *Licensed to Kill,* Sugarloaf doubled for "Cray Cay" in the Bahamas. In the movie *Drop Zone* featuring Wesley Snipes, the airport was the base of operations for the protagonists.

Tiki Bar at the Sugarloaf Lodge

Flying There

Sugarloaf Key is 11 nm northeast of Key West International. Sugarloaf is especially close to the R-2916 Restricted Area, which contains an unmarked, tethered balloon flying up to 14,000 feet. Key West Naval Air Station's Class D airspace lies just a few miles to the west.

Approaches from all directions except the east are over water, and most airway arrivals from the north require crossing the Contiguous United States Air Defense Identification Zone. See "Flying There" under Key West KEYW and/or Marathon KMTH for information and special considerations for flying to the area.

Only the middle twenty feet of the 2,700-foot runway is

paved. The rest is gravel.

The airport is privately owned by the Sugar Loaf Lodge and operated by Skydive Key West. Use of the airport by all other aircraft is limited to registered overnight guests by prior arrangement only. Any guests flying in must receive approval in advance from the skydiving operator in order to deconflict arrivals with jumping operations. Call the lodge at *(305) 745-3211* for reservations and additional airport information.

Getting Around

Walking to the Sugarloaf Lodge from the airport takes about 10 minutes, although if you called the front desk they would most likely pick you up.

If you don't plan on leaving the hotel, then you can probably manage your entire stay on foot. But there are rental cars available if you need to have a vehicle to get out around the keys. **Enterprise** *(877) 410-7393* serves Sugarloaf Key, and you can also arrange a car from the Key West locations of **Thrifty** *(877) 539-5085* or **Hertz** *(305) 294-1039*. Just need an occasional lift?

We-Cycle *(305) 292-3336* has a bike rental program on the Key, and they will deliver a rental bike right to your room for just $10 per day. It's a laid-back and peaceful way to see the rest of the Key, or head down the bike paths along the main highway to check out the other islands at your own self-powered pace.

Things to See and Do at the Lodge

The Sugarloaf Lodge *17001 Overseas Hwy, Sugarloaf Key, FL 33042 (305) 745-* *3211* is the main location for accommodations, activities and dining on this island.

The lodge has a swimming pool and tennis court if you want a little diversion right at home. Every week they run painting classes and yoga sessions too, for a quieter chance to wind down after all your sightseeing. But the bigger activities are found next door at the marina.

Fishing Charters

The Sugarloaf Marina *(305) 745-3135* is next to the lodge, and that's where you'll find all the water sports and activities you could want. The staff at the lodge can help you get everything arranged and organized.

You can head out on your own to explore Sugarloaf Key in a rented kayak, or arrange some charter fishing tours. **Wayward Charters** *(305) 872-0290* has tours for light fishing as well as the more serious game fishing for big trophies. Tarpon and bonefish are the usual culprits. No fishing experience required. **Captain Tim Carlile** *(305) 304-4834* is another choice for the big fish, like barracuda, sharks and sea trout. He also knows where to find the really big snappers.

That's not all. **Double J Charters** *(305) 304-7923* are deep sea specialists that have half-day or full day trips on their schedule to go farther out for bigger fish like cobia or grouper.

At the end of your day, grab a beer at the marina and chat with the locals about the day's fishing. Maybe even show off your catch.

Fishing isn't the only thing the marina can help you organize. The Looe Key Reef is just minutes away, and you'll find some impressive reef and wreck diving there. The reef is 800 yards long, and full of coral and shoals of tropical fish. See how many of the 150 species of fish you can spot. No shell collecting though (it's part of a marine sanctuary, so look but don't touch). In addition to the natural splendor of the reef, the 210-foot long Adolphus Busch was sunk there to add some wreck interest for divers.

Skydiving

One last nearby activity you really need to know about, is the **Skydive Key West** *(305) 745-4386* located at the Sugarloaf Shores Airport where you parked your airplane. Now, don't let the name throw you, the drop zone is actually on Sugarloaf Key not Key West. Words can't describe the feeling of leaping out of a plane from more than two miles in the air, and then falling to the ground for more than five minutes. It's the perfect adventure for a pilot. No experience necessary for a safe but thrilling tandem drop. Cost per dive is $264 (with a discount if you pay in cash).

The Rest of the Keys

If you're out exploring Sugarloaf Key, take a drive down to the mangrove swamps of **Saddlebunch Keys.** It's only 15 minutes away from the lodge, and a great bit of natural landscape. Some of the best wilderness kayaking can be found around here, even just launching your boat by the side of the road.

Still want to check out more

of the Keys? You can be in Key West in under half an hour by car, which is a fantastic way to spend the day without having to actually stay in Key West (the Sugarloaf Key is much more peaceful). Around Key West you can visit the Ernest Hemingway Museum, the Little White House, the butterfly conservatory and Smathers Beach. Or just tour around the island and soak up the wacky lifestyle that Key West seems to thrive on. If you're on Key West at sunset, plan on being around Mallory Square for the island's biggest party.

A short boat trip to the north of Sugarloaf Key will bring you to the **Great White Heron Natural Wildlife Reserve.** The great white heron is extremely rare, and you can see flocks of them on this protected island. It's a beautiful place to see truly untouched wilderness, and you'll need a charter or a rental boat to get out there. Contact the headquarters for the park on Big Pine Key *(305) 872-2239* for more details.

Accommodations

Of course, the rooms and suites are part of your stay at the lodge too. As we've said, the style at the lodge is cute vintage with a Hawaiian touch. All the rooms have private balconies or patios, and they all overlook the water of Lower Sugarloaf Sound. The Lodge is really a bit of old Florida in the Florida Keys. The rooms come in single, double and king size but they are all quite spacious and comfortable. There are fridges in every room so you can keep a few cold drinks handy. If you

need to stay connected during your stay, there is free Wi-Fi too. Rooms start around $120 per night.

Dining and Drinking

The lodge has its own restaurant serving a limited breakfast menu, and pizzas, salad and subs for lunch and dinner. Closed Monday. There is also a busy Tiki Bar on the premises. People from around the Key come to the Tiki for music and drinks every night, it's definitely not just for lodge guests. Live music, a full bar and trivia contests keep the party going until 11 p.m. every night of the week.

Outside the lodge, there are several restaurants you can check out on Sugarloaf Key or on the neighboring Keys. A short drive in either direction along the main Overseas Highway will bring two really good choices to start with.

Two miles to the west is

a new restaurant called **Fish** *3100 Overseas Hwy., Key West FL 33040 (305) 735-4201.* It replaced the very popular Kaya Island Eats, whose owners moved that restaurant to Miami. The early reviews of Fish have been good. They've got a cute patio, and the atmosphere is fun and casual. $$

And about the same distance to the east is **Mangrove Mama's** *19991 Overseas Hwy., Summerland Key, FL 33042 (305) 745-3030* Open from breakfast through dinner, they have a menu of seafood like mahi mahi tacos, crab cake sandwiches, seafood quesadillas and broiled lobster. $$

Both of these restaurants are about five minutes from the lodge by car, and are both around a mid-range for the budget. Note the **Bay Point Market** *(305) 745-3882* is happy to deliver snacks and groceries right to your room door at the lodge.

Retro-feel Room at the Lodge

Sugarloaf Shores

7FA1

CTAF/UNICOM ©122.8

Airport Manager Phone
[305] 745-4386

ASOS at EYW [11 nm SW]: 119.65
[305] 292-4046

Elevation	Traffic Pattern	Flight Service Station
4' MSL	800' MSL [796'AGL]	800-WX-BRIEF

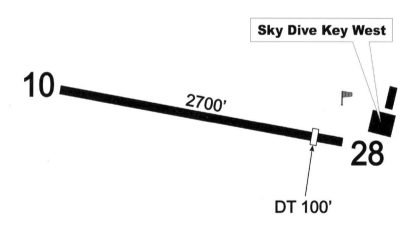

Sky Dive Key West

10

2700'

28

DT 100'

Suwannee River

The reason to fly here is for a true back-to-nature adventure just 15 minutes from the airport. Suwannee River State Park is one of Florida's hidden treasures. It has some of the best back-country canoeing in Florida. Other wilderness areas nearby let you snorkel spring fed ponds or dive sinkholes. Hiking and canoeing are waiting for you all along the Suwannee River.

The town of Live Oak was founded just before the Civil War as a community that sprung up at a junction of two main rail lines. Not surprisingly, there was once a huge oak tree at that point, and that led to the town's name which has stuck ever since. It's not a busy metropolis today by any means, but a very pleasant little city with a quiet small-town attitude.

It's near the northern edge of the state, on the highway between the larger cities of Tallahassee and Jacksonville. Tourists often come through Live Oak as they cross the state, but not everyone knows about the great destinations in the area.

For sights to see, the main one around Live Oak is the big Suwannee River State Park to the west of town. You can easily spend a day or more there, doing all the hiking, canoeing, bird-watching and fishing your heart desires.

Suwannee River State Park

The Suwannee River holds some special meaning to Floridians, as the river is in the opening lyrics of the state song "Old Folks at Home." If you ever wanted to see the real "Suwannee River" for yourself, now's your chance. For a little more Suwannee history, you can see what's on display at the Suwannee Historical Museum right downtown.

Flying There

Suwannee County Airport lies below the Live Oak Military Operations Area, which begins at 8,000 feet MSL. Contact Gainesville Radio on 122.2 for current information on the status of military activities and be alert for high-speed military aircraft operating at low altitudes in the area along charted Military Training Routes. No other airspace or terrain complicates the arrival into 24J.

Runway 25 has a right-hand traffic pattern.

The county-run FBO is open 8 a.m. to 5 p.m. Monday through Friday. No crew cars are available. Self-serve 100LL is available 24/7, as are the restrooms. The code for the restroom door is "12345." Phone number for the FBO is *(386) 362-4200.*

Getting Around

There aren't any car rental outlets at the airport, but there is an **Enterprise** *418 Howard Street W. (386) 364-1515* and a **Hertz** *500 Howard Street W. (386) 219-0347* right in downtown Live Oak. You can also just call a cab from **Gainesville Cab Company** *(352) 371-1515,* they have cars and service around Live Oak too.

Walking Distance Activities

You can reach the outskirts of Live Oak in about 30 minutes walking from the airport and you'll begin seeing places to eat along the main street, Highway 90. **Jay's Family Restaurant** *743 US-90, Live Oak, FL (386) 362-3534* is the first place you'll come to. Their American cuisine has Southern

Divers in Little River Springs

influences and the restaurant has a slightly retro feel. If this doesn't appeal, walk a few more blocks and you'll come across numerous other places to eat.

What to See and Do

Suwannee River State Park *20185 County Road 132, Live Oak, FL 32060 (386) 362-2746* The main attraction near the Suwannee Airport is the big natural area to the northwest, the Suwannee River State Park. It's under 15 minutes by car from the airport.

The park is filled with a whole range of wild landscapes to enjoy, with thick cypress forests along the river and trails running for miles. Watch the water for herons, or climb up the raw stone outcroppings to take in the wider views. Overall, there are five different trail routes, with short 1/4 mile paths to much longer 18 mile trails.

During your walks, you can even see some unique aspects of history in the park. Along the river, there are man-made mounds that were built up as fortifications during the Civil

War. There are also some ruins of a beached 19th century steamboat, and one of the oldest cemeteries in the state. Not too many nature parks offer so many historical points of interest in addition to all the landscapes.

If you want to see the river from the water, the easy flowing river is perfect for canoeing. The park itself doesn't offer canoe rentals, but you can give **Suwannee Canoe Outpost** *(368) 364-4991* a call and arrange a rental with them. They'll meet with you at many points along the river and bring you a canoe.

Fishing is allowed at the park too, as long as you have a Florida fishing license. You'll need to pack your own gear and you can cast from the shore or canoe for catfish, panfish and bass. Other facilities at the park include several places for drinking water and washrooms. Entrance to the park costs $5 per vehicle (with up to eight passengers) and access is open to visitors 365 days a year. The park opens at 8 a.m., and closes at sundown.

Wes Skiles Peacock Springs State Park *18081 185th Road, Live Oak, FL 32060 (386) 776-2194* The Suwannee River Park isn't the only natural area around Live Oaks. About a half hour drive to the south will bring you to the Wes Skiles Peacock Springs State Park. Deep sinkholes and spring-fed ponds bring snorkelers and divers from around the state to explore the underwater landscapes. You'll need cave diving certification for some of the sinkholes (yes, they'll check), but Orange Grove Sink is open enough for any level of diver as well as swimmers. You can also enjoy the park on foot, and walk on the trails to see all the springs from dry land. The park entrance fee is $4 per vehicle.

Spirit of the Suwannee Music Park *3076 95th Drive, Live Oak, FL 32060 (386) 364-1683* Located at a different point along the river than the main nature reserve, this is a music and arts camping park that holds a variety of fun events through the year. There isn't always something happening, but you can watch their schedule to see what's coming up. Music concerts, heritage farm days, holiday light celebrations and more are typical events on the calendar.

Even when there are no events, there are things to see and do at the Spirit of the Suwannee. There is also a woodsy village of craft shops where you can browse some locally-made handicrafts, some nature trails with horseback riding, and the **Boatright Barn Museum** of vintage farming tools.

Canoeing in Suwannee River

Where to Eat

The Brown Lantern *417 Howard St E., Live Oak, FL 32064 (386) 362-1133* Just a couple of blocks past the center of town, the Brown Lantern may look like the local pub on the inside but their menu offers plenty of seafood comfort foods. Grilled fish and rice, fried shrimp sandwiches and BBQ chicken salad are some of the local favorites. You can stop at the Brown Lantern for lunch or dinner, but only on weekdays. They're closed Saturday and Sunday. $$

All Decked Out Cafe *1040 Duval St NE, Live Oak, FL 32064 (386) 362-7752* You'll have to cross town to get there, but the All Decked Out Cafe serves some of the best home-cooked meals in Live Oak.

There is a lot of seafood, like the huge portions of grilled snapper or bay scallops, but the side dishes of fried green tomatoes are a truly Southern touch. And like the name says, there is a nice covered deck outside with picnic tables. Open until 9 p.m., but closed on Sunday and Monday. $$

The 406 *406 Duval St NE, Live Oak, FL 32064 (386) 219-0536* Live Oak has a number of restaurants offering "Country Cooking," and fast food, but if you are looking for something a little more refined try the 406. It is located in the historic Thomas Dowling House. The chefs cook on a wood fire grill with pecan wood. Very fresh seafood with clams from Cedar Key and outstanding steaks.

If you don't want to drive

back to Live Oak from the park to eat, you can bring supplies of your own for a picnic. There are tables and pavilions for eating at the Suwannee River Park, and you can shop for some basic groceries at **Pepe's Grocery** just inside of town at *965 Howard St, Live Oak, FL 32064 (386) 362-2111.*

Where to Stay

Cabins at Suwannee River There are some lovely rustic cabins right in the Suwannee River Park that you can rent for a night or two, for some comfortable wilderness accommodations. Located right on the main hiking trail, these little cottages are spacious enough for six people and have central heat and cooling. Sit out on the screened porch at the end of the day and watch night fall over the forest. You will need to reserve your cabin several months ahead of time, and the rates are $100 per night. Linens and kitchenette utensils are all included. To enhance the relaxation, televisions and phones are not provided. Reservations may be made up to 11 months in advance through **Reserve America** *(800) 326-3521.*

Quality Inn Live Oak *6819 US 129, Live Oak, FL 32060 (855) 849-1513* If you're not staying at the park, you can head up just north of Live Oak for a few other accommodations like the Quality Inn. You can get complimentary breakfast in the morning, and they have a full restaurant for meals later in the day too. Gym, swimming pool and business center are a few of the other amenities you can take advantage of during your stay. The rooms are large, and you can get even more space with a suite. $$

Holiday Inn Express Live Oak *6694 US 129 North, Live Oak, FL 32060 (877) 859-5095*

Also located north of town, the Holiday Inn Express has clean and comfortable rooms with Wi-Fi service throughout. There's a complimentary hot breakfast bar, a gym and a business center with Internet access. The swimming pool also has a lovely hot tub for some extra unwinding. $$

Suwannee County · 24J

CTAF/UNICOM ©**122.8**   AWOS–3 118.225 [386] 362–1731

Airport Manager Phone
[386] 362-3004

Elevation 104' MSL	Traffic Pattern 1300' MSL [1196'AGL]	Flight Service Station 800-WX-BRIEF

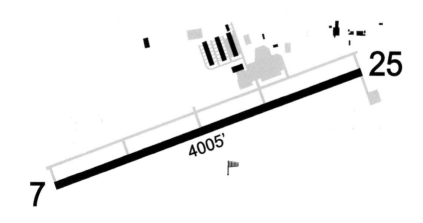

25

4005'

7

Tampa

Tampa is one of the big tourist hubs in Florida, with more attractions at your fingertips than you can list. The airport is close to Amalie Arena, Tampa Convention Center and Raymond James Stadium. In the spring, see the New York Yankees at George M. Steinbrenner Field.

On the west coast of Florida, the city of Tampa is world-class travel destination regardless of what you're interested in. There are amusement parks, zoos, art galleries, nature parks and everything in between.

Located on **David Island** only minutes from Downtown Tampa, Peter O'Knight Airport is a convenient choice for pilots wishing to visit the downtown core, its museums, theaters and entertainment. The airport is just two miles from the **Tampa Convention Center** and **Amalie Arena,** home to the **Tampa Bay Lightning** of the National Hockey League and the **Tampa Bay Storm** of the Arena Football League. The airport is just eight miles from **Raymond James Stadium,** where the **Tampa Bay Buccaneers** play.

Peter O'Knight Airport is adjacent to **Ybor City,** the National Historic Landmark District of Tampa. In 2008, Ybor City's 7th Avenue, was recognized as one of the "10 Great Streets in America" by

Downtown Tampa with Peter O. Knight Airport in the Background

the American Planning Association. For a night on the town, Friday and Saturday evenings are the best, with many places offering live music. The Saturday morning market is popular with lots of local vendors selling a variety of goods.

Flying There

Tampa's first city airport was Peter O. Knight Airport and the main runway was the waters of Tampa Bay for all the seaplanes. There was a classy (long gone) two story terminal, and now the bay is filled with sailboats instead of seaplanes.

TPF is an uncontrolled air-port hemmed in by the Tampa International Class B surface area to the northwest, **MacDill Air Force Base** to the southwest, and a Class B "shelf" at 1,200 feet MSL overhead. The safest plan for arrival is to establish radio contact with Tampa Approach and get clearance to transition the airspace.

Pilots arriving from the southeast must be alert for a cluster of towers reaching over 1,600 feet MSL. Also watch out for large oceangoing ships in the channel east of the airport. A hospital helipad is located one mile north of the field, and traffic there uses radio frequency 122.825. Taxiway E is closed to aircraft with wingspans over 40 feet.

Runways 4 and 36 have right-hand traffic patterns to avoid flight over the residential areas northwest of the airport.

Atlas Aviation is the FBO, located on the south side of the field between the two runways. Services are available from 7 a.m. to 7 p.m. Courtesy cars and **Hertz** rentals available. Call *(813) 251-1752.*

Ybor City

Getting Around

The Hillsborough Area Regional Transit (HART) runs the city's transit system, and there is a good network of buses, heritage street cars and trolley replicas that will take you anywhere in Tampa. Route 9 comes to the north end of Davis Island and will take you to the Marion Transfer Center where you can transfer onto any of the other main routes. Cash fares are $2. For door to door service try the **Yellow Cab Company** *(813) 253-0121.* The standard cab rate to downtown is $25.

Hertz rental cars are available at FBO Atlas Aviation.

Walking Distance Activities

Though located just a short distance south of downtown Tampa, Peter O'Knight is located on **Davis Island** and connected to the mainland via several bridges. A walk into downtown or to the **Florida Aquarium** would take over an hour, while driving from the airport should take around 10 minutes. Adjacent to the airport is a dog beach and park if you traveled with your canine companion, and if you want a bite to eat without heading

into downtown, the Anchor Bar or a Subway restaurant is about 30 minute walk.

What to See and Do

Ybor City is the historic Latin quarter and former center of cigar manufacturing, Ybor City has been designated a National Historic Landmark. With buildings dating to the 1800s, the unique architecture with Spanish tiles and wrought iron balconies looks much like it did when it was built. By day you can enjoy lunching, shopping, cigar shopping and Cuban coffee. At night the city turns into a hot spot where just about anything goes. 7th Avenue is the main street. Start your tour with a visit to the **Cigar Museum and Visitor Center** to learn a little Ybor City history and pick up a map. Be sure to see the **Ybor City State Museum** *1818 Ninth Avenue, Tampa, FL 33605 (813) 247-1434* Along with the history the museum features a tiny fully furnished **Cigar Worker's House,** so you can see how the cigar rollers lived in the late 1800s. Be sure to have a meal at the legendary **Columbia Restaurant** (see "where to eat" below).

The Florida Aquarium

701 Channelside Dr., Tampa, FL 33602 813-273-4000 The Florida Aquarium is a huge marine facility, with a lot more than just the usual tanks of tropical fish. A coral reef can show you a whole new underwater world, or you can stay on land with the wetlands trails. For something a little more daring, take a scuba dive in a tank of sharks (not for scuba novices though). Daily dolphin cruises depart from the aquarium as well. General admission for the aquarium is $24 for adults, with discounts for kids and seniors. Ten minutes from the airport.

Tampa Theatre *711 N. Franklin Street, Tampa, FL 33602 (813) 274-8981* This beautifully restored 1926 movie palace is on the National Register of Historic Places and still plays its Wurlitzer organ before shows. Good for a cozy date night. Arrive early enough to have a wander through the spectacular lobby and balconies with a glass of wine in hand. In addition to movies, they occasionally have live performances.

Wat Mongkolrata Temple, *5306 Palm River Road, Tampa, FL 33619 (813) 621-1669* A fifteen minute drive from the airport, This Buddhist Temple is exquisite and the riverside setting is lovely as well. If you prefer a serene meditative experience, weekday mornings are best. Many people go on Sundays because of the open market. Market hours are every Sunday between approximately 9:30 a.m. and 1 p.m. The market includes a wide variety of Thai food (seasoned to your taste). Cash only. $

CineBistro at Hyde Park Village *Hyde Park, Tampa, FL 33606 (813) 514-8300* A unique and very popular movie and dining experience that is a 10 minute drive from the airport. This is a movie theatre for grown-ups with beer, wine and cocktails, gourmet foods and big comfortable leather chairs with small tables to eat on during the movie. Fun to go on a date night. $$

New York Yankees Baseball is just a 25 minute drive from the airport. Every March the Yankees come to **George M. Steinbrenner Field** to play their spring training games. The dimensions of the field precisely mimic the old Yankee Stadium, and the scalloped grandstand facade is also meant to invoke the spirit of the old ballpark in the Bronx. For 2016 the NY Yankees are scheduled to play the Phillies, Nationals, Rays, Red Sox, Braves, Tigers, Blue Jays, and Astros. When spring training is over, the Tampa Yankees, a Class A Advanced affiliate of the NY Yankees, plays in the park.

Lowry Park Zoo *1101 W Sligh Ave., Tampa, FL 33604 (813) 935-8552* For the animal lover, the Lowry Park Zoo is home to more than 1,000 animals as well as a fun collection

of amusement park rides. It was recognized as the #1 Zoo in the U.S. by Parents Magazine (2009). Spend the afternoon seeing the wildlife of the world on 56 acres of parkland exhibits. Regions of Africa, Australia and Asia are all there as well as several unique spots where you can see Florida wildlife

Museum of Science and Industry IMAX Dome Theater

up close. Tickets are $25 for adults, and they are open every day except Thanksgiving and Christmas. Twenty minutes from the airport.

Museum of Science and Industry *4801 E. Fowler Ave., Tampa, FL 33617 (813) 987-6000* If you want to continue the educational fun, MOSI is filled with interactive science and technology displays that will entertain the grandkids. There are more than 400 exhibits, as well as live presentations all through the day. The facility also holds the Saunders Planetarium as well as an IMAX Dome theater for some extraordinary film experience. Twenty five minutes from the airport.

Busch Gardens *10165 N Malcolm McKinley Dr., Tampa, FL 33612 (888) 800-5447* One of the top attractions in Tampa is the huge Busch Gardens theme park, a thirty minute drive from the airport.

Roller coasters and other thrill rides, along with animal attractions and live shows are spread out over more than 300 acres of African-themed fun. Thrill rides like the Cheetah Hunt, Falcon's Fury and SheiKra are just a few examples of your adrenaline-pumping choices. Every year in October, the Howl-o-Scream event makes Busch Gardens even more fun.

Tampa Museum of Art *120 W Gasparilla Plaza, Tampa, FL 33602 (813) 274-8130* Looking for a little artistic culture while in town? The Tampa Museum of Art has a beautiful collection of art and sculpture, ranging from ancient statuary to very modern art installations. Between the permanent collection and the many traveling exhibits, there is always something new to see. The gallery is open seven days a week, and tickets are $10 for adults. If you're staying for a while, you can get a coffee or a bite to eat at the museum's stylish Sono Cafe.

Beaches and Parks

Along the W. Courtney Campbell Causeway (between Tampa and Clearwater) is the Ben T. Davis Beach. It's across town a bit, but still an easy drive from Peter O'Knight if you want to spend some time on the coast. The beach on the tip of Davis Island, beside the airport, has some great views of the water if you don't mind sharing the space with dogs.

And if you prefer more inland sights, you can go across the city to the north to Trout Creek Park. It's a wilderness area criss-crossed with hiking trails and there are many places for fishing or kayaking.

Where to Eat

Thai Island Restaurant *210 East Davis Blvd., Tampa, FL* Right on Davis Island, this would be a fine choice for a handy meal after you first land and but since it is about a 40 minute walk from the airport you will want to drive. The cuisine is authentic Thai, and the atmosphere of the restaurant is beachy, relaxing and comfortable. The outdoor seating area is compact yet popular. The menu is loaded with curries and lots of vegetable and noodle dishes. $$

The Columbia Restaurant, *2117 E 7th Ave., Tampa, FL 33605 (813) 248-4961* A Ybor city fixture, the Columbia is Florida's oldest restaurant. While other Columbia locations have sprung up over the years, this is where it all started when co-owner Richard Gonzmart's great-grandfather founded it to feed local cigar-rollers in 1905. The stylish decor features Spanish tiles, fountains, and decorative wrought iron. Signature menu items include their "1905" Salad and their Paella "a la Valencia." Outstanding collection of Spanish wines (more than 1,000 different wines). This is

also the only location where they have a Flamenco show Mon-Sat at 7:00 and 9:30 p.m. ($6 cover charge). $$

Jackson's Bistro *601 S Harbour Island Blvd., Suite 100, Tampa, FL 33602 (813) 277-0112* Across the Seddon Channel on Harbour Island, Jackson's Bistro is also just a short drive from the airport. The restaurant features wonderful views of the water but reserve your table ahead of time if you'd like to sit on the patio. Seafood and sushi are on the menu. Open for lunch and dinner, and there is a brunch buffet on Sundays. $$

Zudar's Deli *201 W Platt St., Tampa, FL 33606 (813) 250-6272* For a quick and casual bite to eat, the sandwiches at Zudar's are legendary in Tampa. A big thick Reuben, hot bowl of chowder, or perhaps a Greek salad? If you are on your way to more sight-seeing, they do a very quick takeout too. $$

Al's Finger Licking Good BBQ *1609 Angel Oliva Senior St., Tampa, FL 33605 (813) 956-0675* Only five minutes drive from the Aquarium, Al's Finger Licking Good BBQ is the place to go for old-fashioned southern flavors. It is one of the top rated restaurants in Tampa and their pulled pork always ranks highly. Their mac n' cheese draws a line-up on Fridays! Look for the bright blue and yellow house with the homey patio chairs out on the porch. $

Where to Stay

Hampton Inn & Suites Tampa/Ybor City/Downtown *1301 E 7th Ave, Tampa, FL 33605 855-605-0317* Nice Hampton property at the west

end of Ybor City in Tampa so it is within walking distance to all of Ybor City's attractions. They also have a pre-scheduled courtesy shuttle will take you anywhere within a three-mile radius. (note KTPF is 6 miles away) Very close to downtown Tampa and only 1 block away from the trolley so it is very quick and easy to get to downtown Tampa.

Tampa Marriott Waterside Hotel and Marina *700 S Florida Ave., Tampa, FL 33602 813-221-4900* Just on the mainland from Davis Island is the Tampa Marriott Waterside, about a 10 minute drive from the airport. Being waterside there are lovely views from many of the large and clean rooms. The top-floor lounge provides even better views over the harbor as well as the rest of downtown Tampa. There is a restaurant on-site, as well as a pool and a full service spa. $$$

The Westin Tampa Harbour Island *725 S Harbour Island Blvd., Tampa, FL 33602 813-229-5000* On neighboring Harbour Island, the Westin is also very convenient to the airport. Pet friendly, the hotel has a fitness studio, pool and several restaurants, along with picture-perfect water and city views. $$$

Holiday Inn Express *2807 E Busch Blvd., Tampa, FL 33612 813-936-8200* For accommodations near the famous Busch Gardens, the Holiday Inn Express is right across the street from the theme park and offers a free shuttle for guests. Good, more affordable alternative if you don't want to stay in downtown Tampa and includes complimentary breakfast. $$

Peter O. Knight; *Tampa*   KTPF

CTAF/UNICOM ©122.725

Airport Manager Phone
[813] 807-8735

AWOS–3 118.925 [813] 251–6824

®TAMPA App/Dep 119.9

CLNC DEL 119.8

Elevation	Traffic Pattern	Flight Service Station
8' MSL	908' MSL (900'AGL)	800-WX-BRIEF

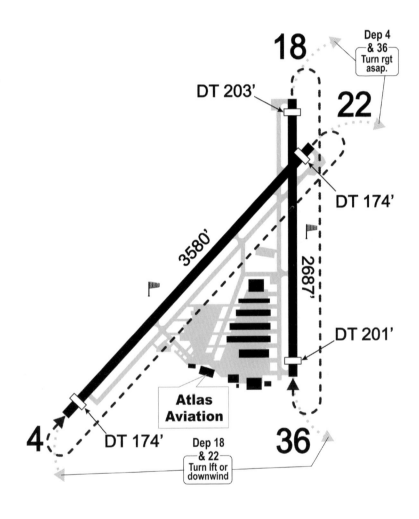

Not for navigation or inflight use | © 2017 Adventus Media LLC

Titusville

Titusville anchors the "Space Coast." KTIX is the closest airport to Kennedy Space Center. But you don't even have to leave the field to see the Warbird Museum.

As a destination, Titusville is a unique mix of fascinating technology and amazing nature. On the technology side there is the nearby **Kennedy Space Center Visitor Complex,** and the **Astronaut Museum.** Connect with nature on the beaches, at the **Merritt Island National Wildlife Refuge** and the **Canaveral National Seashore.** With two runways up to 7,319 feet long, anything you fly will land here.

Known as "Space City, USA," Titusville is your gateway to the Kennedy Space Center and many other related attractions. Next door to the Kennedy Space Center, Titusville is filled to the brim with aeronautical and astronomical attractions. For all flight-lovers, this is a very popular destination with unique sights to see.

Originally called Sand Point, the area was settled after the Seminole Wars, and the post office was founded in 1859. Then a developer named Henry Titus moved in and built the first hotel and saloon. The town was renamed after him when he won a bet

Wildcat at the Valiant Air Command Warbird Museum

on a game of dominoes. Later, one of the islands off the coast became a popular location for military missile testing, which eventually led to the creation of the space exploration complex that is here today. Though the shuttle program has been discontinued, the cape is still busy with launches and private SpaceX projects.

Of course, Titusville isn't only a destination for space fans though. It's a great little town that has a lot of American pride from the success of the space program, and you'll find many shops and services if you just go wandering around the downtown area. Several large conservation areas are outside the city to the west if you prefer some extra green space.

Flying There

The easiest way to get into Titusville is via the V 3 airway from either the north or south. The airway goes between Orlando's Class B to the west and the Restricted Areas over **Cape Canaveral** to the east. Arriving from the west under or through Orlando's airspace, watch out for the Bithlo Towers, which reach as high as 1,749 feet MSL.

Cape Canaveral is still the scene of frequent space

launches, which always create Temporary Flight Restrictions. Space shuttle hangars and launch towers are easily visible from the airway when weather permits.

The R-2935 Restricted Area overlies the entire area from 11,000 feet up to "unlimited," but specifically excludes the Victor Airways.

Atlas V Taking off at Cape Canaveral

Be alert for skydiving activity at the **Arthur Dunn Airpark** just outside TIX's Class D airspace to the north.

Space Coast Tower operates from 7 a.m. to 9 p.m.

Bristow Air Center is located midfield on the east ramp. They provide full-service 100LL and Jet A. Crew cars and rental cars available. Business hours are 7 a.m. to 7 p.m. on weekdays and 8 a.m. to 6 p.m. on weekends. Radio on UNICOM 122.95 or telephone *(321) 567-6000.* Call *(321) 427-7727* to request after-hour services.

Space Coast Jet Center on the west ramp has full-service 100LL and Jet A. Hours are 8 a.m. to 6 p.m. every day, and self-serve 100LL is available

24/7. They have a crew car, Avis rentals, and pilot supplies available. Telephone *(321) 267-8355* or call *(321) 960-1220* to arrange after-hours fueling.

Space Coast Regional is wedged between Orlando airspace to the west and warning areas and military airfields to the east. For pilots approaching from the north or south, flying Victor Airway V3 takes you right over the airport. If you are coming from the south and not flying the airway, all you really need to do is fly up the Indian River and hug its west bank to avoid the Restricted Area surrounding the Space Center. From the west, you'll be dealing with Orlando ATC.

Park at the FBOs. If you are planning to walk to the Warbird Museum, the Bristow Air Center is the closest.

Getting Around

There aren't any car rental outlets right at the airport, but there are **Avis** *(321)268-4467* and **Budget** *(321) 268-5415* locations in Titusville where you can reserve a car. They may

be able to meet you at the airport if you know when you'll be arriving.

Otherwise, you can just call a taxi. **River City Taxi** *(321) 268-1912* is less than 10 minutes from the airport, or the **Space Coast Shuttle Service** *(321) 383-1677* can get you where you need to go. There are public buses serving the Titusville downtown with **Space Coast Area Transit** *(321) 633-1878,* but there isn't any immediate access from the airport.

Walking Distance Activities

The airport is south of Titusville and the main part of town, but some of the best local attractions are within walking distance. **The Valiant Air Command,** the Warbird Museum, is about a 13 minute walk from the **Bristow Air Center.** However you can taxi right up to the museum ramp during their monthly Fly-In breakfast. They hold their Fly-In pancake breakfast for area pilots and passengers on the second Saturday of each month from 8 a.m. to 10:30 a.m. Breakfast and museum entrance is only $8.00.

It is just a half hour walk from the Bristow Air Center to the **American Police Hall of Fame and Museum.**

What to See and Do

Valiant Air Command Warbird Museum *6600 Tico Road, Titusville, FL 32780 (321) 268-1941* Right at the airport, this will probably be your first stop when you get to Titusville. Military aircraft from several eras are collected at the Warbird Museum, as well.

On outdoor display, you can stroll around and see an F14A Tomcat, OV-1D Mohawk, a German Messerschmitt and an A-7A Corsair II. Prefer helicopters? They have those in the collection too, like the UH-1 Huey and UH-19B Sikorsky Chickasaw. They also are busy restoring a TBM-3E Avenger and an F-105D Thunderchief, so you can watch for those two classic planes to be added to their exhibits in the future. For actual air time, the WWII C-47 "TiCo Belle" takes to the sky with visitors aboard. Contact the museum to schedule your own flight on this Normandy veteran.

The museum is open seven days a week, and regular admission is $20 with discounts for seniors, military and children. There is a very large gift shop where you can get some aviation-themed souvenirs.

U.S Astronaut Hall of Fame, *Cape Canaveral FL 32780 (321) 269- 6100* Formerly located near the airport, it has now moved just inside the entrance of the Kennedy Space Center Visitor Complex adjacent to its Rocket Garden making it the first building guests encounter. "Heroes and Legends, featuring the U.S. Astronaut Hall of Fame" brings to life the stories of America's pioneering astronauts by inviting guests to experience their missions through high-tech displays and special effects – including simulated holograms. The highlight of Heroes and Legends is a 3-D omnidirectional theater, designed to make guests feel as though they're floating in space. In the theater, images envelop visitors as Hall of Fame astro-

nauts, including Alan Shepard, John Glenn, Jim Lovell and Neil Armstrong, invite them to join in their historic space journeys. Some of the prior building's astronaut artifacts are also exhibited.

American Police Hall of Fame & Museum *6350 Horizon Dr., Titusville, FL 32780 (321) 264-0911* Dedicated to all officers who have fallen, there is a moving memorial inside the museum and plenty of stories to read as well as some unusual exhibits such as the electric chair and gas chamber, both of which you can sit on and go inside. Kids will enjoy getting to dress up in police uniforms and being locked in a cell. There's also a shooting center on-site that includes a state of the art gun range. They'll even let you shoot a H&K MP-5 machine gun for $40.00. If you are not a U.S. Citizen, you can still use the shooting center, but check their website for the rules. (http://www.aphf.org/) Admission is $13 for adults and free for law enforcement

officers.

Kennedy Space Center *State Road 405, Cape Canaveral, FL 32899 (866) 737-5235* The main attraction for Titusville is the Kennedy Space Center, where you can see many exhibits of vintage space craft, as well as the actual Atlantis space shuttle. Outdoor displays have all the early rockets, including the Atlas and Titan rockets. There is a simulator where you can feel what a shuttle launch was like, or just climb into one of the old Apollo capsules. If you've ever dreamed of flying into space, this might be the closest you get. It's less than a half hour's drive from the airport.

Overall, it's a pretty large facility so you should consider taking the bus tour to really get to see the entire grounds.

Kids in front of an Apollo Saturn rocket at the Kennedy Space Center

Admission to the center is $50 for adults, but there are more tickets to purchase if you want to have lunch with an astronaut or take the Cape Canaveral control center close-up tour. To really appreciate the Space Center and all its attractions you will need to allow yourself a full day here.

Enchanted Forest Sanctuary *444 Columbia Blvd., Titusville, FL 32780 (321) 264-5185* For a peaceful break from the space technology that dominates the attractions around Titusville, you can go for a nature walk through the Enchanted Forest Sanctuary. 10 minutes north of the airport, you can see lots of birds, big gopher tortoises and even some deer. There are miles of trails so you can really stretch your legs. The park is closed on Mondays, and there is a cute little gift shop on site.

Atlantis on Display at Kennedy Space Center

Where to Eat

Crackerjacks Seafood and Tiki Bar *2A Max Brewer Parkway, Titusville, FL 321-264-5065* This is a nice casual place right on the water with a Tiki bar located right beside the Max Brewer bridge in Titusville. GPS doesn't always find it, so keep your eyes open. Eclectic selection of imported and domestic beer on tap and bottle. Great service and excellent food.$$

Wild Ocean Seafood Market *688 S Park Ave., Titusville, FL 32796 (321) 269-1116* One of the best-rated restaurants in Titusville, the Seafood Market is located downtown and it feels like an open-air fish market. It is, in fact, a seafood market but it most certainly is a restaurant as well (even if it doesn't seem like it from outside). All the seafood is incredibly fresh and creatively served. They aren't open very late, only until 6 p.m., so you should plan on staying for lunch or an early dinner. $$

VietRiver *1817 S Washing-ton Ave., Titusville, FL 32780 (321) 600-0880* Heading up toward the main part of Titusville, you can get impressive Asian cuisine at VietRiver. The portions are large, and everything is fresh and tasty. Try the lemongrass chicken with a bowl of pho. They're open for lunch and dinner, and they do take-out if you want to grab some good food on your way to more sightseeing. $$

Moonlight Drive-In *1515 S Washington Ave., Titusville, FL 32780 (321) 267-8222* If you rented a car, drive right in to the 1950s with this unique and classic burger drive-in, complete with trays served to your car window. Burgers, chili cheese fries, thick milkshakes and fried oysters should help fill you up at either lunch or dinner. They're open until 9 p.m. but closed on Mondays and Sundays.

Where to Stay

Casa Coquina Bed & Breakfast *4010 Coquina Avenue, Titusville, FL 32780 (321) 268-4653* Right on the coast, the Casa Coquina Bed & Breakfast is lovely as well as convenient. Looking like an Italian villa brimming with an-tiques, it's a very comfortable place to stay if you enjoy a little extra beauty in your accommodations. Rumor has it that Al Capone may have stayed at the Casa Coquina, so there is a little notoriety there that you won't get at many other hotels. $$

The Inn at Cocoa Beach *4300 Ocean Beach Blvd., Cocoa Beach, FL 32931 (321) 799-3460* The Inn at Cocoa Beach is over on Cape Canaveral. There is a great hot breakfast bar each morning, and you are steps from the beach. It feels like a very expensive resort, yet the prices are very reasonable. Hang out for evening happy hour, and enjoy a glass of wine with the other residents. $$

Travel Inn of Titusville *7503 S US Hwy 1, Titusville, FL 32780 (321) 267-7774* The Travel Inn is one of the closest hotels to the airport, and the place is great when you're on a tight budget. It's not fancy, but the rooms are clean and quiet. The grounds of this little one-story motel are always tidy. Not only is it near the airport, but being on Hwy 1 means you are just a short drive from everything else too. $

Space Coast Regional; *Titusville*   KTIX

SPACE COAST TOWER ©**118.9**
[0700-2100]

Ground Control **121.85**

Control Tower Phone
[321] 267-0204

Airport Manager Phone
[321] 267-8780

AWOS-3 at X21 [6.6 N]: 119.725
[321] 385-0383

ATIS 120.625

®ORLANDO App/Dep 134.95

UNICOM 122.95

Elevation 34' MSL	Traffic Pattern 1000' MSL [966'AGL]	Flight Service Station ST PETERSBURG TITUSVILLE RCO 123.6

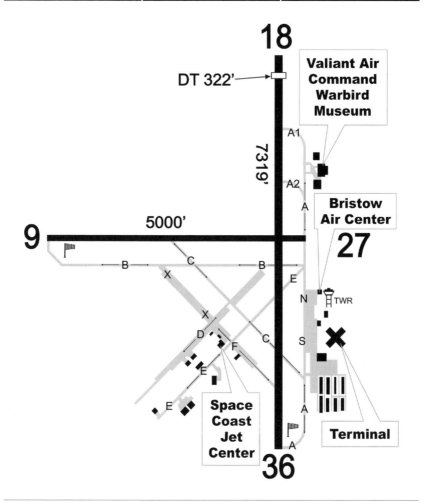

18

DT 322'→

Valiant Air
Command
Warbird
Museum

A1

7319'

A2

A

Bristow
Air Center

27

9

5000'

B   C   B

X

E

N   TWR

X

S

D

F

C

E

A

Space
Coast
Jet
Center

E

A   A

Terminal

36

KVNC

Venice

Venice has some gorgeous waterfront views, beaches and boating all right by the airport. For pilots, there is an excellent restaurant at the FBO, and the famous Sharky's on the Pier restaurant is just a few minutes away.

The first settling of Venice was as a family homestead owned by Richard Roberts in the 1870s. Roberts Bay is still named for the family today. Citrus farms grew up in the area, though it was the fishing industry that helped the area thrive. It was named Venice after the famous city in Italy.

Today it's a busy little city that does a big tourism business due to the long sandy beach that makes up the entire western edge of town. The architecture of Venice is quaint, and visitors often enjoy just walking around town to see the urban sights when they're not on the beach.

As the unofficial "shark's tooth capital of the world," many people come to Venice to hunt for teeth and fossils. If you're a shark tooth enthusiast, you should plan to visit during the annual **Shark Tooth Festival** *(941) 412-0402* held each spring to celebrate the local fossils. They've been holding the event for more than 20 years, and it draws amateur

Pier at Venice

archaeologists from around the world.

Flying There

Venice in an un-towered airport that lies well-outside the Sarasota Class C airspace to the north. Pilots arriving from the northeast should avoid flight below 2,000 feet AGL over the Myakka River State Park and

below 1,500 feet AGL in the area east of the airport.

The neighborhoods around the airport are noise sensitive. When able, pilots are requested to use runway 5 for arrivals and runway 23 for departures. Runway 13 has a right-hand traffic pattern.

Keep an eye out for parasailing along the beach to the west.

Suncoast Air Center is on the eastern end of the north ramp. The Suncoast Cafe is located in the FBO. Full-service fueling for 100LL and Jet A during business hours from 7:30 a.m. to 7:30 p.m. Self-serve 100LL also available under the Phillips 66 sign east of the FBO. Radio 131.3 or telephone *(941) 485-1799.*

Florida Flight Maintenance on the west end of the ramp also offers self-serve 100LL. Call *(941) 485-1149.*

Getting Around

Renting a car is an option, and the airport has both **Hertz** and **Enterprise** *(866) 315-9155.* Getting a taxi from the airport is easy too, with a quick call to **Venice Yellow Cab** *(941) 480-9222.*

There is a good public bus system that services Venice, the Sarasota County Area Transit (SCAT), though access to and from the airport is limited. You can get to downtown Venice via route 90X.

Walking Distance Activities

The **Suncoast Café** is right at the **Suncoast Air Center.** This aviation-themed restaurant overlooks the runways at the Venice Airport. The food and presentation are very good. If you sit at the bar, you'll probably get a chance to talk with Chef Tony and you'll find he has a million stories. Open 7 days a week from 7:30 until 2:00. They serve breakfast all day Sunday.

A 20-minute walk from the airport will bring you to the coast and **Caspersen Beach** if you'd like a little beach time. Here you'll also find **Sharky's**

On the Pier, a popular restaurant and Tiki bar and local landmark, as well as the **Lake Venice Golf Club** across the street. If you call Sharky's, and they aren't too busy, they may pick you up.

What to See and Do

Venice Fishing Pier *1600 Harbor Dr. S., Venice, FL 34285* The Venice Fishing Pier is located at **Brohard Park** due west of the airport. It's about a two-minute drive or a 20-minute walk from the airport. The 700-foot Pier is a great location for fishing and to end the day watching a beautiful sunset.

Connected to Sharky's restaurant, you can walk or fish from the Pier for free. It is open 24 hours a day and 7 days a week. If you need to rent a rod and reel or purchase live or frozen bait, go to Papa's Bait Shop located midway down the Pier. It opens at 6 a.m., seven days a week. Papa's also sells coffee. Nearby are six picnic shelters, two sand volleyball courts, and public restrooms.

Myakka River State Park *13208 State Road 72, Sarasota, FL 34241 (941) 361-6511*

A 30-minute drive by car will take you out into a natural paradise of river delta, wetland and forests. There are hiking trails all through the Myakka River State Park, as well as a high suspension walkway that lets you see some of the forest from tree-top vantage points. It's the best way to see the birds. Bike rentals are available if you want to pedal your way through the park, and they also offer airboat rides so you can see even more alligators.

Shamrock Park and Nature Center *3900 Shamrock Dr.,*

Venice, FL 34293 (941) 486-2706 For some closer green space, the Shamrock Park has nature trails and a nice picnic area near the water. If you don't have time for the longer drive to Myakka River, this might fit your schedule better.

Shopping

The Venice Main Street is the hot-spot in town for fun shopping, with all sorts of little boutiques, cafes, art galleries and more. If you want to see the heart of Venice, this is it. And don't let the "Main Street" name get you confused. You're looking for West Venice Avenue, right downtown. Just take the South Tamiami Trail from the airport to West Venice and you're there.

The Historic Architecture

Venice has a number of buildings that are listed on the National Register of Historic Places, and wandering around to see the historic architecture is a popular activity. There are several Historic Districts within the city, plus specific buildings such as the former Hotel Venice and the Blalock House.

The Beaches

Not only will you find the usual sun and sand, Venice is known for the shark teeth that wash up on shore. Go collecting a few unique souvenirs while walking along any of the local beaches.

Caspersen Beach on Harbor Drive is one of the closest, and you can get there easily from the airport. Closer to downtown is Venice Beach, running all along the coast. It's quite a long beach so there tends to be plenty of room although it can get crowded on nice days. It is a great spot for shark tooth hunting which many people visit for. There are plenty of places to eat and park all along the beach. At the very southern end of the beach (and right next to the airport!) is the Venice Fishing Pier 1600 Harbor Drive S. (see above).

Boat Tours

Whether you want head out on a power boat or just paddle close to shore in a kayak, there are boat charters and rentals to suit. **Aristakat Charters** *(941) 321-0852* will take you out on a catamaran for tours as well as diving for shark teeth. They know where all the best sites are for wreck diving and tooth collecting.

For a more peaceful boating excursion, hook up with **Easy Kayaking** *304 Warfield Ave. #17, Venice, FL 34285 (941) 960-5505* Take a tour up the coast or stay closer to Venice through the various bays and islands. Tell them what you want to see, and they'll know where to go. Sailboat charters are available with **SailVenice** *(941) 554-2190* or **Black Duck Charters** *(941) 929-6584* if you prefer a bit more of an old-school boating experience. They take a maximum of six people on this small two masted sailboat.

Deer Prairie Creek Horseback Riding *7001 Forbes Trail, Venice, FL 34292 (941) 907-7272* Not everything in Venice takes place on the water. If you want a change of landscape, you can stay inland and do some horseback riding at Deer Prairie Creek. It's a little farther out than the other activities mentioned, but it does make a splendid day trip whether you're an experienced rider or just a horseback novice.

Where to Eat

Sharky's on the Pier *1600 Harbor Drive S., Venice, FL 34285 (941) 488-1456* Mentioned above in our "Walking Distance Activities," the restaurant is located right at the Pier on Venice Beach. Great views of the beach and gulf as you enjoy a relaxing meal. It has a real beachy vibe and the menu has something for everyone. Air-conditioned inside or ask to be seated in the small outdoor seating area next to the bar for some of the best views and the perfect spot for watching the sunset. $$

Robbi's Reef *775 US Hwy 41 Bypass S., Venice, FL 34285 (941) 485-9196* One of the best rated restaurants in Venice is just a 10 minute drive from the airport, where you can get huge portions of seafood galore. It's located in a strip mall so there isn't a lot of ambiance but the service is friendly and casual. $$

Cassariano Italian Eatery *313 W Venice Ave., Venice, FL 34285 (941) 485-0507* A night of fine dining is waiting for you at Cassariano's in downtown Venice. The cuisine is Italian and the overall atmosphere is high-end gourmet. Veal ravioli, linguine with seafood and chicken piccata are a few of the options that the locals rave about. They have a lovely dining room as well as a patio outside and it's open fairly late (10 p.m.) for that special night out. $$$

Wee Blew Inn Restaurant *590 US Highway 41 Bypass S., Venice, FL 34285 (941) 484-*5616 Not looking to spend that much? Then have a meal at the Wee Blew Inn. If you're arriving in Venice early, you'll get a breakfast to remember and it's just minutes from the airport. It's not just for breakfast though. You can get burgers and huge portions of fried fish here too. $

Where to Stay

Kon-Tiki Motel *1487 Tamiami Trl S., Venice, FL 34285 (941) 485-9696* This is one of the closest motels to the airport, and you can be unpacking your bags after just a 15-minute walk. It's simple, clean and easy to get to. If you want any advice about Venice or have questions, talk to the staff. They seem to know everything about the town. $$

Inn at the Beach *725 West Venice Avenue, Venice, FL 34285* Great location next to main Venice beach. Nothing too fancy but certainly has what you need for a little beach getaway. The hotel offers umbrellas, chairs and towels for your trip to the beach. Walking distance to all the restaurants and shops on Venice Ave. Friendly staff; good breakfast; nice pool and hot tub. Ask for a room that faces the water for a great sunset view.

Venice Beach Villas *501 W Venice Ave., Venice, FL 34285 (941) 488-1580* If you'd rather stay near the beaches than the airport, you can get some budget accommodations at the Venice Beach Villas. Even though the prices are low, you get tons of space with a private and fully-equipped villa. They have a pool and free Wi-Fi, and you are within walking distance of Venice Beach. $

Venice Municipal Airport — KVNC

CTAF/UNICOM ©122.725

Airport Manager Phone
(941) 486-2711

AWOS–3 119.275

®TAMPA App/Dep 119.65
App/Dep 124.95

CLNC DEL 118.075

Elevation	Traffic Pattern	Flight Service Station
17' MSL	1017' MSL (1000'AGL)	800-WX-BRIEF

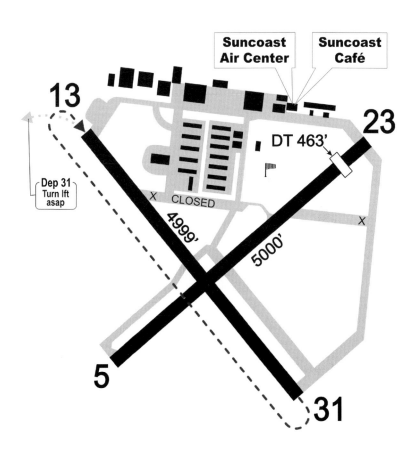

Suncoast Air Center

Suncoast Café

13

23

DT 463'

Dep 31 Turn lft asap

X CLOSED

4999'

5000'

X

5

31

Vero Beach

Vero Beach is the home of Piper Aircraft and a great airport restaurant. You can fly in for a tour of Piper, for a romantic getaway, beach fun, or to get out into the wetlands for some boat tours. Far from the crowds of south Florida, you'll find the best of the East Coast here.

Vero Beach is part of the famed Treasure Coast, and its appeal is such that more active and retired Fortune 500 CEOs have homes here than anywhere else in the country.

The beaches are only part of the appeal. Kayaking by manatees or taking an exciting airboat tour through the alligator and bird populated wetlands will add more dimension to your trip. One visitor described Vero Beach as having a Hampton's ambiance in Florida. Wandering by the cozy shops and restaurants on Ocean Drive will have you agreeing.

Vero Beach Sunrise

Piper Aircraft moved to Vero Beach in the 1950s. Originally a research center, it developed the successful Piper Cherokee, which has been manufactured here since 1960. Eventually all airplane production moved here and today they build eight different models, from the Cherokee derived Archer to the turbine powered M-Class. Take the five minute walk to Piper for their factory tour and a look at their gift shop (see details below).

Flying Here

The only other controlled airspace in the vicinity of Vero Beach is the St. Lucie County International Airport's Class D in Fort Pierce to the south. The airports have similar runway sizes and orientations, and pilots should be careful to approach the right one.

Vero Beach is home to two very-active flight schools and the Piper Aircraft factory. During peak times, VFR arrivals may encounter delays getting into the Class D airspace. Trainer traffic is most concentrated in the area between the airport and Blue Cypress Lake and around

State Route 60. The highway has a long, easily-recognizable straightaway running due west out of Vero Beach.

Arrivals from the north need to be alert in the Sebastian area for traffic along the beach and the lagoon. Avoid overflying the Sebastian Municipal Airport (X26) due to frequent skydiving activity.

Sun Aviation is the FBO on the central ramp next to the terminal. Normal hours are 6 a.m. to 9 p.m. A courtesy van is available. Full-service 100LL and Jet A are available along with self-serve 100LL. Radio on UNICOM 122.95 or telephone *(772) 562-9257.*

Corporate Air operates an FBO on the west ramp. Full-service 100LL and Jet A, and courtesy cars. Open from 7 a.m. to 7 p.m. or by appointment. Call *(772) 569-8473.*

Paris Air on the west ramp is primarily a flight school, but also offers FBO services and sells pilot supplies. They have full-service 100LL and a self-serve 100LL pump off of taxiway C near the run-up area for runway 12R. Radio 122.875 or call *(772) 770-2708.* Line service hours are 8 a.m. to 7 p.m. Monday through Saturday and 8 a.m. to 6 p.m. on Sunday.

Getting Around

Sun Aviation's offices are right next to the Vero Terminal and they have **Hertz** rental cars *(772) 794-9960.* Or go with **Enterprise** *(772) 770-0811* from the Corporate Air terminal. **Avis** has a desk inside the main terminal. Either one can have a car waiting for you when you arrive.

GoLine has a bus system for Vero Beach that is free

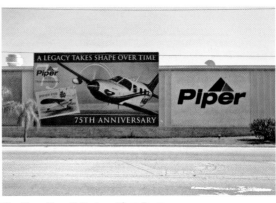

The Piper Aircraft Factory Gives Tours

for riders (a donation would be appreciated though). The main connecting hub for all the city's routes is at the airport. A two minute walk from the terminal lets you easily grab a bus to go anywhere in town including over to the island and the beach. There are many taxi companies in the area, but **ABC Cab** *(772) 231-8321* is one of the best for service from the airport.

Walking Distance Activities

There is a restaurant, **C.J Cannon's,** right at the airport. It is considered one of the best airport restaurants in Florida, and you can taxi right up to it. (see the "Where to Eat" section below). You can also take a tour of **Piper Aircraft.** The entrance is just a five-minute walk from the Vero Beach Airport terminal. Piper also has a **Gift Shop** with all kinds of things for Piper fans. It is next to the Piper entrance. **Flight Safety,** the famous flight school, is located here, and they have a Pilot Shop that is open to the public. It is a four-minute walk from the terminal.

What to See and Do

Piper Aircraft Factory Tour *2926 Piper Drive, Vero Beach, FL 32960 (772) 567-4361* A must-do for all aviation enthusiasts. The factory tour is a guided tour of Piper's manufacturing facility in which you get to see the different stages of airplane construction, from the beginning through to final assembly. Tours are free, though offered only by reservation on Tuesdays, Wednesdays and Thursday at 9:30 a.m. and 12:30 p.m., so call ahead to arrange your tour.

Airboat Excursions

The Blue Cypress Conservation Area is a 24-minute drive west from the airport. A trip here will give you a classic wetlands airboat tour you won't soon forget. **Captain Bob's Airboat Adventure Tours** *(772) 633-7849* is one of the best. Capt. Bob Montuoro originated the idea of using airplane-style headsets so that he could narrate the tour over the loud airboat engine. He encourages you to ask him questions. You'll love seeing the birds, flowers, water and gators. You really should book in advance in order to be sure of a seat.

Vero Beach Museum of Art *3001 Riverside Park Drive, Vero Beach, FL 32963 (772) 231-0707* Their mixed media collection of art is quite contemporary, including a number of creative modern sculptures out on the museum grounds. The permanent collection has nearly 900 pieces, and there are temporary exhibits from around the country all the time. After your artistic browsing, check out the lovely wares at the gift shop or stop for a coffee at the Museum Cafe. They are open seven days a week, except Mondays and are closed during the summer months. Admission to the museum is $10.

Nature Reserves

Besides the Blue Cypress area, there are a number of other popular natural areas around Vero Beach that you should try to visit. The **Round Island Beach Park** *2201 Highway A1A, Vero Beach, FL 32963 (772) 492-2412* has lots of nature trails and open waters for kayaking or paddleboarding. This location is legendary for spotting manatees but also watch for turtles, herons, stingrays, ospreys, pelicans and even occasional dolphins. The park has good washroom facilities, a lovely sandy beach for swimming and picnic tables if you've brought some food along. **Orchard Island Bikes and Kayaks** *(772) 299-1286* has a guided Round Island Kayak tour available. **Adventure Kayaking** *(772) 567-0522* has Stand-Up Paddle Board Tours also available here.

A peaceful 30 minute drive

up the island will bring you to the **Pelican Island National Wildlife Refuge** *4055 Wildlife Way, Vero Beach, FL 32963 (772) 581-5557*. Bird watchers will love the chance to see the flocks of pelicans that make their home here. Other than that, you can explore the trails, watch the water and see a slice of untouched Florida nature.

Historical & Ghost Walking Tours *3150 Ocean Drive, Vero Beach, FL 32963 (772) 559-5966* For a creative way to see the historical side of Vero Beach, try a ghost walking tour.

Blue Cypress Conservation Area

A 90-minute walking tour will show you many landmarks on the island, and the guide is filled with tales of ocean-going pirates and other spooky stories of the region. You can also find out more about the original native residents of the barrier islands. Tickets are $12 each, and you should call to book a spot.

If you just want sandy

beaches, **South Beach** and **Humiston Park** are very popular spots on the island.

Where to Eat

C.J. Cannon's *3414 Cherokee Rd., Vero Beach, FL 32960 (772) 567-7727* You can taxi right up to the terminal location of C.J. Cannon's. Big windows let you have a great view over the runway where you'll see everything from Piper Cherokees, test aircraft from Piper and corporate jets, to the Coast Guard's 36,000 pound CG-711 coming in for lunch. With an airport-themed lobby, they've got a great breakfast menu, and the lunch menu has some more sophisticated salads and entrees in addition to classic American comfort foods like burgers, meatloaf, tuna melts and pork chops. They also serve dinner. $$

The Ocean Grill *1050 Sexton Plaza, Vero Beach, FL 32963 (772) 231-5409* An

Captain Bob's Airboat Adventure Tours

icon in Vero Beach, this old time oceanfront restaurant is always packed during the season. Built by Vero Beach's legendary Waldo Sexton (who also built the Driftwood Inn), the dark wood interior features salvaged architectural artifacts that he incorporated in the construction. The views are very good if you get a table by the windows or are in the cozy bar.

Casey's Place *917 Azalea Ln., Vero Beach, FL 32963 (772) 231-4790* For outside dining or takeout, this restaurant is just a block back from the beach so tourists usually do not find it, but they have some of the best burgers and sandwiches in town. There are picnic tables in a shaded courtyard if you are eating there. $

Johnny D's Market & Bistro *1409 Highway A1a, Vero Beach, FL 32963 (772) 234-4181* Most restaurants on the islands are costly, but you can get great Italian-style deli eats at Johnny D's without spending a fortune. It's just south of the 17th street bridge and near the Round Island Beach Park. Try a Mediterranean-grilled veggie sandwich, mussels over pasta,

or huge portions of chicken Parmesan. If you are on your way to a beach rendezvous, they'll happily pack you some take-out. $$

Where to Stay

Costa d'Este Beach Resort *3244 Ocean Drive, Vero Beach, FL 32963 (772) 562-9919* For accommodations over on the island, you can't get much nicer than the Costa d'Este Beach Resort. Owned by famous musicians Gloria and Emilio Estefan, the oceanfront rooms have a terrific view over the beach, and everything has a sophisticated Miami modern feel. Whether you go for the standard room or a luxury suite, you'll be pampered for your entire stay. You can dine at their signature restaurant, **The Wave,** or get a more casual meal at the **Cabana Bar and Grill.** For activities, you can hang out at the pool or get out into the ocean and do some scuba diving with the **Sharkbait** dive club. Located on Ocean Drive alongside many cozy shops and restaurants. $$$

Vero Beach Hotel and Spa, *3500 Ocean Drive, Vero Beach,*

FL 32963 (772) 231-5666 This is a world-class oceanfront hotel and spa that will make your visit relaxing. They have an oceanside pool and two restaurants (both with outdoor seating). A fire pit, overlooking the ocean, makes relaxing with an adult beverage dinner drink a special moment. You can walk to all the shops and restaurants on Ocean Drive easily. $$$

Driftwood Resort *3150 Ocean Dr., Vero Beach, FL 32963 (772) 231-0550* Built in the early 1900s by Waldo Sexton, it was named to the National Registry of Historic Places in 1994. Much of the original facade was built of salvaged wood giving the resort an "ambiance of the sea" eclectic charm. If you are used to staying at four-star or better resorts, this is a little different. The resort has a great location, beautiful beach and a fun bar and pool. The rooms are clean and comfortable with a place to cook and spend time by the ocean. It is downtown in the oceanside village where there are lots of shops and places to dine and it's right on the ocean. It also has its own **Waldo's Restaurant,** right on the ocean with a nice bar and occasional live entertainment. $$

Sea Spray Inn *965 East Causeway Blvd, Vero Beach, FL 32963 (800) 827-0181* Also by the beaches, the little Sea Spray Inn lets you stay near the sand without paying the big resort prices. Their rooms are big and clean, with Wi-Fi and access to their heated swimming pool. Lots of shops and restaurants around, and you can walk to the beach in just a few minutes. $$

Vero Beach Municipal · KVRB

TOWER ©**126.3, 133.15**
(0700-2100)

Ground Control **127.45**

Control Tower Phone
(772) 299-0129

Airport Manager Phone
(772) 978-4930

ASOS (772) 978–9535

ATIS 120.575

®PALM BEACH App/Dep 123.625

UNICOM 122.95

Elevation 23' MSL	Traffic Pattern 1023' MSL (1000'AGL)	Flight Service Station ST PETERSBURG 122.2 122.5 122.1R 122.3T

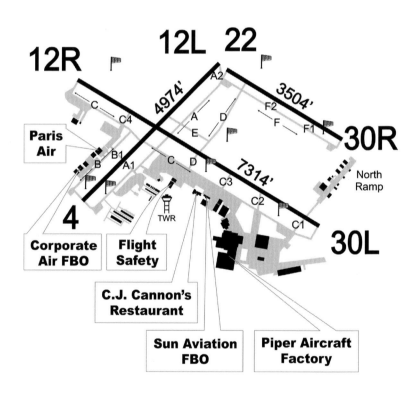